THE LONGMAN DICTIONARY OF

SPANISH
GRAMMAR
AND IDIOMS

ANDRÉ HURTGEN

Longman

**The Longman Dictionary of Spanish Grammar
and Idioms**

Longman, 95 Church Street, White Plains, N.Y. 10601

Associated companies:
Longman Group Ltd., London
Longman Cheshire Pty., Melbourne
Longman Paul Pty., Auckland
Copp Clark Pitman, Toronto

Executive editor: Lyn McLean
Production editor: Dee Amir Josephson
Text design: Dee Amir Josephson
Cover design: Joseph de Pinho
Production Supervisor: Joanne Jay

ISBN 0-8013-0626-4 (ppr)
      0-8013-0627-2 (csd)

1 2 3 4 5 6 7 8 9 10-MA-969594939291

INTRODUCTION

This is a dictionary, not a textbook or a workbook. Its aim is to provide clear and convenient assistance to students and other users or lovers of the Spanish language who are unsure of, or have completely forgotten, a rule of grammar, an irregular verb, an idiomatic construction, etc.

Language is a complex set of rules, conventions, and idioms, some of them logical, others seemingly flouting common sense. Learning them—or even looking them up—in isolation is no recipe for mastery of a language. It makes no more sense to memorize idioms or grammatical rules out of context than it does to commit to memory lists of vocabulary items. Language must be considered and studied as a whole. This is best done by *living* the language, the way all of us learned our mother tongue.

In practice and by necessity, however, most foreign-language teaching and learning takes place in the artificial context of a classroom. Rules are learned piecemeal, drilled and practiced, and then gradually forgotten as additional material is accumulated. The same is true of vocabulary, much of which the student memorizes, uses a little, and then gradually forgets. But here the problem is readily overcome: the forgotten word can be looked up in the dictionary. What to do, though, when a grammar rule has been forgotten? Looking it up in an old first- or second-year textbook (if these are still on hand) is no simple task. The material therein is generally presented in small segments. Conjugations, irregular verbs, rules of syntax, idioms, etc., are scattered all over the book and certainly not listed in alphabetical order.

This dictionary is designed to help solve this problem. It lists alphabetically (in both Spanish and English) the following types of items:

Common Spanish and English abbreviations
Common Spanish and English idioms
Conjugations of regular and irregular verbs
Definitions of grammatical terms
Spanish and English conjunctions and prepositions
Function-related expressions and structures
Letter-writing conventions
Punctuation rules, diacritical marks, and accents
Rules of Spanish grammar and syntax
The metric system and Celsius/Fahrenheit scales

The entries in this work do not pretend to be an exhaustive treatment of the subject. Rules and common exceptions are stated succinctly and as clearly as possible. Examples in Spanish (with English translations) are provided in every case. Cross-references direct the user to all other entries in the dictionary where the same point is discussed.

Suppose, for instance, that the user has forgotten how to say "ago" in Spanish. The user may look it up under that word. If the question occurs in the form: "What does *Hace diez minutos* mean?," the answer can be found under the headings *HACER* + **TIME EXPRESSION** and **TIME EXPRESSIONS**.

Other examples: a user who is confused as to the difference between *a cause de* and *porque* will find help under *A CAUSA DE* vs. *PORQUE* and also under **BECAUSE vs. BECAUSE OF**. One who is not sure how to convey *would* in Spanish will find help under the headings **WOULD, IMPERFECT TENSE**, and **CONDITIONAL TENSES**.

ACKNOWLEDGMENTS

The existence of this dictionary is due to repeated proddings over many years by my students, whose persistent questions and repeated requests for explanations and clarifications kept reminding me that the grammar of a foreign language is hard to learn and easy to forget. But this book is not my work alone. Besides my students, who provided the inspiration for it, I wish to thank also Robert J. Blake, associate professor of Spanish at the University of Rochester, and Roberto

Véguez, professor of Spanish at Middlebury College, who read the drafts with utmost care and thoroughness, and caught many inconsistencies and confusing entries. Their careful and meticulous attention improved the manuscript immeasurably. Terrence A. Wardrop's indispensable technical assistance, always generously proffered, rescued me on more than one occasion when it seemed that my word processor had irretrievably lost large chunks of the manuscript. My editor Lyn McLean's unfailing cheerfulness and support helped me to overcome the numerous hurdles, both large and small, involved in writing a work of this sort.

Any and all remaining errors and omissions are, of course, my own. I ask that readers kindly bring these to my attention so that any failings may be corrected in later editions.

André Hurtgen

A

A

(Preposition). *A* has many meanings, depending on the context. Its most common uses are to express: (a) direction: to, (b) distance: from, (c) position: at, (d) time: at, (e) manner: in, on, (f) instrument or means: by, in, on, (g) price or rate: by, at, (h) the dative: to, for, from, off, on.

E.g.: (a) *Vamos a Barcelona.*
Let's go to Barcelona.

(b) *Toledo está a 50 kilómetros de Madrid.*
Toledo is 50 kilometers from Madrid.

(c) *Están sentados a la mesa.*
They are seated at the table.

(d) *Vendrán a las seis.*
They will come at six o'clock.

(e) *Viajé a caballo.*
I traveled on horseback.

(f) *La carta está escrita a mano.*
The letter is handwritten.

(g) *Se venden a cien pesetas el kilo.*
They sell for a hundred pesetas a kilo.

(h) *Le escribo a Juan.*
I am writing to John.

Le compré un regalo a Marta.
I bought a present for Martha.

NOTE:

With the verbs *comprar* (to buy), *pedir* (to request), *robar* (to steal), and *quitar* (to remove), it means "from."

E.g.: *Compraron el coche a Pedro.*
They bought the car from (or for) Peter.

See **A (personal)**

A (personal)

The preposition *a* must be placed before a noun which refers to known persons or to things personified and functions as the direct object. It is not translated into English.

E.g.: *Conozco a María.*
I know Mary.

EXCEPTIONS:

(1) The personal *a* is not used with (a) the verb *tener* or (b) direct object pronouns referring to persons.

E.g.: (a) *Tengo un amigo.*
I have a friend.

(b) *Lo conozco.*
I know him.

(2) However, the personal *a is* used before the indefinite pronouns *alguien* and *nadie.*

E.g.: *No veo a nadie.*
I don't see anyone.

Encontré a alguien en la calle.
I met somebody in the street.

1

(3) The personal *a* is frequently omitted when the noun does not refer to a specific person. Its use depends upon the individuality attached to the object by the speaker.

> E.g.: *Encontré un hombre.*
> I met a man (unknown).
> *Encontré a un hombre.*
> I met a man (known).

A, AN

See **ARTICLES, INDEFINITE**

A or DE + INFINITIVE

See **PREPOSITIONS + INFINITIVE**

A vs. EN

(Prepositions). While both frequently correspond to the English preposition "at," they are not interchangeable.

(1) *A* generally means "To, at."

> E.g.: *Vendré a las diez.*
> I shall come at ten o'clock.

(2) *En* generally means "In, into."

> E.g.: *La llave está en el cajón.*
> The key is in the drawer.

See **A**

See also **EN**

A + INFINITIVE

See **PREPOSITIONS + INFINITIVE**

A CAUSA DE vs. PORQUE

(1) *A causa de* (Prepositional construction) = "Because of."

> E.g.: *No pudo salir a causa de la nieve.*
> He was not able to go out because of the snow.

(2) *Porque* (Conjunction) = "Because."

> E.g.: *No pudo salir porque nevaba.*
> He was not able to go out because it was snowing.

A ESO DE

(Prepositional construction) = "About, around (+ time of day)."

E.g.: *Volverán a eso de las cinco.*
> They will return at about five o'clock.

See **ALREDEDOR DE**

A FIN DE vs. A FIN DE QUE

(1) *A fin de* (Prepositional construction) = "In order to."

> E.g.: *Fui al Prado a fin de ver las pinturas de Goya.*
> I went to the Prado in order to see the paintings of Goya.

(2) *A fin de que* + subjunctive (Conjunctional construction) = "In order that, so that."

> E.g.: *Enviaron a su hijo a Portugal a fin de que aprenda la lengua.*
> They sent their son to Portugal in order that he might learn the language.

A FINES DE

(Adverbial idiom) = "Toward the end, late in."
E.g.: *Volverán a fines de julio.*
They will return toward the end of July.

A FONDO

(Adverbial idiom) = "Thoroughly."
E.g.: *Estudió el problema a fondo.*
He studied the problem thoroughly.

A FUERZA DE

(Prepositional construction) = "By dint of, by force of."
E.g.: *Llegó a ser presidente a fuerza de campañas políticas.*
He got to be president by dint of political campaigns.

A LA DERECHA

(Adverbial idiom) = "To the right, on the right side."
E.g.: *El museo está a la derecha de la estación.*
The museum is to the right of the station.
See **A LA IZQUIERDA** below.

A LA IZQUIERDA

(Adverbial idiom) = "To the left, on the left side."
E.g.: *Mi oficina está a la izquierda del pasillo.*
My office is to the left of the hallway.
See **A LA DERECHA** above.

A LA VEZ

(Adverbial idiom) = "At the same time."
E.g.: *No comprendo lo que dicen porque hablan todos a la vez.*
I don't understand what they are saying because they are all speaking at the same time.

A LITTLE

(1) (Adverbial expression) = *Un poco.*
E.g.: *Estoy un poco cansado.*
I am a little tired.
(2) (Expression of quantity) = *Un poco de.*
E.g.: *Dame un poco de vino.*
Give me a little wine.

A LO LEJOS

(Adverbial idiom) = "Far away, in the distance."
E.g.: *Se ve un castillo a lo lejos.*
One can see a castle in the distance.

A LO MEJOR

(Adverbial idiom) = "Probably."
It is generally followed by the subjunctive mood.
E.g.: *A lo mejor lleguen pronto.*
They will probably arrive soon.

A LOT OF, LOTS OF

Muchos (-as) (Adjective).
E.g.: *Tengo muchos libros.*
    I have a lot of books.

A MENOS QUE

(Conjunctional construction) + subjunctive = "Unless."
E.g.: *Irá a Santiago a menos que sus padres estén enfermos.*
    He will go to Santiago unless his parents are ill.

A MENUDO

(Adverbial idiom) = "Often."
E.g.: *Vamos al museo a menudo.*
    We go to the museum often.

A MI (TU, SU, etc.) PARECER

(Idiomatic expression) = "In my (your, his, etc.) opinion."
E.g.: *A mi parecer no hay peligro.*
    In my opinion, there is no danger.

A PARTIR DE

(Prepositional expression) = "From . . . on, starting on . . ."
E.g.: *La película se proyectará a partir del lunes.*
    The movie will be shown from Monday on (starting on Monday).

A PESAR DE (QUE)

(1) *A pesar de* (Prepositional construction) = "Despite."
    E.g.: *Salieron a pesar de la nieve.*
        They went out despite the snow.
(2) *A pesar de que* (Conjunctional construction) + indicative = "Despite the fact that."
    E.g.: *Ella cantó anoche a pesar de que tenía un resfriado.*
        She sang last night despite the fact she had a cold.

A PIE

(Adverbial idiom) = "To walk, to go on foot."
E.g.: *Voy a la universidad a pie.*
    I walk to the university.

A PRINCIPIOS DE

(Prepositional construction) = "At the beginning of, early in."
E.g.: *Saldremos a principios de agosto.*
    We shall leave at the beginning of August.

A SOLAS

(Adverbial idiom) = "Alone, by oneself."
E.g.: *Estoy a solas.*
   I am by myself.

A TIEMPO

(Adverbial idiom) = "On time."
E.g.: *Hay que llegar a tiempo.*
   You have to arrive on time.
See **EN PUNTO**

A TRAVÉS DE

(Prepositional construction) = "Through, across."
E.g.: *Entró en Francia a través de los Pirineos.*
   He entered France through the Pyrenees.

ABAJO vs. ABAJO DE

(1) *Abajo* (Adverb) = "Below, down, underneath, downstairs."
  E.g.: *Dejaron sus maletas abajo.*
    They left their suitcases downstairs.
(2) *Abajo de* (Prepositional construction) = Below, under."
  E.g.: *El garaje está situado abajo del edificio.*
    The garage is located under the building.
See **DEBAJO vs. DEBAJO DE**

ABBREVIATIONS

Some **Spanish** abbreviations with their English equivalents:

a. de C.	= *antes de Cristo*	= B.C. (Before Christ)
a. de J.C.	= *antes de Jesucristo*	= B.C.
A. E. C. E.	= *Asociación Española de Cooperación Europea*	= Spanish Association for European Economic Cooperation
A.P.	= *apartado postal*	= post office box
apto.	= *apartamento*	= apartment
A.R.	= *Alteza Real*	= Royal Highness
Arz.	= *Arzobispo*	= Archbishop
ato., ata.	= *atento, atenta*	= used with *servidor* in courtesy formulas in correspondence
Av., Avda.	= *Avenida*	= Avenue
AVIANCA	= *Aerovías Nacionales de Colombia*	= Colombian National Airlines
B.I.C.	= *Brigada de Investigación Criminal*	= Spanish equivalent of FBI (USA); CID (GB)
b.l.m.	= *besa las manos*	= kiss the hand (courtesy formula)
C.	= *calle*	= street
C.A.	= *Corriente eléctrica alterna*	= A.C. current
C.D.	= *Corriente eléctrica directa*	= D.C. current
Cía	= *Compañía*	= Company
D.	= *Don*	= title used before masc. first names
Da.	= *Doña*	= title used before fem. first names
d. de. J.C.	= *después de Jesucristo*	= A.D. (anno Domini)
D.F.	= *Distrito Federal*	= Federal District

D.G.T.	= *Dirección General del Turismo*	= General Tourist Administration
EE.UU.	= *Estados Unidos*	= United States
ej.	= *ejemplo*	= example
ENESA	= *Empresa Nacional de Electricidad, Sociedad Anónima*	= Spanish Electric Utility Service
Fr.	= *Fray*	= Friar
g.p.	= *giro postal*	= money order
Gral.	= *General*	= General
Hnos.	= *Hermanos*	= Brothers
izq.	= *izquierda*	= left
J.C.	= *Jesucristo*	= Jesus Christ
km/h.	= *kilómetros por hora*	= kilometers per hour
l.	= *litro*	= liter
Na. Sra.	= *Nuestra Señora*	= Our Lady
NN.UU.	= *Nacionas Unidas*	= United Nations
no.	= *número*	= number
N.S.	= *Nuestro Señor*	= Our Lord
O.E.A.	= *Organización de Estados Americanos*	= OAS (Organization of American States)
ONU	= *Organización de las Naciones Unidas*	= UN (United Nations)
Op.D.	= *Opus Dei*	= (a Spanish Catholic lay order)
OTAN	= *Organización del Tratado del Atlántico Norte*	= NATO (North Atlantic Treaty Organization)
OVNI	= *Objeto volante no identificado*	= UFO (Unidentified Flying Object)
P.	= *Padre*	= Father
p.c.	= *por ciento*	= percent
p.ej.	= *por ejemplo*	= e.g. (for example)
pta., ptas.	= *peseta, pesetas*	= Spanish currency unit
p.v.p.	= *precio de venta al público*	= (used after the price in some stores)
PYRESA	= *Prensa y Radio Española, Sociedad Anónima*	= Spanish Press Agency
RENFE	= *Red Nacional de los Ferrocarriles Españoles*	= Spanish National Railroads
R.N.E.	= *Radio Nacional de España*	= Spanish National Radio
R.P.	= *Reverendo padre*	= Reverend Father
S.A.	= *Sociedad Anónima*	= Corporation, Inc.
S.A.R.	= *Su Alteza Real*	= His/Her Royal Highness
SIDA	= *síndrome de inmuno-deficiencia adquirida*	= AIDS
S.M.	= *Su Majestad*	= His/Her Majesty
Sr.	= *Señor*	= Mr.
Sra.	= *Señora*	= Mrs.
Sres., Sras.	= *Señores, Señoras*	= Messrs., Mesdames
Srta.	= *Señorita*	= Miss
S.	= *San, Santo, Santa*	= Saint
s.s.s.	= *su seguro servidor*	= your faithful servant (courtesy formula)
Sto., Sta.	= *Santo, Santa*	= Saint
TVE	= *Televisión Española*	= Spanish Television
Ud., Uds.	= *usted(es)*	= you (formal)
Vd., Vds.	= *usted(es)*	= you (formal)

Some **English** abbreviations with their Spanish equivalents:

AC	= alternating current	= *C.A.*
A.D.	= Anno Domini	= *d. de J.C.*

AIDS	= acquired immune deficiency syndrome	= *SIDA*
Atty.	= attorney	= *abogado diplomado*
Ave.	= Avenue	= *Avda.*
B.A.	= Bachelor of Arts	= *Lic. en Fil. y Let. (Licienciado en filosofía y letras)*
B.C.	= Before Christ	= *a.de J.C.*
Bros.	= Brothers	= *Hnos.*
Co.	= Company	= *Cía.*
Corp.	= Corporation	= *S.A. (Sociedad Anónima)*
D.C.	= Direct current	= *C.D.*
D.D.S.	= Doctor of Dental Surgery	= *Dentista diplomado*
DJ	= Disc Jockey	= *Presentador de discos*
e.g.	= exempli gratia	= *p. ej.*
encl.	= enclosure	= *adjunto*
Esq.	= Esquire	= *Don* (used before masc. first name)
F.M.	= Frequency modulation	= *M.F.*
G.B.	= Great Britain	= *Gran Bretaña*
GNP	= Gross National Product	= *Producto nacional bruto*
G.P.	= General Practicioner	= *Médico general*
HMS	= Her (His) Majesty's Ship	= *Buque de guerra británico*
H.R.H.	= His (Her) Royal Highness	= *S.A.R.*
Inc.	= Incorporated	= *S.A.*
IQ	= Intelligence Quotient	= *Cociente intellectual*
Jr.	= Junior	= *hijo*
M.A.	= Master of Arts	= *Maestro de artes*
M.D.	= Medicinae Doctor	= *Médico diplomado*
Messrs.	= Messieurs	= *Sres.*
misc.	= miscellaneous	= *vario, diverso*
m.p.g.	= miles per gallon	= the equivalent is in liters per 100 km. *(litros por 100 km.)*
m.p.h.	= miles per hour	= the equivalent is in kilometers per hour *(kilómetros por hora)*
Mr.	= Mister	= *Sr.*
Mrs.	= Mistress	= *Sra.*
NATO	= North Atlantic Treaty Organization	= *OTAN*
N.B.	= Nota bene, note well	= *Nótese bien*
OAS	= Organization of American States	= *O.E.A.*
Ph.D.	= Doctor of Philosophy	= *Doctor en Filosofía*
PTO	= Please turn over	= *Véase al dorso*
RN	= Registered nurse	= *Enfermera diplomada*
RSVP	= Please reply	= *S.R.C. (Se ruega contestación)*
Secy.	= Secretary	= *Secretario (-a)*
Sen.	= senior	= *padre*
sq.	= square	= *cuadrado*
sq. ft.	= square feet	= *pies cuadrados*
UFO	= Unidentified flying object	= *OVNI (Objeto volante no identificado)*
UN	= United Nations	= *NN.UU.*
US	= United States	= *EE.UU.*
USSR	= Union of Soviet Socialist Republics	= *U.R.S.S.*
VIP	= Very important person	= *personaje importante*
Xmas	= Christmas	= *Navidad*
yr.	= year	= *año*
yrs.	= yours	= *suyo*

to be ABLE

(Verbal expression) = *Poder* or *Saber.*
(1) In general, *poder* means "To have the capacity, the ability."
    E.g.: *Ella puede correr más rápidamente que yo.*
        She is able to run faster than I.
(2) *Saber* means "to have the knowledge."
    E.g.: *Ella sabe contar en chino.*
        She is able (knows how) to count in Chinese.
See **SABER vs. CONOCER vs. PODER**

ABOUT

(1) (Preposition) meaning "relating to" = (a) *acerca de* or (b) *con respecto a.*
    E.g.: (a) About that story . . . .
           Acerca de este cuento . . .
      (b) About the child, he will come with us.
           Con respecto al niño, vendrá con nosotros.
(2) (Adverb) meaning (a) "approximately" = *a eso de* or (b) "almost" = *casi.*
    E.g.: (a) We'll return about three o'clock.
           Volveremos a eso de las tres.
      (b) I have about finished the book.
           Casi he terminado el libro.

ABOUT (hear about, read about, write about, etc.)

(1) It's about = *Se trata de.*
    This book is about = *Este libro trata de.*
    E.g.: *Don Quijote trata de las aventuras de un hombre quien . . .*
        Don Quijote is about the adventures of a man who . . .
(2) To ask about = *Preguntar por.*
    E.g.: *Pedro preguntó por la situación política.*
        Peter asked about the political situation.
See **PREGUNTAR (POR)**
(3) To hear about = (a) *Oír hablar de* (+ noun or pronoun) or (b) *Oír decir que* (+ clause).
    E.g.: (a) *¿Has oído hablar de esa película?*
           Have you heard about that movie?
      (b) *He oído decir que es muy buena.*
           I have heard that it is very good.
See **OÍR HABLAR DE**
See **OÍR DECIR QUE**
(4) To talk about = *Hablar de.*
    E.g.: *Estábamos hablando de su hermano.*
        We were talking about his brother.
(5) To write about = *Escribir sobre.*
    E.g.: *Escriba Ud. sobre sus vacaciones.*
        Write about your vacation.
(6) To tell about = *Contar* or *hablar.*
    E.g.: *Mi hermana me contó sus aventuras del año pasado.*
        My sister told me about her adventures of last year.
See **A ESO DE**

ABOUT TO + verb

(Idiomatic construction).
(1) To indicate an action to be performed immediately = *Estar para* + infinitive.
E.g.: *Estábamos para salir.*
We were about to leave.
(2) To indicate an action yet to be performed = *Estar por* + infinitive.
E.g.: *La reunión está por terminar.*
The meeting is about to end.
See **ESTAR PARA + infinitive**
See also **ESTAR POR + infinitive**

ABOVE

(1) (Adverb) = *Encima, por encima, arriba.*
E.g.: *La torre está arriba.*
The tower is above.

La torre está por encima.
The tower is above.
(2) (Preposition) = *Encima de.*
E.g.: *El techo está encima de la guardilla.*
The roof is above the attic.

ABRAZAR

(Transitive verb) = "To embrace, to hug."
Conjugated like **cruzar.**

ABRIR

(Transitive verb) = "To open."
PRES.: *abr-o, -es, -e, -imos, -ís, -en.*
IMPERF.: *abr-ía, -ías, -ía, -íamos, -íais, -ían.*
PRET.: *abr-í, -iste, -ió, -imos, -isteis, -ieron.*
FUT.: *abrir-é, -ás, -á, -emos, -éis, -án.*
CONDIT.: *abrir-ía, -ías, -ía, -íamos, -íais, -ían.*
SUBJ. PRES.: *abr-a, -as, -a, -amos, -áis, -an.*
SUBJ. IMPERF. 1: *abri-era, -eras, -era, -éramos, -erais, -eran.*
SUBJ. IMPERF. 2: *abri-ese, -eses, -ese, -ésemos, -eseis, -esen.*
INFORMAL IMPERAT.: *abre (tú), no abras (tú); abrid (vosotros), no abráis (vosotros).*
FORMAL IMPERAT.: *abra (Vd.); abramos; abran (Vds.).*
PRES. PARTIC.: *abriendo.*
PAST PARTIC.: *abierto.*

ABSOLUTE CONSTRUCTION

The past participle may be used as an absolute, i.e., separate from the rest of the sentence. It then has the value of a clause of cause, condition, manner, or means.
E.g.: *Terminado el trabajo, se marcharon.*
The work (being) finished, they departed.

ABSOLUTE SUPERLATIVE
See **SUPERLATIVE, ABSOLUTE**

ACABAR

(Transitive and intransitive verb) = "To complete, to end, to finish."
E.g.: *La palabra acaba con D.*
    The word ends with D.
NOTES:
(1) The reflexive *acabarse* = "to come to an end."
    E.g.: *¡Se acabó!*
        It's finished!
(2) Note the idiom with an indirect object:
    E.g.: *Se me acabó el café.*
        I ran out of coffee.

ACABAR CON + noun or pronoun

(Intransitive verb) = "To put an end to, to end in."
E.g.: *Acabó con la revolución.*
    He put an end to the revolution.

ACABAR DE + infinitive

(Verbal idiom) = "To have just + past participle."
E.g.: *Acabamos de llegar.*
    We have just arrived.
This construction is called the "recent past."
NOTE:
In a past context, this construction will always be in the imperfect because it describes a state of affairs, not an action.
E.g.: *Acabábamos de llegar cuando llamaste.*
    We had just arrived when you called.
See **HAVE JUST + past participle**

ACABAR POR + infinitive

(Intransitive verb) = "To finally + verb, to end up by."
E.g.: *Acabaron por abandonar la lucha.*
    They finally gave up the struggle.

ACASO

(Adverb) = "Perhaps."
It is followed by:
(a) the indicative if certainty is implied.
    E.g.: *Acaso vienen pronto.*
        Perhaps (= probably) they will arrive soon.
(b) the subjunctive if uncertainty is implied.
    E.g.: *Acaso lleguen mañana.*
        Perhaps they might arrive tomorrow.

ACCENTS

An accent *(un acento)* [´] is a diacritical mark used:
(a) to indicate where the stress falls when it does not follow the normal rule.
    E.g.: *fantástico; hábil; lápiz.*

(b) to distinguish between two words spelled alike bu whose meanings are different.

E.g.: *si—sí; mas—más; el—él.*

See **STRESS**

See also **DIACRITICAL MARKS**

ACERCARSE A + noun or pronoun

(Reflexive verb) = "To approach, to near."

E.g.: *El ladrón se acercó a la casa.*

The burglar approached the house.

ACERTAR

(Transitive verb) = "To hit upon, to figure out."

PRES.: *aciert-o, -as, -a, -amos, -áis, -an.*

IMPERF.: *acert-aba, -abas, -aba, -ábamos, -abais, -aban.*

PRET.: *acert-é, -aste, -ó, -amos, -asteis, -aron.*

FUT.: *acertar-é, -ás, -á, -emos, -éis, -án.*

CONDIT.: *acertar-ía, -ías, -ía, -íamos, -íais, -ían.*

SUBJ. PRES.: *aciert-e, -es, -e, -emos, -éis, -en.*

SUBJ. IMPERF. 1: *acert-ara, -aras, -ara, -áramos, -arais, -aran.*

SUBJ. IMPERF. 2: *acert-ase, -ases, -ase, -ásemos, -aseis, -asen.*

IMFORMAL IMPERAT.: *acierta (tú), no aciertes (tú); acertad (vosotros), no acertéis (vosotros).*

FORMAL IMPERAT.: *acierte (Vd.); acertemos; acierten (Vds.).*

PRES. PARTIC.: *acertando.*

PAST PARTIC.: *acertado.*

to ACHIEVE

(Transitive verb) = (a) *lograr,* (b) *conseguir,* (c) *llevar a cabo,* or (d) *realizar.*

E.g.: (a) *Siempre logra todo lo que quiere.*

He always achieves what he wants.

(b) *No consiguieron su objetivo*

They did not achieve their goal.

(c) *Llevaremos a cabo esta tarea.*

We shall achieve this task.

(d) *Nunca realizarán nada si no trabajan.*

They will never achieve anything if they don't work.

ACONSEJAR

(Transitive verb) = "To advise."

E.g.: *Le aconsejé que no fuera a clase porque estaba tan cansado.*

I advised him not to go to class because he was so tired.

NOTE:

Although the normal rule is that a clause is required when there is a change of subject between the main clause and the subordinate clause, *aconsejar* may take the infinitive, especially when the object of the verb is a pronoun.

E.g.: *Le aconsejé no ir a clase.*

I advised him not to go to class.

See **SUBJUNCTIVE vs. INFINITIVE**

ACORDARSE DE + noun or pronoun

(Reflexive verb) = "To remember, to recall."
E.g.: *No me acuerdo de tu cumpleaños.*
     I don't remember your birthday.

ACOSTARSE

(Reflexive verb) = "To go to bed."
Conjugated like *contar.*

ACROSS

(1) (Adverb) = *Al través.*
    E.g.: *No vaya por aquí, vaya al través.*
        Don't go this way, go across.
(2) (Preposition)
    (a) meaning "through" = *A través de* or *por.*
      E.g.: *Hay que pasar a través del* (or *por el) parque.*
        You have to go through the park.
    (b) meaning "opposite" = *Al otro lado de.*
      E.g.: *La iglesia está al otro lado de la calle.*
        The church is across the street.

ACTIVE VOICE

The active voice *(la voz activa)* indicates that the subject performs the action of the verb. It is the voice most frequently used in normal written or spoken language.
E.g.: *El hombre maneja el coche.*
    The man drives the car.
    Cristóbal Colón descubrió las Américas.
    Christopher Columbus discovered the Americas.
    Lloverá mañana.
    It will rain tomorrow.

ACTUAR

(Transitive verb) = "To act."
PRES.: *actúo, actúas, actúa, actuamos, actuáis, actúan.*
IMPERF.: *actu-aba, -abas, -aba, -ábamos, -abais, -aban.*
PRET.: *actu-é, -aste, -ó, -amos, -asteis, -aron.*
FUT.: *actuar-é, -ás, -á, -emos, -éis, -án.*
CONDIT.: *actuar-ía, -ías, -ía, -íamos, -íais, -ían.*
SUBJ. PRES.: *actúe, actúes, actúe, actuemos, actuéis, actúen.*
SUBJ. IMPERF. 1: *actu-ara, -aras, -ara, -áramos, -arais, -aran.*
SUBJ. IMPERF. 2: *actu-ase, -ases, -ase, -ásemos, -aseis, -asen.*
INFORMAL IMPERAT.: *actúa (tú), no actúes (tú); actuad (vosotros), no actuéis (vosotros).*
FORMAL IMPERAT.: *actúe (Vd.); actuemos; actúen (Vds.).*
PRES. PARTIC.: *actuando.*
PAST PARTIC.: *actuado.*

ADELGAZAR

(Transitive verb) = "To make thin, to become slender."
Conjugated like *cruzar.*

ADJECTIVE

An adjective *(un adjetivo)* is a word which qualifies a noun by describing its nature, size, qualities, etc.

E.g.:   *Una mesa grande.*
   A *big* table.
   Un libro difícil.
   A *difficult* book.

See **ADJECTIVES, AGREEMENT OF**
See also **ADJECTIVES, POSITION OF**

ADJECTIVE + ENOUGH + verb

"*Bastante* + adjective + *para* + infinitive."

E.g.:   *Eres bastante inteligente para comprender esto.*
   You are intelligent enough to understand this.

ADJECTIVES

FEMININE OF ADJECTIVES:
(1) Many adjectives end in *-o* in the masculine singular. The ending changes to *-a* in the feminine.
   E.g.:   *cómico → cómica*   funny
       antiguo → antigua   ancient
(2) Adjectives which do not end in *-o* keep the same ending in the feminine.
   E.g.:   *dulce → dulce*   sweet
       fácil → fácil   easy
       joven → joven   young
BUT:
(3) Adjectives ending in a consonant and which indicate geographical origin add *-a* to form the feminine.
   E.g.:   *español → española*   Spanish
       alemán → alemana   German
(4) Adjectives ending in *-án* and *-ón* add *-a* in the feminine.
   E.g.:   *holgazán → holgazana*   lazy
       preguntón → preguntona   inquisitive
(5) Adjectives ending in *-or* and which are not comparative forms add *-a* to form the feminine.
   E.g.:   *encantador → encantadora*   enchanting
   BUT: *peor → peor*   worse
PLURAL OF ADJECTIVES:
(1) Adjectives ending in a vowel add *-s*:
   E.g.:   *cierto → ciertos*   certain (masc.)
       cierta → ciertas   certain (fem.)
(2) Adjectives ending in a consonant add *-es*:
   E.g.:   *popular → populares*   popular
       elemental → elementales   elementary
NOTES:
(1) Adjectives ending in *-z* change the *z* to *c* in the plural.
   E.g.:   *Feliz → felices*   happy
(2) Some adjectives must add or drop a written accent in order to maintain the same stress as in the singular.
   E.g.:   *joven → jóvenes*   young
       francés → franceses   French
       alemán → alemanes   German
       cortés → corteses   courteous

ADJECTIVES OF COLOR

As all adjectives, they normally agree with the noun they modify. However:
(1) Compound adjectives of color are invariable.
    E.g.: *Una falda azul claro.*
        A light blue skirt.

        Zapatos blanco y negro.
        Black and white shoes.
(2) Nouns used as adjectives are invariable.
    E.g.: *Una falda naranjo.*
        An orange skirt.

ADJECTIVES, ABSOLUTE SUPERLATIVE OF

The absolute superlative expresses the English "very, extremely, exceedingly." It is constructed by adding *-ísimo(-a, -os, -as)* as follows:
(a) directly to the adjectives ending in a consonant.
    E.g.: *fácil → facilísimo*
        cruel → cruelísimo
(b) if the adjective ends in a vowel, by first dropping this final vowel.
    E.g.: *alto → altísimo*
        complicado → complicadísimo
(c) after first making the following spelling changes: *-z → -c; -co → -qu, -go → -gu; -ble → -bil.*
    E.g.: *feliz → felicísimo*
        rico → riquísimo
        largo → larguísimo
        agradable → agradabilísimo.

ADJECTIVES, AGREEMENT OF

(1) Adjectives agree in number and gender with the noun they modify.
    E.g.: *Margarita es guapa.*
        Margaret is pretty.

        Los automóviles modernos.
        The modern cars.
(2) An adjective which modifies two or more nouns of different gender is in the masculine plural.
    E.g.: *María y Pedro son perezosos.*
        Mary and Peter are lazy.
APOCOPATION OF ADJECTIVES:
(1) The following adjectives drop the final *-o* when they precede the noun:
    (a) *uno* = a(n), one
        E.g.: *Un hombre.*
            A man.
    (b) *bueno* = good
        E.g.: *Un buen amigo.*
            A good friend.
    (c) *malo* = bad
        E.g.: *Un mal libro.*
            A bad book.

(d) *primero* = first
    E.g.: *El primer día.*
        The first day.

(e) *tercero* = third
    E.g.: *El tercer día.*
        The third day.

(f) *alguno* = some
    E.g.: *Algún día.*
        Some day.

(g) *ninguno* = no, not any
    E.g.: *No hay ningún problema.*
        There is no problem.

(2) *Santo* shortens to *San* when it precedes the name, unless the name begins with *Do-* or *To-*.
    E.g.: *San José.*
        Saint Joseph.

        San Juan.
        Saint John.

    BUT: *Santo Tomás.*
        Saint Thomas.

        Santo Domingo.
        Saint Dominic.

        Santo Toribio.
        Saint Toribio.

(3) *Grande* shortens to *gran* when it precedes the noun.
    E.g.: *Un gran héroe.*
        A great hero.

        Una gran hazaña.
        A great deed.

(4) *Ciento* shortens to *cien* when followed by a noun (masculine or feminine) or by *mil* or *millones*
    E.g.: *Cien personas.*
        A hundred people.

        Cien mil pesetas.
        A hundred thousand pesetas.

        Cien millones.
        One hundred million.

    BUT: There is no change with multiples of *ciento*:
    E.g.: *Trescientas pesetas.*
        Three hundred pesetas.

ADJECTIVES, COMPARISON OF

(1) *Comparisons of quality:* "as . . . as" = *tan . . . como.*
    E.g.: *María es tan inteligente como Guillermo.*
        Mary is as intelligent as William.

(2) *Comparisons of superiority:* "more . . . than" = *más . . . que.*
    E.g.: *Los gatos son más grandes que los ratones.*
        Cats are bigger than mice.

NOTE:

Before numbers:

(a) In affirmative constructions use *de:*
    E.g.: *Ella tiene más de diez años.*
        She is more than ten years of age.

(b) In negative constructions, note the difference in meaning between *de* and *que*:

E.g.: *No tengo más de quinientas pesetas.*

   I have no more (perhaps less) than five hundred pesetas.

   No tengo más que quinientas pesetas.

   I have only five hundred pesetas (no more, no less).

(3) *Comparisons of inferiority:* "less . . . than" = *menos . . . que.*

E.g.: *Pedro es menos fuerte que Juan.*

   Peter is less strong than John.

NOTE:

Before numbers use *de*

E.g.: *Tengo menos de mil pesetas.*

   I have less than a thousand pesetas.

But the two negative constructions have different meanings:

E.g.: *Ella no tiene más de cien pesetas.*

   She has no more (perhaps less) than a hundred pesetas.

   Ella no tiene más que cien pesetas.

   She has only a hundred pesetas (no more, no less).

SPECIAL CASES:

Comparative form of *bueno* = *mejor*

         good = better

Comparative form of *pequeño* = *menor*

         small = smaller (or younger)

Comparative form of *malo* = *peor*

         bad = worse

E.g.: *El té es mejor que el café.*

   Tea is better than coffee.

   Juan es el menor de los cuatro muchachos.

   John is the smallest (or youngest) of the four boys.

   La gripe es peor que un catarro.

   The flu is worse than a cold.

ADJECTIVES, DEMONSTRATIVE

Demonstrative adjectives *(los adjetivos demostrativos)* point (really or figuratively) to the noun which follows.

FORMS:

While there are only two forms of demonstrative adjectives in English ("this" and "that"), there are three forms in Spanish:

(a) "This" (near the speaker)

(b) "That" (near the listener)

(c) "That" (remote from both the listener and the speaker)

ADJECTIVES, DEMONSTRATIVE

		Masculine	Feminine
(a)	This (near me)	*este*	*esta*
	These (near me)	*estos*	*estas*
(b)	That (near you)	*ese*	*esa*
	Those (near you)	*esos*	*esas*
(c)	That (over there)	*aquel*	*aquella*
	Those (over there)	*aquellos*	*aquellas*

E.g.: (a) *Esta falda que llevo es vieja.*
      This skirt I am wearing is old.
      (b) *Quiero esos libros que tienes.*
      I want those books which you have.
      (c) *Déme aquella blusa que está en el cuarto de Margarita.*
      Give me that blouse which is in Margaret's room.

NOTE:

The definite article is sometimes used instead of the demonstrative adjective:

(1) before a phrase beginning with *de.*
    El (la, los, las) de . . .
    That (those) of, the one(s) of (in, with) . . .
(2) to express a possessive construction in English.
    E.g.: *Mi libro y el de Patricia.*
        My book and Patricia's.
        La del vestido rojo.
        The one in the red dress.
        El de los ojos morenos.
        The one with the brown eyes

ADJECTIVES, DESCRIPTIVE

Descriptive adjectives *(los adjetivos calificativos)* describe nouns by stating their color, size, type, etc.

E.g.: *La casa blanca.*
      The white house.
      Un edificio enorme.
      An enormous building.
      Una alfombra persa.
      A Persian rug.

ADJECTIVES, EXCLAMATIVE

For exclamations use the interrogative *qué* (with no article [as opposed to the English construction]).

E.g.: *¡Qué mujer!*
      What a woman!

See **EXCLAMATIONS**

ADJECTIVES, FEMININE OF

See **ADJECTIVES**

ADJECTIVES, INDEFINITE

(Los adjetivos indefinidos). These are adjectives which indicate a rather vague concept of quantity, quality, identity, resemblance, or difference. The most common indefinite adjectives are:

(a) *Algún (alguna, -os, -as)* = Any, some
    E.g.: *¿Tienes algún diccionario?*
        Do you have a (any) dictionary?
(b) *Cada* (invariable) = Each, every
    E.g.: *Cada día.*
        Every day.
(c) *Cualquier(a), cualesquier(a)* = Any
    E.g.: *En cualquier momento.*
        Any time.

(d) *Ningún, ninguno (-a, -os, -as)* = No
    E.g.: *Ninguna mujer.*
        No woman.
(e) *Todos los (todas las)* = All
    E.g.: *Todas las casas.*
        All the houses.
(f) *Todo el (toda la)* = All, the whole
    E.g.: *Toda la noche.*
        The whole night.
(g) *Un (-o, -a, -os, -as)* = A, some, a few
    E.g.: *Unas flores.*
        Some flowers.

ADJECTIVES, INTERROGATIVE

(Los adjetivos interrogativos). These adjectives indicate that the noun they refer to is the topic of a question as to its quality, identity, or rank.

FORMS:

(a) *¿Qué?* = What, which?
    E.g.: *¿Qué libro estás leyendo?*
        What (= which) book are you reading?

NOTE:

Qué is also used in exclamations.
E.g.: *¡Qué imaginación!*
    What an imagination!

See **ADJECTIVES, EXCLAMATIVE**

(b) *¿Cuánto (-a, -os, -as)?* = How much, how many?
    E.g.: *¿Cuántas hermanas tiene?*
        How many sisters does he have?
REMEMBER that all interrogatives have a written accent.

ADJECTIVES, PLURAL OF

See **ADJECTIVES**

ADJECTIVES, POSITION OF

(1) Descriptive adjectives generally follow the noun.
    E.g.: *Una muchacha encantadora.*
        A charming girl.

        La casa rosada
        The pink house.
(2) Adjectives placed before the noun indicate an evaluative meaning rather than a descriptive meaning.
    E.g.: *Cervantes era un gran escritor.*
        Cervantes was a great writer (not: a big writer).

NOTE:

The following adjectives have a different meaning depending on their position:

	AFTER THE NOUN	BEFORE THE NOUN
(a) *antiguo (-a, -os, -as)*	ancient, old	former, old
	E.g.: *Un palacio antiguo.*	*Mi antiguo profesor.*
	An ancient palace.	My former teacher.

	AFTER THE NOUN	BEFORE THE NOUN
(b) *cierto (-a, -os, -as)*	sure, true E.g.: *Un método cierto.* A sure method.	a certain *Una cierta idea.* A certain idea.
(c) *grande(s)*	large E.g.: *Una casa grande.* A large house.	great *Un gran héroe.* A great hero.
(d) *mismo (-a, -os, -as)*	self E.g.: *Yo mismo.* I myself.	same *El mismo día.* The same day.
(e) *nuevo (-a, -os, -as)*	new E.g.: *Un coche nuevo.* A new car.	another, different *Una nueva política.* A new (= different) policy.
(f) *pobre(s)*	poor E.g.: *Una mujer pobre.* A poor woman.	unfortunate *El pobre animal.* The unfortunate animal.
(g) *puro (-a, -os, -as)*	pure, unadulterated E.g.: *Un vaso de agua pura.* A glass of pure water.	sheer *Fue una pura casualidad.* It was sheer chance.
(h) *simple(s)*	silly, simple-minded E.g.: *Un muchacho simple.* A simple-minded boy.	simple, mere. *Quiero tu simple palabra.* I merely want your word.

(3) Limiting adjectives (such as numbers, possessives, demonstratives, adjectives of quantity) generally go before the noun:

E.g.: *Cuatro amigos.*
      Four friends.
      Mis padres.
      My parents.
      Esta escuela.
      This school.
      Más trabajo.
      More work.

The common adjectives of quantity are:
alguno (-a, -os, -as) = some
cada (invariable) = each, every
cuanto (-a, -os, -as) = as much, as many
más = more
menos = less, fewer
mucho (-a, -os, -as) = much, many
ninguno (-a, -os, -as) = no, not any
numeroso (-a, -os, -as) = numerous
poco (-a, -os, -as) = few, little
tanto (-a, -os, -as) = so many, so much
todo (-a, -os, -as) = all, every
unos (-as) = some, a few
varios (-as) = several

ADJECTIVES, POSSESSIVE

(Los adjetivos posesivos). These adjectives indicate the possessor of the noun they refer to.

ADJECTIVES, POSSESSIVE	
SHORT FORMS (placed before the noun):	
mi(s)	my
tu(s)	your
su(s)	his, her, your
nuestro (-a, -os, -as)	our
vuestro (-a, -os, -as)	your
su(s)	their, your
LONG FORMS (placed after the noun):	
mío (-a, -os, -a)	of mine
tuyo (-a, -os, -as)	of yours
suyo (-a, -os, -as)	of his, of hers, of yours
nuestro (-a, -os, -as)	of ours
vuestro (-a, -os, -as)	of yours
suyo (-a, -os, -as)	of theirs, of yours

NOTES:

(1) Possessive adjectives agree in number and gender with the noun they modify.

E.g.: *Nuestra escuela.*

Our school.

Nuestros libros.

Our books.

(2) Spanish possessive adjectives do not indicate the gender of the possessor.

E.g.: *Su padre* = "his father" or "her father" or "your father."

(3) Do not use the possessive adjective for parts of the body when the context makes clear who the possessor is. Use the definite article instead.

E.g.: *Me lavo el pelo.*

I wash my hair.

Ella se cortó el dedo.

She cut her finger.

(4) To avoid ambiguity or confusion *suyo (-a, -os, -as)* can be replaced by *de él, de ella, de ellos, de ellas, de Ud., de Uds.*

E.g.: *Un amigo de él.*

A friend of his.

El hermano de Ud.

Your brother.

ADJECTIVES, SUPERLATIVE OF

The superlative of adjectives is formed by adding *el (la, los, las)* + *más* + adjective + *de.*

E.g.: *La Ciudad de México es las más grande del mundo.*

Mexico City is the largest in the world.

NOTES:

(1) When there is a noun in the superlative expression, it is placed between the article and the adjective:

E.g.: *La ciudad más artística.*

The most artistic city.

(2) After a superlative, "in" is expressed by *de*.

E.g.: *La ciudad más artística de España.*

The most artistic city in Spain.

(3) IRREGULAR FORMS:

Bueno (-a, -os, -as) → *el (la, los, las) mejor(es)* = the best

Malo (-a, -os, -as) → *el (la, los, las) peor(es)* = the worst

Menos grande)s) → *el (la, los, las) menos grand(es)* = the least large

Más grande(s) → *el (la, los, las) más grand(es)* = the largest

Pequeño (-a, -os, -as) → *el (la, los, las) menor(es)* = the least, the youngest

Más pequeño (-a, -os, -as) → *el (la, los, las) menos pequeño (-a, -os, -as)* = the smallest

Menos pequeño (-a, -os, -as) = the least small

ADVANTAGE (to take advantage of)

(1) *Aprovechar* (Transitive verb).

E.g.: *Arturo aprovechó la oportunidad de hacer el viaje.*

Arthur took advantage of the opportunity to make the trip.

(2) *Aprovecharse de* (Reflexive verb).

E.g.: *Voy a aprovecharme de esta oportunidad*

I am going to take advantage of this opportunity.

ADVERBS

An adverb *(un adverbio)* is an invariable word which modifies the meaning of a verb, an adjective, or another adverb.

E.g.: *Comen rápidamente.*

They eat fast.

Ella es muy guapa.

She is very pretty.

Escribes demasiado lentamente.

You write too slowly.

FORMATION:

GENERAL RULE: (1) Add *-mente* to the feminine singular form of the adjective.

E.g.: *Claro* → *clara* → *claramente*   Clearly

Hábil → *hábil* → *hábilmente*   Skillfully

Gracioso → *graciosa* → *graciosamente*   Gracefully

NOTES:

(1) When there is a string of two or more adverbs, the ending *-mente* is used only on the last of the series.

E.g.: *Diana escribe rápida y claramente.*

Diane writes quicky and clearly.

(2) A few adverb forms are different from the corresponding adjectives:

Bueno → *bien*   Well

Malo → *mal*   Badly

(3) The following are both adjectives and adverbs:

Demasiado enough   *Mucho* much
Más more   *Peor* worse
Mejor better   *Poco* little
Menos less, fewer

E.g.: *Arturo es más* (adverb) *inteligente, pero Pedro tiene más* (adjective) *dinero.*
Arthur is more intelligent but Peter has more money.

Tengo mucho (adjective) *trabajo y leo mucho* (adverb).
I have a lot of work and I read a lot.

ADVERBS, COMPARATIVE AND SUPERLATIVE OF

GENERAL RULES:

(a) COMPARISONS OF INEQUALITY: *Más* (or *menos*) + adverb + *que.*
E.g.: *Gabriel conduce más* (or *menos*) *rápidamente que yo.*
Gabriel drives faster (less fast) than I.

(b) COMPARISON OF EQUALITY: *Tan* + adverb + *como.*
E.g.: *Andrés trabaja tan rápidamente como yo.*
Andrew works as rapidly as I.

(c) SUPERLATIVE: *Lo más* (or *menos*) + adverb.
E.g.: *Pedro dibuja lo más artísticamente.*
Peter draws the most artistically.

NOTES:

(1) The article used before adverbs is the neuter *lo*, since adverbs have no gender and do not modify nouns.

(2) If a context is given for the superlative, it is preceded by the preposition *de* (corresponding to the English "in").
E.g.: *Pedro dibuja lo más artísticamente de toda la clase.*
Peter draws the most artistically in the whole class.

(3) Before a number:

(a) In the affirmative, the second term of the comparison is introduced by *de:*
E.g.: *Tenemos más de mil libros.*
We have more than a thousand books.

(b) In the negative, the two constructions have different meanings:
E.g.: *No tenemos más que mil libros.*
We have no more than a thousand books.

No tenemos más de mil libros.
We have no more (perhaps fewer) than a thousand books.

(4) If the second part of the comparison is a clause, it is preceded by the construction *de lo que.*
E.g.: *Comió más de lo que le recomendó el médico.*
He ate more than the doctor recommended.

IRREGULAR FORM:

Bien → mejor → lo mejor
Well → better → the best

E.g.: *Ella habla mejor que yo.*
She speaks better than I.

ADVERBS, INTERROGATIVE

(1) *¿Cómo?* = How?
(2) *¿Para qué?* = Why (= for what purpose?)
(3) *¿Por qué?* = Why (= for what reason, because of what?)
(4) *¿Dónde?* = Where?

(5) *¿Cuándo?* = When?

E.g.: *¿Cómo estás?*

How are you?

¿Para qué necesitas dinero?

Why (for what purpose) do you need money?

¿Por qué no tienes dinero?

Why (for what reason) do you have no money?

¿Dónde están tus padres?

Where are your parents?

¿Cuándo llegarás a Toledo?

When will you arrive in Toledo?

REMEMBER: All interrogatives have a written accent.

ADVERBS, POSITION OF

There are no firm rules for the position of adverbs, but generally:

(a) the adverb immediately follows the verb it modifies.

E.g.: *Corre rápidamente.*

He runs fast.

(b) the adverb immediately precedes the adjective or adverb it modifies.

E.g.: *Canta muy bien.*

She sings very well.

NOTE:

When an adverb stands alone in a negative statement, *no* follows the adverb. This is the opposite of the English construction.

E.g.: *Ahora no.*

Not now.

ADVERBS, SUPERLATIVE OF

See **ADVERBS, COMPARATIVE AND SUPERLATIVE OF**

ADVERTIR

(Transitive verb) = "To advise."

Conjugated like *sentir.*

ADVISING

Several expressions may be used to give advice:

(a) *Aconsejar (a uno)* + infinitive.

E.g.: *Te aconsejo guardar cama.*

I advise you to stay in bed.

(b) *Recomendar (a uno) que* + subjunctive.

E.g.: *Le recomiendo a Ud. que no vaya allá.*

I recommend that you not go there.

AFRAID (OF)

See *TENER MIEDO (DE)*

AFTER + verb (-ing)

(Idiomatic construction) = "*Después de* + infinitive."

E.g.: *Se acostaron después de comer.*

They went to bed after eating.

AGE

See **YEARS OLD**

AGENT

The "agent" *(el agente)* is the person or thing by whom the action of the verb is performed. It is preceded by the preposition *por* (sometimes by *de* with verbs of feeling or emotion).

E.g.: *El ladrón fue prendido por la policía.*

The robber was arrested by the police.

La princesa es amada de su pueblo.

The princess is loved by her people.

AGO

(Idiomatic construction) = "*Hace* + time expression."

E.g.: *Hace una hora.*

An hour ago.

NOTE:

When "ago" is part of a clause, two constructions are possible:

(a) "Clause + *hace* + time expression."

E.g.: *Llegaron hace una hora.*

They arrived an hour ago.

(b) "*Hace* + time expression + *que* + clause."

E.g.: *Hace una hora que llegaron.*

They arrived an hour ago.

REMEMBER: The tense usage is quite different from the English construction:

(1) If the situation or state of affairs still exists, the present tense is used.

E.g.: *Hace diez minutos que estoy aquí.*

I have been here ten minutes (and I am still here).

(2) If the situation or state of affairs was going on when something happened, the imperfect is used.

E.g.: *Hacía diez minutos que estaba aquí cuando ella entró.*

I had been here ten minutes when she came in.

REMEMBER that *hace* changes to *hacía* in a past context.

NOTE:

If the verb states an action (as opposed to a situation), it is in the preterite.

E.g.: *Me rompí la pierna hace una semana.*

I broke my leg a week ago.

See **SINCE + time expression**

See also **HACER + time expression**

AGRADAR

(Transitive and intransitive verb) = "To please, to be pleasing."

NOTE:

In the idiomatic construction *Agradarle a uno una cosa*, the thing which pleases is the subject, while the person is the indirect object.

E.g.: *Esta decisión no le agrada a Marta.*

This decision doesn't please Martha.

AGRADECER

(Transitive verb) = "To thank."

Conjugated like **conocer**.

NOTE:
In the construction *Agradecerle a uno una cosa,* the person is the indirect object, while the thing is the direct object.

E.g.: *Le agradecí al profesor su ayuda.*
   I thanked the teacher for his help.

to AGREE (WITH)

(Idiomatic construction) = *Estar de acuerdo (con).*

E.g.: *Estoy de acuerdo con ellos.*
   I agree with them.

AGREEMENT OF ADJECTIVES

See **ADJECTIVES, AGREEMENT OF**

AGREEMENT OF PAST PARTICIPLES

See **PAST PARTICIPLES, AGREEMENT OF**

AGREEMENT OF TENSES

See the following entries: **CUANDO, DESPUÉS vs. DESPUÉS DE, vs. DESPUÉS DE QUE, "SI" CLAUSES, SUBJUNCTIVE MOOD**

AHOGAR vs. *AHOGARSE*

(1) *Ahogar* (Transitive verb) = "To drown."
   E.g.: *Ahogaron a los pobres gatitos.*
      They drowned the poor kittens.
(2) *Ahogarse* (Reflexive verb) = "To drown, to suffocate."
   E.g.: *Se ahogó en el lago cerca de su casa.*
      He drowned in the lake near his house.
Conjugated like **llegar**.

AHORA MISMO

(Adverbial expression) = "At once, immediately, right away."

E.g.: *¡Ven aquí ahora mismo!*
   Come here at once!

AHORA NO

(Adverbial expression) = "Not now."

E.g.: *¿Ir al centro? Ahora no puedo.*
   Go downtown? I can't now.

AJENO

(Adjective) = "Somebody else's, other people's."

E.g.: *Es una casa ajena.*
   It is somebody else's house.

AL

See **CONTRACTION: *A* + *EL***

AL + INFINITIVE

(Idiomatic construction). This is the equivalent of the English "Upon (or on) + present participle."
E.g.: *Al llegar a Madrid.*
        Upon arriving in Madrid.
See **UPON + verb (-ing)**

AL AIRE LIBRE

(Adverbial expression) = "In the open air, outdoors."
E.g.: *Cuando hace buen tiempo, me gusta comer al aire libre.*
        When the weather is nice, I like to eat outdoors.

AL AMANECER

(Adverbial expression) = "At daybreak, in the early morning."
E.g.: *Nos levantamos al amanecer.*
        We get up at daybreak.

AL ANOCHECER

(Adverbial expression) = "At nightfall."
E.g.: *Hace frío al anochecer.*
        It's cold at nightfall.

AL CABO (DE)

(Prepositional construction) = "At the end (of)."
E.g.: *Al cabo de un año, llegaron a su destinación.*
        They reached their destination at the end of a year.

AL FIN

(Adverbial expression) = "Finally, at last."
E.g.: *Al fin, abandonó la lucha.*
        Finally, he gave up the struggle.
See **POR FIN**

AL PARECER

(Adverbial expression) = "Apparently, seemingly."
E.g.: *Al parecer van a quedarse en Chile.*
        Apparently, they are going to stay in Chile.

AL REVÉS

(Adverbial expression) = "Upside down, inside out, backwards."
E.g.: *Se puso el suéter al revés.*
        He put on his sweater inside out.
        Tienes el libro al revés.
        You are holding the book upside down.

ALCANZAR

(Transitive verb) = "To reach."
Conjugated like ***cruzar***.

ALEGRARSE (DE)

(Reflexive verb) = "To rejoice, to be glad (of or to)."
E.g.: *Se alegró de la noticia.*
    He was glad of the news.
    Me alegro de verte.
    I am glad to see you.

ALEJARSE (DE)

(Reflexive verb) = "To go away (from)."
E.g.: *Se alejaron de la montaña.*
    They went away from the mountain.

ALGO

(1) (Indefinite pronoun) = "Something, anything."
    E.g.: *Marta quiere comprar algo nuevo.*
        Martha wants to buy something new.
(2) (Adverb) = "Rather, somewhat."
    E.g.: *Está algo sorprendida.*
        She is rather surprised.

ALGUIEN

(Indefinite pronoun) = "Someone, somebody, anyone, anybody."
E.g.: *Alguien quiere hablarte.*
    Somebody wants to speak to you.
NOTE:
The personal *a* is needed before *alguien* when it is direct object.
E.g.: *Encontró a alguien en la calle.*
    He met someone in the street.

ALGÚN, ALGUNO (-A, -OS, -AS)

(1) (Adjective) = "Some, any."
    E.g.: *¿Tiene Vd. algún amigo allá?*
        Do you have some friend over there?
NOTE:
When placed after the noun, *alguno (-a)* means "any (at all)."
E.g.: *Ella no tiene amiga alguna.*
    She doesn't have any friend.
(2) (Pronoun) = "Some, one, someone."
    E.g.: *Alguno vale la pena, pero la mayoría no.*
        One is worth the trouble, but most are not.

ALL (= everything)

(1) Used as subject = *Todo.*
    E.g.: *Todo está muy bien hecho.*
        Everything is very well done.
(2) Used as object = *Lo . . . todo.*
    E.g.: *Lo comió todo.*
        He ate everything.

ALL (OF) THE + noun

Todo (-a, -os, -as) (Adjective).
E.g.: *Toda la universidad.*
       All the university (the whole university).
       Toda la ciudad.
       The whole town.
       Todos los niños.
       All the children.
       Todas las mujeres.
       All the women.

ALLÍ vs. *ALLÁ*

(Adverbs).
(1) *Aquí* and *acá* both mean "here" and refer to a place near the speaker.
    (a) *Aquí* is used when there is no movement.
        E.g.: *Aquí se pueden comprar discos.*
              One can buy records here.
    (b) *Acá* is used with verbs of motion.
        E.g.: *Manuel, ¡Ven acá!*
              Manuel, come here!
(2) *Allí* and *allá* both mean "there" and refer to a place far from the speaker.
    (a) *Allí* is used when there is no movement.
        E.g.: *Mi tío vive en Cuernavaca, pero mi sobrino no vive allí.*
              My uncle lives in Cuernavaca, but my nephew doesn't live there.
    (b) *Allá* is used with verbs of motion.
        E.g.: *Tú vas a Cuernavaca pero yo no quiero ir allá.*
              You are going to Cuernavaca, but I don't want to go there.
See *AQUÍ* vs. *AHÍ* vs. *ALLÍ*

ALMORZAR

(Transitive verb) = "To have lunch."
PRES.: *alm-uerzo, -uerzas, -uerza, almorzamos, almorzáis, almuerzan.*
IMPERF.: *almorz-aba, -abas, -aba, -ábamos, -abais, -aban.*
PRET.: *almorcé, almorzaste, almorzó, almorzamos, almorzasteis, almorzaron.*
FUT.: *almorzar-é, -ás, -á, -emos, -éis, -án.*
CONDIT.: *almorzar-ía, -ías, -ía, -íamos, -íais, -ían.*
SUBJ. PRES.: *almuerc-e, -es, -e, almorcemos, almorcéis, almuercen.*
SUBJ. IMPERF. 1: *almorz-ara, -aras, -ara, -áramos, -arais, -aran.*
SUBJ. IMPERF. 2: *almorz-ase, -ases, -ase, -ásemos, -aseis, -asen.*
INFORMAL IMPERAT.: *almuerza (tú), no almuerces (tú); almorzad (vosotros), no almorcéis (vosotros).*
FORMAL IMPERAT.: *almuerce (Vd.); almorcemos; almuercen (Vds.).*
PRES. PARTIC.: *almorzando.*
PAST PARTIC.: *almorzado.*

ALMOST + verb

(1) (Adverb) = *Casi.*
    E.g.: *El trabajo está casi terminado.*
          The job is almost finished.
(2) (Idiomatic construction) = *Por poco* + verb.
    E.g.: *Por poco me corté el dedo.*
          I almost cut my finger.
See *POR POCO*

ALPHABET

In addition to the letters used in English, the Spanish alphabet uses the letters *ch, ll, ñ,* and *rr,* which represent single sounds and are considered single letters. The vowels are of two types: strong vowels *(a, e, o)* and weak vowels *(i, u).*
The names of letters are all feminine. They are:
a, be, ce, che, de, e, efe, ge, hache, i, jota, ka, ele, elle, eme, ene, eñe, o, pe, cu, ere, erre, ese, te, u, ve (or *uve), doble ve, equis, i griega, zeta.*

ALREADY

(Adverb) = *Ya.*
E.g.: *Ya hemos visto esta obra.*
    We have already seen this play.

ALREDEDOR DE

(Prepositional construction) = ''About, around (+ time of day).''
E.g.: *Volvieron alrededor de las nueve.*
    They returned around nine o'clock.
See **A ESO DE**

ALSO

También, además (Adverbs).
E.g.: *Visitaron también Machu Picchu.*
    They also visited Machu Picchu.

ALTHOUGH

(Conjunction) = *Aunque.* It is followed by:
(1) the indicative if there is no uncertainty.
    E.g.: *Fue a su despacho aunque estaba enfermo.*
        He went to his office although he was ill.
(1) the subjunctive if there is uncertainty.
    E.g.: *Iremos a la playa aunque llueva.*
        We'll go to the beach although it might rain.
See **SUBJUNCTIVE MOOD**

AMBOS (-AS)

(Plural adjective) = ''Both.''
E.g.: *Fidel tiene dos hijos; ambos tienen el pelo rubio.*
    Fidel has two children; they both have blond hair.

AMONG(ST)

(Preposition) = *Entre, en medio de.*
E.g.: *Pusieron el lobo entre las ovejas.*
    They put the wolf among(st) the sheep.

AMPLIAR

(Transitive verb) = "To enlarge."
Conjugated like **cambiar**.

ANDAR

(Intransitive verb) = "To go, to walk."
PRES.: *and-o, -as, -a, -amos, -áis, -an.*
IMPERF.: *and-aba, -abas, -aba, -ábamos, -abais, -aban.*
PRET.: *anduv-e, -iste, -o, -imos, -isteis, -ieron.*
FUT.: *andar-é, -ás, -á, -emos, -éis, -án.*
CONDIT.: *andar-ía, -ías, -ía, -íamos, -íais, -ían.*
SUBJ. PRES.: *and-e, -es, -e, -emos, -éis, -en.*
SUBJ. IMPERF. 1: *anduvi-era, -eras, -era, -éramos, -erais, -eran.*
SUBJ. IMPERF. 2: *anduvi-ese, -eses, -ese, -ésemos, -eseis, -esen.*
INFORMAL IMPERAT.: *anda (tú), no andes (tú); andad (vosotros), no andéis (vosotros).*
FORMAL IMPERAT.: *ande (Vd.); andemos; anden (Vds.).*
PRES. PARTIC.: *andando.*
PAST PARTIC.: *andado.*

ANOCHE

(Adverb) = "Last night, yesterday evening."
E.g.: *Me acosté temprano anoche.*
    I went to bed early last night.

ANOTHER

(Adjective) = *Otro (-a, -os, -as).*
E.g.: *Quiero leer otra revista.*
    I want to read another magazine.

ANTE

(Preposition) = "In front of, before (a person), in the presence of."
E.g.: *Tiene que ir ante el juez.*
    He has to go before the judge.

ANTECEDENT

An antecedent *(el antecedente)* is the noun or pronoun to which a pronoun refers.
E.g.: *El libro que me compré ayer.*
    The book (that) I bought yesterday.
El libro is the antecedent of the relative pronoun *que.*

ANTES, ANTES DE, ANTES DE QUE

All three are translated as "Before," but note the differences:
(a) *Antes* (Adverb).
    E.g.: *Iremos al cine, pero haremos el trabajo antes.*
        We shall go to the movies, but we shall do the work before (we go).
(2) *Antes de* (Prepositional construction + noun, pronoun, or infinitive).
    E.g.: *Mi hermano se graduó antes de mí.*
        My brother graduated before me.

        Fueron al cine antes de hacer su trabajo.
        They went to the movies before doing their work.
(3) *Antes de que* (Conjunctional construction + subjunctive).
    E.g.: *Salieron antes de que llegáramos.*
        They left before we arrived.

ANTES DE vs. *DELANTE DE*

(Prepositional constructions).
(a) *Antes de* = "Before," used for temporal relationships.
(b) *Delante de* = "In front of," used for spatial relationships.
> E.g.: (a) *Se levantan antes de las ocho.*
> They get up before eight o'clock.

> (b) *La silla está delante de la mesa.*
> The chair is in front of the table.

ANY

(1) Affirmative indefinite adjective = *Algún, alguna.*
> E.g.: *¿Tienes algún dinero?*
> Do you have any money?
(2) Partitive (not translated into Spanish).
> E.g.: *¿Tiene Ud. plátanos?*
> Do you have any bananas?
(3) Meaning "No matter which" = *Cualquier(a).*
> E.g.: *Tome Ud. cualquier libro que le guste.*
> Take any book (no matter which one) you like.
(4) Negative indefinite adjective "No, not any" = *Ningún, ninguna.*
> E.g.: *Ninguna revista me interesa.*
> I am not interested in any magazine.
(5) Affirmative indefinite pronoun = *Alguno (-a, -os, -as).*
> E.g.: *¿Hay algunos que prefieren pescado?*
> Are there any who prefer fish?
(6) Negative indefinite pronoun "Not any" = *Ninguno (-a, -os, -as).*
> E.g.: *¿Las bailarinas? No he visto a ninguna.*
> The ballerinas? I haven't seen any.

ANYHOW

(Adverb).
(1) Meaning "At any rate" = *De todas formas, de todos modos.*
> E.g.: *No podré ir contigo de todos modos* (or *de todas formas*).
> I will not be able to go with you anyhow.
(2) Meaning "In any way whatever, any old way" = *De cualquier modo.*
> E.g.: *Hace su tarea de cualquier modo.*
> He does his homework any (old) way.

ANYONE, ANYBODY

(Indefinite pronoun).
(1) In an affirmative sentence = *Alguien, alguno.*
> E.g.: *Alguno puede entrar.*
> Anyone may enter.
(2) In a negative sentence ("not . . . anyone, not . . . anybody") = *Nadie, ninguno.*
> E.g.: *No veo a nadie* (or *ninguno*).
> I don't see anybody.
(3) In an interrogative sentence = *Alguien, alguno.*
> E.g.: *¿Hay alguien* (or *alguno) aquí?*
> Is anybody here?
(4) Meaning "Anybody whatsoever" = *Cualquiera.*
> E.g.: *Cualquiera puede explicártelo.*
> Anybody can explain it to you.

ANYTIME

(Adverbial expression) = *Cuando quieras* or *en cualquier momento.*
E.g.: *Puedes entrar cuando quieras.*
　　　You may enter anytime.

ANYWAY

See **ANYHOW**

ANYWHERE

(Adverb).
(1) In an affirmative sentence: *En todas partes, en* (or *a*) *cualquier parte,* or *dondequiera.*
　　E.g.: *Esto se puede encontrar en todas partes* (or *dondequiera*).
　　　　This can be found anywhere.
　　　　Puedes andar dondequiera.
　　　　You may walk anywhere.
(2) In a negative sentence:
　　(a) *En ninguna parte* (if there is no movement).
　　　　E.g.: *No la encontré en ninguna parte.*
　　　　　　I didn't find her anywhere.
　　(b) *A ninguna parte* (if there is movement).
　　　　E.g.: *No voy a ninguna parte.*
　　　　　　I'm not going anywhere.

APAGAR

(Transitive verb) = "To put out, to extinguish, to turn off."
Conjugated like **llegar**.

APARECER

(Intransitive verb) = "To appear."
Conjugated like **conocer**.

APENAS

(1) (Adverb) = "Barely, hardly, scarcely."
　　E.g.: *Apenas podía andar.*
　　　　He could hardly walk.
(2) (Conjunction) = "No sooner . . ." (generally placed at the beginning of the sentence).
　　E.g.: *Apenas había terminado que me dieron más trabajo.*
　　　　No sooner had I finished than they gave me more work.

APOCOPATION

Apocopation *(el apócope)* is the dropping of a word ending.
See **ADJECTIVES, AGREEMENT OF**

APODERARSE

(Reflexive verb) = "To take possession (by force) of."
E.g.: *Los enemigos se apoderaron de la fortaleza.*
　　　The enemy took possession of the fortress.

APOLOGIZING

Apologies are conveyed by the following expressions:
(a) *Disculparse de* (for) *con* (to).
   E.g.: *Tendrás que disculparte del insulto con Pedro.*
      You will have to apologize to Peter for the insult.
(b) *Pedir perdón (a).*
   E.g.: *Le pido perdón a Ud. por llegar tarde.*
      I apologize to you for arriving late.
(c) *Presentar sus excusas.*
   E.g.: *Le presenté mis excusas a mi vecino por haber hecho tanto ruido.*
      I apologized to my neighbor for having made so much noise.
(d) *¡Perdón!* or *¡Disculpe!*
   Sorry!
(d) *Lo siento mucho.*
   I'm very sorry.
(f) *Sentí mucho que* + subjunctive.
   I was sorry that . . .

APOYAR, APOYARSE (EN)

(1) *Apoyar* (Transitive verb) = "To lean."
   E.g.: *Apoyé la cabeza en la mesa.*
      I leaned my head on the table.
(2) *Apoyarse en* (Reflexive verb) = "To lean on, to rely on."
   E.g.: *Me apoyé en la pared.*
      I leaned against the wall.

   Me apoyo en ti para terminar el trabajo.
   I am relying on you to finish the job.

APPOSITIVE

An appositive *(un apositivo)* is a noun or pronoun placed beside another noun or pronoun to explain or identify it. The definite and indefinite articles are usually omitted before appositives.
E.g.: *El señor Rodríguez, presidente de la compañia, se jubilará el año próximo.*
   Mr. Rodríguez, *the presdient of the company*, will retire next year.

APROVECHAR

(Transitive verb) = "To take advantage of."
NOTE:
The preposition "of" is included in the verb.
E.g.: *Aprovechamos la oportunidad de aprender la lengua.*
   We took advantage of the opportunity to learn the language.

AQUEL, AQUELLA (-OS, -AS)

(Demonstrative adjective) = "That . . . (over there)."
E.g.: *¿Ven Uds. aquel castillo a lo lejos?*
   Do you see that castle in the distance?
NOTE:
The corresponding demonstrative pronoun has a written accent.
See **AQUÉL, AQUÉLLA (-OS, -AS)**

AQUÉL, AQUÉLLA (-OS, -AS)

(Demonstrative pronoun) = "That . . . that one (over there)."
E.g.: *Conozco a esta muchacha pero no a aquélla.*
    I know this girl, but not that one.
NOTE:
The corresponding demonstrative adjective has no written accent.
See **AQUEL, AQUELLA (-OS, -AS)**
See also **FORMER . . . LATTER**

AQUELLO

(Neuter demonstrative pronoun) = "That (thing, business, matter)." It is used to refer to abstract ideas or things which have not been previously identified.
E.g.: *Aquello de su viaje a Portugal me sorprendió mucho.*
    That (matter about) his trip to Portugal surprised me very much.
See **ESO**
See also **ESTO**

AQUÍ vs. ACÁ

AQUÍ vs. AHÍ vs. ALLÍ

(Adverbs).
(a) *Aquí* = "Here," referring to a place near the speaker.
(b) *Ahí* = "There," referring to a place not very far from the speaker.
    E.g.: (a) *Pedro está aquí conmigo.*
           Peter is here with me.
       (b) *¡Deja tu abrigo ahí en el pasillo!*
           Leave your coat there in the hallway.
(c) *Allí* = "There," referring to a place far from the speaker.
    E.g.: *Mi hermano se ha ido a Chile y ahora vive allí.*
         My brother has gone to Chile and now he lives there.

ARGÜIR

(Transitive verb) = "To argue."
Conjugated like **construir**.

ARITHMETICAL OPERATIONS

The terminology for arithmetical expressions is:
(1) Addition *(la adición* or *la suma)*:
    E.g.: *Cuatro y tres son siete.*
       Four and three make seven.
(2) Subtraction *(la sustracción* or *la resta)*:
    E.g.: *Siete menos tres son cuatro.*
       Seven minus three makes four.
(3) Multiplication *(la multiplicación)*:
    E.g.: *Tres por cinco son quince.*
       Three times five is fifteen.
(4) Division *(la división)*:
    E.g.: *Diez dividido por cinco son dos* or *Diez entre cinco son dos.*
       Ten divided by five is two.

AROUND

(1) *Alrededor* (Adverb).
E.g.: *Hay una casa y un jardín alrededor.*
There is a house and a garden around (it).
(2) *Alrededor de* (Preposition).
E.g.: *Plantaron unas flores alrededor de la casa.*
They planted some flowers around the house.
(3) *A eso de* (Preposition meaning "approximately").
E.g.: *Llegarán a eso de las tres.*
They will arrive around three o'clock.
See **A ESO DE**

ARREPENTIRSE (DE)

(Reflexive verb) = "To repent (for)."
E.g.: *El verdadero criminal nunca se arrepiente de sus crímenes.*
The true criminal never repents for his crimes.

ARTICLE

An article *(un artículo)* is a word placed before a noun to give it definiteness or indefiniteness. In Spanish the article also indicates the number and the gender of the noun.
See **ARTICLES, DEFINITE**
See also **ARTICLES, INDEFINITE**

ARTICLE, NEUTER

The neuter article *lo* is used before adjectives or past participles to form abstract nouns or ideas.
E.g.: *Lo mejor de la comida fue el postre.*
The best (part) of the meal was the dessert.

Lo dicho es un secreto.
What was said is a secret.

ARTICLES, CONTRACTION OF

see **CONTRACTION: A + EL**
See also **CONTRACTION: DE + EL**

ARTICLES, DEFINITE

(Los artículos definidos). They are words which come before the noun to give them specificity, and correspond to "the" in English.
FORMS:
Masculine singular: *el*
Feminine singular: *la*
Masculine plural: *los*
Feminine plural: *las*
Neuter: *lo*
USAGE:
The definite article is used:
(a) Before a noun taken in the general sense.
E.g.: *Los deportes son muy populares.*
Sports are very popular.

(b) Before names of languages (except after *hablar* and the preposition *en*), and after verbs meaning to learn *(aprender)*, to practice *(practicar)*, to read *(leer)*, to write *(escribir)*, to study *(estudiar)*.

    E.g.: *El inglés es difícil.*
        English is difficult.

    BUT: *Hablamos español.*
        We speak Spanish.

        Estudian alemán.
        They study German.

NOTE:

The article *is* used if there is an adverb between the verb and the name of the language.

E.g.: *Hablan bien el alemán.*
     They speak German well.

(c) Before a title, except when addressing the person.

    E.g.: *El general Duarte.*
        General Duarte.

        El profesor Méndez.
        Professor Méndez.

    BUT: *Buenos días, señor Villegas.*
        Hello, Mr. Villegas.

NOTE:

No article is used before *Don, Doña, San, Santo, Santa.*

E.g.: *Don Pedro.*
     Peter.

     Doña María.
     Mary.

     Santo Tomás.
     Saint Thomas.

     San Juan.
     Saint John.

     Santa María.
     Saint Mary.

(d) Before days of the month.

    E.g.: *El tres de agosto.*
        The third of August.

(e) With days of the week (except after *ser*), but only in the sense of repeated or habitual times.

    E.g.: *No vamos a la universidad el sábado.*
        We don't go to the university on Saturdays.

    BUT: *Iré al teatro sábado.*
        I shall go to the theater on Saturday.

(f) Before days of the week modified by *antes* or *siguiente*.

    E.g.: *Fuimos al centro el martes antes de la fiesta.*
        We went downtown the Tuesday before the party.

        Vinieron el viernes siguiente.
        They came the following Friday.

(g) With the names of seasons.

    E.g.: *Me gusta el invierno.*
        I like winter.

(h) Sometimes, before infinitives used as nouns.

    E.g.: *El viajar es agradable.*
        Traveling is pleasant.

    BUT: *Fumar es malo para la salud.*
        Smoking is bad for your health.

(i) The neuter article *lo* is used with adjectives used as nouns to express an abstract idea or a quality.

> E.g.: *Lo peligroso me atrae.*
>
>> That which is dangerous attracts me.

NOTES:

(1) *Lo* + adjective or adverb + *que* = "How (to what extent)."

> E.g.: *Yo comprendo lo difícil que es.*
>
>> I understand how difficult it is.

(2) Since *lo* is neuter, it is invariable.

(j) With parts of the body or articles of clothing.

> E.g.: *Se lavan las manos.*
>
>> They wash their hands

(k) Before a phrase beginning with *de*, instead of the possessive pronoun.

> E.g.: *Mi chaqueta y la de mi hermano.*
>
>> My jacket and my brother's (the one of my brother).

(l) To form possessive pronouns: *el mío, la mía, los nuestros,* etc.

> E.g.: *Tu coche es americano pero el suyo es japonés.*
>
>> Your car is American, but his is Japanese.

See **PRONOUNS, POSSESSIVE**

OMISSION OF THE DEFINITE ARTICLE

The definite article is not used:

(a) Before a title when one is addressing the person.

> E.g.: *Buenos días, profesor Méndez.*
>
>> Hello, Professor Méndez.

(b) After the verb *hablar* and verbs meaning to learn *(aprender)*, to practice *(practicar)*, to read *(leer)*, to write *(escribir)*, to study *(estudiar)* before the name of a language.

> E.g.: *Ella habla chino.*
>
>> She speaks Chinese.
>
> *Escribo japonés.*
>
>> I write Japanese.

(c) After the preposition *en* before the name of a language.

> E.g.: *El libro está escrito en ruso.*
>
>> The book is written in Russian.

(d) With the verb *ser* and a profession or nationality.

> E.g.: *Es ingeniero.*
>
>> He is an engineer.
>
> *Son ingleses*
>
>> They are English.

(e) Before nouns placed in apposition.

> E.g.: *Madrid, capital de España, está situada a orillas del río Manzanares.*
>
>> Madrid, the capital of Spain, is situated on the banks of the Manzanares River.

(f) Before the number following the name of a monarch or a pope.

> E.g.: *Alfonso XIII.*
>
>> Alphonse XIII.
>
> *Juan XXIII.*
>
>> John XXIII.

ARTICLES (IN APPOSITIVES)

See **APPOSITIVES**

ARTICLES, INDEFINITE

(Los artículos indefinidos). They are words which come before the nouns to indicate that they are taken in an unidentified or unidentifiable sense, and correspond to "a, an, or some" in English.

FORMS:

Masculine singular: *un*

Feminine singular: *una*

Masculine plural: *unos*

Feminine plural: *unas*

NOTES:

(1) The singular forms *un, una* also mean the numeral "one."

E.g.: *Tengo una hermana.*

I have one sister.

(2) The indefinite article must be repeated before each noun in a series.

E.g.: *Había un elefante, un tigre y una jirafa.*

There was an elephant, a tiger, and a giraffe.

(3) The plural forms *unos, unas* also mean "a few, several, some."

E.g.: *Tengo unas amigas en el colegio.*

I have a few friends at school.

OMISSION OF THE INDEFINITE ARTICLE:

The indefinite article is omitted:

(1) when it is not emphasized.

E.g.: *Hay libros y periódicos en la biblioteca.*

There are books and newspapers in the library.

(2) after the verb *ser* and before nouns of nationality, profession, or religion.

E.g.: *Ella es boliviana.*

She is Bolivian.

Es profesor.

He is a professor.

Somos católicos.

We are Catholic.

ARTICLES, OMISSION OF
See **ARTICLES, DEFINITE**
See also **ARTICLES, INDEFINITE**

ARTICLES REFERRING TO PREVIOUSLY STATED NOUNS

The definite article may be used to refer back to a noun stated previously in the sentence.

E.g.: *He encontrado a las amigas de Juana y las de Carolina.*

I met Joan's friends and Caroline's (those of Caroline).

ARTICLES WITH GEOGRAPHICAL NAMES
See **GEOGRAPHICAL NAMES**

ARTICLES WITH NAMES OF SEASONS
See **SEASONS**

ARTICLES WITH WEIGHTS AND MEASURES
See **WEIGHTS AND MEASURES**

AS

(1) (Conjunction) "as" in comparisons = *Tan . . . como.*
    E.g.: *No es tan alto como yo.*
        He is not as tall as I.
        Corre tan rápidamente como yo.
        He runs as fast as I.
(2) (Conjunction) "as" meaning "when, while" = *Cuando.*
    E.g.: *Cuando entraba en mi casa vi a un ladrón salir por la ventana.*
        As I was entering my house, I saw a thief going out the window.
(3) (Conjunction) "as" meaning "because, since" = *Desde que, ya que,* or *puesto que.*
    E.g.: *Ya que estoy enfermo no puedo salir.*
        As I am ill, I can't go out.
(4) (Preposition) "as" meaning "in the capacity of" = *Como.*
    E.g.: *Hablo como padre de dos hijos.*
        I am speaking as a father of two children.
(5) (Preposition) "as" meaning "because" = *Como.*
    E.g.: *Como no hablo inglés, no lo comprendo.*
        As I don't speak English, I don't understand him.

AS IF, AS THOUGH

(Idiomatic construction) = *Como si* + imperfect or pluperfect subjunctive.
E.g.: *Come como si estuviera muerto de hambre.*
    He eats as if he were dead (= dying) of hunger.
    Gritaba como si hubiera visto un tigre.
    He was screaming as though he had seen a tiger.
See **COMO SI**
See also **"SI" CLAUSES**

AS MUCH + NOUN + AS

(Idiomatic construction) = *Tanto* + noun + *como.*
E.g.: *Tienes tanto dinero como yo.*
    You have as much money as I.

AS MUCH AS

(Adverb) = *Tanto como.*
E.g.: *María trabaja tanto como Pedro.*
    Mary works as much as Peter.

ASÍ QUE

(Conjunctional construction).
(1) = "As soon as." It is followed by:
    (a) the indicative if there is no doubt or uncertainty:
        E.g.: *Siempre me levanto así que suena mi despertador.*
            I always get up as soon as my alarm clock rings.
    (b) the subjunctive if there is uncertainty or doubt.
        E.g.: *Me despertaré así que me llames.*
            I shall wake up as soon as you call me. [but you may never call me]
(2) = "So, you see . . ."
    E.g.: *Estoy muy ocupado, así que no pienso ir contigo.*
        I am very busy so, you see, I don't think I'll go with you.

ASISTIR (A)

(1) *Asistir a* (Intransitive verb) = "To attend, to be present at."
    E.g.: *No asistimos a misa.*
        We did not attend mass.
(2) *Asistir* (Transitive verb) = "To help, to attend to."
    E.g.: *El médico que le asiste es muy bueno.*
        The doctor who attends to him is very good.

ASK vs. ASK ABOUT vs. ASK FOR

See **HACER UNA PREGUNTA**
See also **PEDIR vs. PREGUNTAR**

ASOMARSE (A)

(Reflexive verb) = "To appear, to show up."
E.g.: *Julieta se asomó a la ventana para hablar con Romeo.*
      Juliet appeared at the window to speak with Romeo.

AT

(Preposition). Its translation depends on the context:
(a) Indicating position = *en, a.*
    E.g.: *Estamos en la cumbre de la colina.*
        We are at the top of the hill.

        Están sentados a la mesa.
        They are seated at the table.
(b) Indicating time = *a.*
    E.g.: *Ella llegará a las cinco.*
        She will arrive at five o'clock.
(c) Expressing price = *a.*
    E.g.: *Esto se vende a cuatrocientas pesetas la libra.*
        This sells at four hundred pesetas a pound.

AT THAT TIME

(1) Meaning "At that moment" = *En aquel momento.*
    E.g.: *En aquel momento llegó la policía.*
        At that time (moment), the police arrived.
(2) Meaning "In those days" = *En esa época.*
    E.g.: *En esa época había muchas enfermedades.*
        At that time (in those days), there were many diseases.

AT THE SAME TIME

(Idiomatic expression) = *Al mismo tiempo.*
E.g.: *Carmen y Juana estudiaron en la universidad al mismo tiempo.*
      Carmen and Jean studied at the university at the same time.

ATENDER

(Transitive verb) = "To pay attention, to attend to, to heed."
Conjugated like **perder**.

ATREVERSE A

(Reflexive verb) = "To dare."
E.g.: *No me atrevo a saltar en el agua.*
      I don't dare jump in the water.

AUGMENTATIVE ENDINGS

Augmentative endings are added to nouns to convey the idea of large size or, sometimes, of clumsiness, awkwardness, or unpleasantness. The most common augmentative endings are:
(a) *-acho (-a, -os, -as).*
    E.g.: *Un (hombre) rico* = a rich man
           Un (hombre) ricacho = a filthy rich man (pejorative)
(b) *-azo (-a, -os, -as).*
    E.g.: *Una madre* = a mother
           Una madraza = a very indulgent mother (pejorative)
(c) *-ote (-a, -es, -as).*
    E.g.: *Una conferencia larga* = a long lecture
           Una conferencia largota = an unbearably long lecture (pejorative)
(d) *-ón (-ona)*
    E.g.: *Un hombre* = a man
           Un hombrón = a big man
(e) *-ucho (-a, -os, -as).*
    E.g.: *Una casa* = a house
           Una casucha = a shack (pejorative)

AUN CUANDO

(Idiomatic construction) = "Even if, even though." It is followed by the indicative.
E.g.: *Vamos a la piscina aun cuando llueve.*
      We go to the swimming pool even if it rains.

AUN vs. AÚN

(1) (Adverb) *Aun* = "Even."
    E.g.: *Los leí todos, aun los escritos en español.*
          I read them all, even those written in Spanish.
(2) (Adverb) *Aún* = "Still, yet."
    E.g.: *Aún no sé si vendrán.*
          I still don't know if they will come.

AUNQUE

(Conjunction) = "Although." It is followed by: (a) the indicative, if there is no doubt or uncertainty, or (b) the subjunctive, if there is doubt, uncertainty, anticipation, or indefiniteness.
E.g.: (a) *No habla inglés aunque vive en Londres desde 1975.*
          He does not speak English although he has been living in London since 1975.
     (b) *Aunque viva en Londres por veinte años nunca aprenderá el inglés.*
          Although he might live in London for twenty years, he will never learn English.

AUXILIARY VERB

See **VERBS, AUXILIARY**
See also **PROGRESSIVE TENSES; TENSES, COMPOUND**

AVERGONZAR

(Transitive verb) = ''To shame.''
PRES.: *avergüenz-o, -as, -a, avergonzamos, avergonzáis, avergüenzan.*
IMPERF.: *avergonz-aba, -abas, -aba, -ábamos, -abais, -aban.*
PRETER.: *avergoncé, avergonz-aste, -ó, -amos, -asteis, -aron.*
FUT.: *avergonzar-é, -ás, -á, -emos, -éis, -án.*
CONDIT.: *avergonzar-ía, -ías, -ía, -íamos, -íais, -ían.*
SUBJ. PRES.: *avergüenc-e, -es, -e, avergoncemos, avergoncéis, avergüencen.*
SUBJ. IMPERF. 1: *avergonz-ara, -aras, -ara, -áramos, -arais, -aran.*
SUBJ. IMPERF. 2: *avergonz-ase, -ases, -ase, -ásemos, -aseis, -asen.*
INFORMAL IMPERAT.: *avergüenza (tú), no avergüences (tú); avergonzad (vosotros), avergoncéis (vosotros).*
FORMAL IMPERAT.: *avergüence (Vd.); avergoncemos; avergüencen (Vds.).*
PRES. PARTIC.: *avergonzando.*
PAST PARTIC.: *avergonzado.*
NOTE:
The reflexive verb *avergonzarse* = ''To be ashamed.''

AVERIGUAR

(Transitive verb) = ''To ascertain, to find out.''
PRES.: *averigu-o, -as, -a, -amos, -áis, -an.*
IMPERF.: *averigu-aba, -abas, -aba, -ábamos, -abais, -aban.*
PRETER.: *averigü-é, -aste, -ó, -amos, -asteis, -aron.*
FUT.: *averiguar-é, -ás, -á, -emos, -éis, -án.*
CONDIT.: *averiguar-ía, -ías, -ía, -íamos, -íais, -ían.*
SUBJ. PRES.: *averigü-e, -es, -e, -emos, -éis, -en.*
SUBJ. IMPERF. 1: *averigu-ara, -aras, -ara, -áramos, -arais, -aran.*
SUBJ. IMPERF. 2: *averigu-ase, -ases, -ase, -ásemos, -aseis, -asen.*
INFORMAL IMPERAT.: *averigua (tú), no averigües (tú); averiguad (vosotros), no averigüéis (vosotros).*
FORMAL IMPERAT.: *averigüe (Vd.); averigüemos; averigüen (Vds.).*
PRES. PARTIC.: *averiguando.*
PAST PARTIC.: *averiguado.*

B

BACK

(1) The noun ''the back'' = *Las espaldas.*
    E.g.: *Me duelen las espaldas.*
        I have a backache.
(2) The adjective ''back'' = *último (-a, -os, -as).*
    E.g.: *La última fila de asientos.*
        The back row of seats.
(3) The adverb ''back'' = *atrás.*
    E.g.: *Los niños están atrás.*
        The children are in back.

(4) The idiom "to go back" = *volver*.

E.g.: *Volvieron a España.*

They went back to Spain.

(5) The idiom "to be back" = *estar de vuelta*.

E.g.: *Manuel no está de vuelta.*

Manuel is not back.

(6) The idiom "to send back" = *devolver*.

E.g.: *Voy a devolver el libro.*

I'm going to send the book back.

BAJO

(Preposition) = "Under."

NOTE:

It is never used in the physical sense of "underneath." This is expressed by the prepositional construction *Debajo de*.

E.g.: *España era muy conservadora bajo el gobierno de Franco.*

Spain was very conservative under the government of Franco.

See **ABAJO DE**

See also **DEBAJO DE**

BASTANTE

(1) The adverb *bastante* = "Enough."

E.g.: *He estudiado bastante.*

I have studied enough.

(2) The advective *bastante* (plural *bastantes*).

E.g.: *Tenemos bastantes libros.*

We have enough books.

BASTANTE + adjective + PARA + infinitive

This construction means "adjective + enough + verb."

E.g.: *Eres bastante inteligente para comprender el problema.*

You are intelligent enough to understand the problem.

BASTAR

(Intransitive verb) = "To suffice, to be enough."

NOTE:

The person is an indirect object.

E.g.: *Me bastan cinco horas para hacer esto.*

Five hours are enough for me to finish this.

to BE HAVING . . . + past participle

(Idiomatic construction)

E.g.: *Hago reparar mi coche.*

I am having my car repaired.

See **HACER + infinitive**

BECAUSE vs. BECAUSE OF

(1) The conjunction "Because" = *Porque*. It is followed by a clause in the indicative mood.
   E.g.: *Me quedé en la cama porque tenía un resfriado.*
      I stayed in bed because I had a cold.
(2) The preposition "Because of" = *A causa de*. It is followed by a noun or pronoun.
   E.g.: *Me quedé en la cama a causa de mi resfriado.*
      I stayed in bed because of my cold.

NOTE:

Avoid using *porque* at the beginning of a sentence. Use *como* instead.
E.g.: *Como estaba cansado se quedó en casa.*
      As he was tired he stayed home.

to BECOME

(1) *Hacerse* + noun or adjective (indicating that a serious effort is involved).
   E.g.: *Quiero hacerme médico.*
      I want to become a doctor.

      Pienso hacerme famoso tocando la guitarra.
      I intend to become famous playing the guitar.
(2) *Llegar a ser* (stressing the final result).
   E.g.: *Llegó a ser almirante.*
      He became an admiral.
(3) *Ponerse* + adjective or past participle (indicating an emotional, physical or mental change).
   E.g.: *Ella se puso muy enferma.*
      She became very ill.
(4) *Volverse* (indicating a violent or radical change).
   E.g.: *Se volvió loco.*
      He became mad.
(5) *Meterse a* (indicating an unexpected change of job or profession).
   E.g.: *Enseñó por ocho años, luego se metió a abogado.*
      He taught for eight years then he became a lawyer.

BEFORE + VERB (BEFORE + -ing)

(1) *Antes de* + infinitive.
   E.g.: *Ella se peinó antes de salir.*
      She combed her hair before going out.
(2) *Antes de que* + subjunctive.
   E.g.: *Ella se peinó antes de que volvieran sus padres.*
      She combed her hair before her parents returning.
                  (= before her parents returned.)

to BELONG

(a) *Pertenecer a*.
   E.g.: *Este coche pertenece a Miguel.*
      This car belongs to Michael.
(b) *Ser de*.
   E.g.: *Este coche es de Miguel.*
      This car is Michael's.

BESIDE

(Prepositional construction) = *Junto a.*
E.g.: *Se sentó junto a mí.*
      She sat down beside me.

BESIDES

(Adverbial expression) = *Además.*
E.g.: *Estoy cansado y además tengo dolor de cabeza.*
      I am tired and besides I have a headache.

it is BETTER to

(Idiomatic construction) = *Más vale* + infinitive.
E.g.: *Más vale leer que mirar la televisión.*
      It is better to read than to watch television.

BIEN

(Adverb) = "Well, very, much."
E.g.: *No lo comprendo bien.*
      I don't understand it well.
      Bien habéis trabajado.
      You have worked much.

BILLION

(Masculine noun) = *Billón, billones* or *mil millones.*
NOTE:
It requires the preposition *de* when followed by a noun.
E.g.: *Tres billones de personas.*
      Three billion people.

to be BORN

(Intransitive verb) = *Nacer.*
NOTE:
Since it refers most frequently to a past action it is generally encountered in the preterite.
E.g.: *Cervantes nació en 1547.*
      Cervantes was born in 1547.
The past participle is *nacido.*
E.g.: *Cervantes, nacido en 1547, es un escritor famoso.*
      Cervantes, born in 1547, is a famous writer.

BULLIR

(Transitive and intransitive verb) = "To boil."
PRES.: *bull-o, -es, -e, -imos, -ís, -en.*
IMPERF.: *bull-ía, -ías, -ía, -íamos, -íais, -ían.*
PRETER.: *bull-í, -iste, -ó, -imos, -isteis, -eron.*
FUT.: *bullir-é, -ás, -á, -emos, -éis, -án.*
CONDIT.: *bullir-ía, -ías, -ía, -íamos, -íais, -ían.*
SUBJ. PRES.: *bull-a, -as, -a, -amos, -áis, -an.*
SUBJ. IMPERF. 1: *bull-era, -eras, -era, -éramos, -erais, -eran.*
SUBJ. IMPERF. 2: *bull-ese, -eses, -ese, -ésemos, -eseis, -esen.*
INFORMAL IMPERAT.: *bulle (tú), no bullas (tú); bullid (vosotros), no bulláis (vosotros).*
FORMAL IMPERT.: *bulla (Vd.); bullamos; bullan (Vds.).*
PRES. PARTIC.: *bullendo.*
PAST PARTIC.: *bullido.*

BURLARSE DE

(Reflexive verb) = "To make fun of."
E.g.: *¡No te burles de mí!*
      Don't make fun of me!

BUSCAR

(Transitive verb) = "To look for, to seek."
PRES.: *busc-o, -as, -a, -amos, -áis, -an.*
IMPERF.: *busc-aba, -abas, -aba, -ábamos, -abais, -aban.*
PRETER.: *busqué, buscaste, buscó, buscamos, buscasteis, buscaron.*
FUT.: *buscar-é, -ás, -á, -emos, -éis, -án.*
CONDIT.: *buscar-ía, -ías, -ía, -íamos, -íais, -ían.*
SUBJ. PRES.: *busqu-e, -es, -e, -emos, -éis, -en.*
SUBJ. IMPERF. 1: *busc-ara, -aras, -ara, -áramos, -arais, -aran.*
SUBJ. IMPERF. 2: *busc-ase, -ases, -ase, -ásemos, -aseis, -asen.*
INFORMAL IMPERAT.: *busca (tú), no busques (tú); buscad (vosotros), no busquéis (vosotros).*
FORMAL IMPERAT.: *busque (Vd.); busquemos; busquen (Vds.).*
PRES. PARTIC.: *buscando.*
PAST PARTIC.: *buscado.*
NOTE:
No preposition is needed since it is a transitive verb.
E.g.: *Gabriela busca su cartera.*
      Gabriela is looking for her purse.

BUT

(Conjunction). There are two very different equivalents for "but" in Spanish.
(1) Meaning "nevertheless" = *Pero.*
    E.g.: *Es pobre pero es feliz.*
          He is poor but he is happy.
(2) Indicating a contradiction between the two parts of the sentence = *Sino.* In this case the first
    half of the sentence is always in the negative.
    E.g.: *No es inglés sino americano.*
          He is not English but American.
NOTE:
When the second part of the sentence is a new clause, use *sino que.*
E.g.: *No se quedaron en casa sino que salieron temprano.*
      They didn't stay at home but left early.

BY

(Preposition). Its translation depends on the context:
(1) Indicating the agent or the manner = *Por.*
    E.g.: *El libro fue escrito por Ortega y Gasset.*
          The book was written by Ortega y Gasset.

          Hay que pagar por cheque.
          You have to pay by check.
(2) Indicating proximity = *Cerca de.*
    E.g.: *El despacho está cerca de mi casa.*
          The office is by (near) my house.
(3) Meaning "across, by way of, through" = *Por.*
    E.g.: *Pasaron por España.*
          They went through (across) Spain.

(4) To express the time limit in the future = *Para.*
    E.g.: *Terminaremos el trabajo para mañana.*
          We shall finish the job by tomorrow.
(5) Expressing measurement = *Por.*
    E.g.: *10 metros por 12.*
          10 meters by 12.
(6) Followed by a gerund it is not translated:
    E.g.: *Se aprende una lengua viviendo en el país.*
          One learns a language by living in the country.

BY + VERB (BY + -ing)

The English construction "By + present participle" is translated by using the present participle alone in Spanish.
E.g.: *Empezando ahora podremos terminarlo pronto.*
    By starting now we shall be able to finish it promptly.
Do not use *por* or *para* for this construction.

C

CABER

(Intransitive verb) = "To fit, to be contained in."
PRES.: *quepo, cab-es, -e, -emos, -éis, -en.*
IMPERF.: *cab-ía, -ías, -ía, -íamos, -íais, -ían.*
PRETER.: *cup-e, -iste, -o, -imos, -isteis, -ieron.*
FUT.: *cabr-é, -ás, -á, -emos, -éis, -án.*
CONDIT.: *cabr-ía, -ías, -ía, -íamos, -íais, -ían.*
SUBJ. PRES.: *quep-a, -as, -a, -amos, -áis, -an.*
SUBJ. IMPERF. 1: *cupi-era, -eras, -era, -éramos, -erais, -eran.*
SUBJ. IMPERF. 2: *cupi-ese, -eses, -ese, -ésemos, -eseis, -esen.*
INFORMAL IMPERAT.: *cabe (tú), no quepas (tú); cabed (vosotros), no quepáis (vosotros).*
FORMAL IMPERAT.: *quepa (Vd.); quepamos; quepan (Vds.).*
PRES. PARTIC.: *cabiendo.*
PAST PARTIC.: *cabido.*

CADA

(Invariable adjctive) = "Each, every."
E.g.: *Cada frase.*
    Each sentence.
    Cada día.
    Every day.

CADA VEZ MÁS (MENOS)

(Idiomatic expressions) = "More and more; less and less."
E.g.: *Tengo cada vez más trabajo pero gano cada vez menos dinero.*
    I have more and more work but I earn less and less money.

CAER

(Intransitive verb) = "To fall."
PRES.: *caigo, caes, cae, caemos, caéis, caen.*
IMPERF.: *ca-ía, -ías, -ía, -íamos, -íais, -ían.*
PRETER.: *caí, caíste, cayó, caímos, caísteis, cayeron.*
FUT.: *caer-é, -ás, -á, -emos, -éis, -án.*
CONDIT.: *caer-ía, -ías, -ía, -íamos, -íais, -ían.*
SUBJ. PRES.: *caig-a, -as, -a, -amos, -áis, -an.*
SUBJ. IMPERF. 1: *cay-era, -eras, -era, -éramos, -erais, -eran.*
SUBJ. IMPERF. 2: *cay-ese, -eses, -ese, -ésemos, -eseis, -esen.*
INFORMAL IMPERAT.: *cae (tú), no caigas (tú); caed (vosotros), no caigáis (vosotros).*
FORMAL IMPERAT.: *caiga (Vd.); caigamos; caigan (Vds.).*
PRES. PARTIC.: *cayendo.*
PAST PARTIC.: *caído.*

CALLARSE

(Reflexive verb) = "To keep silent, to keep quiet."
E.g.: *Los alumnos se callan cuando el maestro entra.*
     The students keep quiet when the teacher enters.

CAMBIAR (DE)

(Transitive and intransitive verb) = "To change."
PRES.: *cambi-o, -as, -a, -amos, -áis, -an.*
IMPERF.: *cambi-aba, -abas, -aba, -ábamos, -abais, -aban.*
PRETER.: *cambi-é, -aste, -ó, -amos, -asteis, -aron.*
FUT.: *cambiar-é, -ás, -á, -emos, -éis, -án.*
CONDIT.: *cambiar-ía, -ías, -ía, -íamos, -íais, -ían.*
SUBJ. PRES.: *cambi-e, -es, -e, -emos, -éis, -en.*
SUBJ. IMPERF. 1: *cambi-ara, -aras, -ara, -ásemos, -aseis, -asen.*
INFORMAL IMPERAT.: *cambia (tú), no cambies (tú); cambiad (vosotros), no cambiéis (vosotros).*
FORMAL IMPERAT.: *cambien (Vd.); cambiemos; cambien (Vds.).*
PRES. PARTIC.: *cambiando.*
PAST PARTIC.: *cambiado.*
NOTES:
(1) The transitive verb *Cambiar* = "To change."
    E.g.: *Han cambiado el color del edificio.*
         They've changed the color of the building.
(2) The intransitive construction *Cambiar de* = "To change one thing for another."
    E.g.: *He cambiado de camisa.*
         I have changed shirts.
Note that the noun following *de* is singular.

CAN

(1) Meaning "Able to" = *Poder.*
    E.g.: *Pedro puede acompañarnos.*
         Peter can accompany us.
(2) Meaning "Know how" = *Saber.*
    E.g.: *¿Sabes conducir?*
         Can you drive?

CAN'T HELP

(Idiomatic construction).
(a) "It can't be helped" = *No hay remedio.*
(b) "Can't help + present participle" = *No poder menos de* + infinitive.
    E.g.: *No puedo menos de reír.*
        I can't help laughing.

CAPITALIZATION

The rules for using capital letters *(las mayúsculas)* in Spanish are the same as in English EXCEPT in the following cases:
(1) Only proper names and the first word of a sentence are capitalized.
(2) The pronoun *yo* is not capitalized (except at the beginning of a sentence).
(3) Days of the week and months are not capitalized.
    E.g.: *El martes, doce de febrero.*
        Tuesday, February twelfth.
(4) Names of languages are not capitalized.
    E.g.: *Hablan portugués.*
        They speak Portuguese.
(5) Adjectives of nationality and religion are not capitalized.
    E.g.: *Un general americano.*
        An American general.

        Son católicos.
        They are Catholic.
(6) Titles are not capitalized except when abbreviated.
    E.g.: *El señor Fuster.*
        Mister Fuster.
    BUT: *El Sr. Fuster.*
        Mr. Fuster.
(7) Such words as *avenida, calle, lago, mar, océano* are not capitalized when they are part of a place name.
    E.g.: *El océano Pacífico.*
        The Pacific Ocean.

        La calle Ortega.
        Ortega Street.
(8) In the titles of novels, plays, films, etc., only the first word and proper nouns are capitalized.
    E.g.: *La casa de Bernarda Alba.*
        The House of Bernarda Alba (a play by Federico García Lorca).

        La muerte de la emperatriz de la China.
        The Death of the Empress of China (a story by Rubén Darío).

CARDINAL NUMBERS
See **NUMBERS, CARDINAL**

CARECER DE + noun or pronoun

(Intransitive verb) = "To lack, to need."
E.g.: *Carecemos de medios para terminar el trabajo.*
    We lack the means to finish the job.

CASAR

(Transitive verb) = "To marry off."
E.g.: *Casamos a nuestra hija el mes pasado.*
    We married off our daughter last month.
See *CASARSE CON*

CASARSE CON

(Reflexive verb) = "To marry, to get married, to wed."
E.g.: *Julia se casó con Pedro.*
    Julie married Peter.
See **CASAR**

CAUSATIVE CONSTRUCTIONS WITH *HACER*

The "*Hacer* + infinitive" construction expresses the idea that someone causes an action to be performed by somebody or something else.
E.g.: *El profesor hace trabajar a los alumnos.*
    The teacher makes the students work.

    Hicieron arreglar el horno.
    They had the furnace fixed.
NOTE:
If there is only one object it is direct.
E.g.: *El profesor le hizo marcharse.*
    The teacher made him leave.

CERRAR

(Transitive verb) = "To close."
PRES.: *cierr-o, -as, -a, cerramos, cerráis, cierran.*
IMPERF.: *cerr-aba, -abas, -aba, -ábamos, -abais, -aban.*
PRETER.: *cerr-é, -aste, -ó, -amos, -asteis, -aron.*
FUT.: *cerrar-é, -ás, -á, -emos, -éis, -án.*
CONDIT.: *cerrar-ía, -ías, -ía, -íamos, -íais, -ían.*
SUBJ. PRES.: *cierr-e, -es, -e, cerremos, cerréis, cierren.*
SUBJ. IMPERF. 1: *cerr-ara, -aras, -ara, -áramos, -arais, -aran.*
SUBJ. IMPERF. 2: *cerr-ese, -ases, -ase, -ásemos, -aseis, -asen.*
INFORMAL IMPERAT.: *cierra (tú), no cierres (tú); cerrad (vosotros), no cerréis (vosotros).*
FORMAL IMPERAT.: *cierre (Vd.); cerremos; cierren (Vd.).*
PRES. PARTIC.: *cerrando.*
PAST PARTIC.: *cerrado.*

CH

Ch is the fourth letter of the Spanish alphabet. In Spanish dictionaries words beginning with *ch* are therefore listed under this heading, not after words beginning with *ce*.

CIEN(TO)

The numerical *ciento* ("hundred") drops the ending *-to* before a noun (masculine, feminine, singular or plural).
E.g.: *Libros de matemáticas, tiene por lo menos ciento.*
    Mathematics books, he has at least a hundred.
BUT: *Tiene por lo menos cien libros de matemáticas.*
    He has at least a hundred mathematics books.

CLASSROOM EXPRESSIONS

USEFUL CLASSROOM EXPRESSIONS

"How do you say ⎯⎯ in Spanish?"	= « *¿Cómo se dice ⎯⎯ en español?* »
"Please explain!"	= « *¡Explique (Vd.), por favor!* »
"Please translate!"	= « *¡Traduzca (Vd.), por favor!* »
"How do you spell ⎯⎯?"	= « *¿Cómo se escribe ⎯⎯?* »
"What does ⎯⎯ mean?"	= « *¿Qué significa ⎯⎯?* »
"Would you explain ⎯⎯?"	= « *¿Me quiere explicar ⎯⎯?* »
"What is the word for ⎯⎯?"	= « *¿Cómo se dice ⎯⎯?* »
"Please repeat!"	= « *¡Repita (Vd.), por favor!* »
"I don't understand."	= « *No comprendo.* »

CLAUSE

A clause *(una oración)* is a group of words which contains a subject and a predicate. It is:
(a) independent *(independiente)*:
   E.g.: *Irás a Costa Rica.*
         You will go to Costa Rica.
(b) subordinate *(subordinada)*:
   E.g.: *Si te dan permiso, irás a Costa Rica.*
         If they give you permission, you will go to Costa Rica.
(c) relative *(relativa)*, which is a subordinate clause beginning with a relative pronoun:
   E.g.: *Conozco al profesor que te enseña el español.*
         I know the teacher who teaches you Spanish.

COCER

(Transitive verb) = "To cook."
PRES.: *cuezo, cueces, cuece, cocemos, cocéis, cuecen.*
IMPERF.: *coc-ía, -ías, -ía, -íamos, -íais, -ían.*
PRETER.: *coc-í, -iste, -ió, -imos, -isteis, -ieron.*
FUT.: *cocer-é, -ás, -á, -emos, -éis, -án.*
CONDIT.: *cocer-ía, -ías, -ía, -íamos, -íais, -ían.*
SUBJ. PRES.: *cuez-a, -as, -a, cozamos, cozáis, cuezan.*
SUBJ. IMPERF. 1: *coci-era, -eras, -era, -éramos, -erais, -eran.*
SUBJ. IMPERF. 2: *coci-ese, -eses, -ese, -ésemos, -eseis, -esen.*
INFORMAL IMPERAT.: *cuece (tú), no cuezas (tú); coced (vosotros), no cozáis (vosotros).*
FORMAL IMPERAT.: *cueza (Vd.); cozamos; cuezan (Vds.).*
PRES. PARTIC.: *cociendo.*
PAST PARTIC.: *cocido.*

COGER

(Transitive verb) = "To seize, to grasp, to gather."
PRES.: *cojo, coges, coge, cogemos, cogéis, cogen.*
IMPERF.: *cog-ía, -ías, -ía, -íamos, -íais, -ían.*
PRETER.: *cog-í, -iste, -ió, -imos, -isteis, -ieron.*
FUT.: *coger-é, -ás, -á, -emos, -éis, -án.*
CONDIT.: *coger-ía, -ías, -ía, -íamos, -íais, -ían.*
SUBJ. PRES.: *coj-a, -as, -a, -amos, -áis, -an.*
SUBJ. IMPERF. 1: *cogi-era, -eras, -era, -éramos, -erais, -eran.*
SUBJ. IMPERF. 2: *cogi-ese, -eses, -ese, -ésemos, -eseis, -esen.*
INFORMAL IMPERAT.: *coge (tú), no cojas (tú); coged (vosotros), no cojáis (vosotros).*
FORMAL IMPERAT.: *coja (Vd.); cojamos; cojan (Vds.).*
PRES. PARTIC.: *cogiendo.*
PAST PARTIC.: *cogido.*

COLLECTIVE SUBJECT

When the subject of a verb is collective, the predicate is generally singular.

E.g.: *Vivimos nuestra vida en la tierra.*

      We live our lives on earth.

NOTE:

This contrasts with the English construction, which requires the plural.

COMENZAR

(Transitive verb) = "To begin, to commence."

PRES.: *comienzo, comienzas, comienza, comenzamos, comenzáis, comienzan.*

IMPERF.: *comenz-aba, -abas, -aba, -ábamos, -abais, -aban.*

PRETER.: *comencé, comenzaste, comenzó, comenzamos, comenzasteis, comenzaron.*

FUT.: *comenzar-é, -ás, -á, -emos, -éis, -án.*

CONDIT.: *comenzar-ía, -ías, -ía, -íamos, -íais, -ían.*

SUBJ. PRES.: *comience, comiences, comience, comencemos, comencéis, comiencen.*

SUBJ. IMPERF. 1: *comenz-ara, -aras, -ara, -áramos, -arais, -aran.*

SUBJ. IMPERF. 2: *comenz-ase, -ases, -ase, -ásemos, -aseis, -asen.*

INFORMAL IMPERAT.: *comienza (tú), no comiences (tú); comenzad (vosotros), no comencéis (vosotros).*

FORMAL IMPERAT.: *comience (Vd.); comencemos; comiencen (Vds).*

PRES. PARTIC.: *comenzando.*

PAST PARTIC.: *comenzado.*

NOTE:

Comenzar takes the preposition *a* before an infinitive.

COMER

(Transitive verb) = "To eat."

PRES.: *com-o, -es, -e, -emos, -éis, -en.*

IMPERF.: *com-ía, -ías, -ía, -íamos, -íais, -ían.*

PRETER.: *com-í, -iste, -ió, -imos, -isteis, -ieron.*

FUT.: *comer-é, -ás, -á, -emos, -éis, -án.*

CONDIT.: *comer-ía, -ías, -ía, -íamos, -íais, -ían.*

SUBJ. PRES.: *com-a, -as, -a, -amos, -áis, -an.*

SUBJ. IMPERF. 1: *comi-era, -eras, -era, -éramos, -erais, -eran.*

SUBJ. IMPERF. 2: *comi-ese, -eses, -ese, -ésemos, -eseis, -esen.*

INFORMAL IMPERAT.: *come (tú), no comas (tú); comed (vosotros), no comáis (vosotros).*

FORMAL IMPERAT.: *coma (Vd.); comamos; coman (Vds.).*

PRES. PARTIC.: *comiendo.*

PAST PARTIC.: *comido.*

COMMANDS

See **IMPERATIVE MOOD**

COMMANDS, INDIRECT

See **INDIRECT COMMANDS**

COMO

(1) the adverb *Como* = "As, like."

    E.g.: *Atrevido como un león.*

        Brave as a lion.

(2) The conjunction *Como* = "As, inasmuch as."

    E.g.: *Como es pobre no puede comprar un coche.*

        As he is poor, he cannot buy a car.

¡CÓMO NO!

(Idiomatic expression) = "Of course, obviously."

E.g.: *¿Vienes con nosotros? - ¡Cómo no!*
    "Are you coming with us?" "Of course!"

COMO SI

(Conjunctional construction) = "As if." *Como si* expresses a contrary-to-fact condition. It takes:

(a) the imperfect subjunctive to express a present condition.

(b) the pluperfect subjunctive to express a past condition.

    E.g.: (a) *Habla como si fuera el director.*

          He talks as if he were the director.

      (b) *Viven como si hubieran ganado un millón.*

          They live as if they had won a million.

See *"SI"* CLAUSES

COMPARATIVE AND SUPERLATIVE OF ADVERBS

See ADVERBS, COMPARATIVE AND SUPERLATIVE OF

COMPARISON OF ADJECTIVES

See ADJECTIVES, COMPARISON OF

COMPOUND TENSES

See TENSES, COMPOUND

COMPRAR

(Transitive verb) = "To buy."

NOTE:

The thing one buys is the direct object. The person from whom one buys is the indirect object.

E.g.: *Le compró un terreno a su vecino.*

    He bought a piece of land from his neighbor

    (or, depending on the context, for his neighbor.)

CON

(Preposition) = "With."

E.g.: *Los Ramos se han ido con sus hijos.*

    Mr. and Mrs. Ramos have left with their children.

NOTE:

Con combines with the personal pronouns *mí, ti,* and *sí* to form *conmigo, contigo,* and *consigo.*

E.g.: *Llevo la maleta conmigo.*

    I take the briefcase with me.

    Quiero ir contigo.

    I want to go with you.

    Hay que llevar el pasaporte consigo.

    You have to have the passport with you.

CON + infinitive

See PREPOSITIONS + infinitive

CON TAL QUE

(Conjunctional construction) = "Provided that." It is followed by the subjunctive.

E.g.: *Saldré mañana temprano con tal que me despiertes.*

I shall leave early tomorrow provided that you wake me up.

CONDITIONAL CLAUSES

See **"SI" CLAUSES**

CONDITIONAL TENSES

The conditional *(el potencial)* tenses present the action of the verb as:

(a) possible.

E.g.: *Este hombre trabajaría todo el tiempo.*

This man would work all the time.

(b) dependent upon some condition.

E.g.: *Este hombre trabajaría si pudiera.*

This man would work if he could.

There are two conditional tenses:

PRESENT CONDITIONAL:

FORMATION:

Same stem as that used for the future + *ía, ías, ía, íamos, íais, ían.*

E.g.: Infinitive: *Hablar* → Future: *Hablaré* → Conditional: *Hablaría.*

Venir →   *Vendré* →   *Vendría.*

NOTE:

If the future stem is irregular, the conditional stem has the same irregularity.

USAGE:

(a) To state a future action in a past context. That is, if the main verb is in a past tense and the subordinate verb is in the future in relation to the main verb, then the subordinate verb is in the conditional.

E.g.: *Pienso que ella vendrá.* → *Yo pensaba que ella vendría.*

I think she will come. → I thought that she would come.

Dicen que llegarán mañana. → *Dijeron que llegarían mañana.*

They say they will arrive tomorrow. → They said they would arrive tomorrow.

(b) In the result clause of a condition introduced by "*si* + imperfect subjunctive."

E.g.: *Si tuviera mucho dinero, compraría un coche.*

If I had a lot of money, I would buy a car.

PAST CONDITIONAL:

FORMATION:

Conditional of the auxiliary verb *haber* + past participle.

E.g.: *Habría comido.*

I would have eaten.

USAGE:

(a) In the result clause of an unrealized condition introduced by "*si* + pluperfect subjunctive."

E.g.: *Si hubiera ganado el premio, habría comprado un coche.*

If I had won the prize, I would have bought a car.

(b) To express conjecture or speculation in the past.

E.g.: *Habría robado la pintura.*

The rumor is that he stole the painting (He probably robbed the painting).

¿Quién sería?

I wonder who it was (Who could it have been?).

See **"SI" CLAUSES**

CONDUCIR

(Transitive verb) = "To drive, to conduct, to lead."
PRES.: *conduzco, conduc-es, -e, -imos, -ís, -en.*
IMPERF.: *conducía, -ías, -ía, -íamos, -íais, -ían.*
PRETER.: *conduj-e, -iste, -o, -imos, -isteis, -eron.*
FUT.: *conducir-é, -ás, -á, -emos, -éis, -án.*
CONDIT.: *conducir-ía, -ías, -ía, -íamos, -íais, -ían.*
SUBJ. PRES.: *conduzc-a, -as, -a, -amos, -áis, -an.*
SUBJ. IMPERF. 1: *conduj-era, -eras, -era, -éramos, -erais, -eran.*
SUBJ. IMPERF. 2: *conduj-ese, -eses, -ese, -ésemos, -eseis, -esen.*
INFORMAL IMPERAT.: *conduce (tú), no conduzcas (tú); conducid (vosotros), no conduzcáis (vosotros).*
FORMAL IMPERAT.: *conduzca (Vd.); conduzcamos; conduzcan (Vds.).*
PRES. PARTIC.: *conduciendo.*
PAST PARTIC.: *conducido.*

CONJUGATIONS, REGULAR
See **REGULAR VERBS**

CONJUNCTIONS

A conjunction *(una conjunción)* is an invariable word which serves to link two clauses or two words in a sentence. Examples of conjunctions are: *antes de que, a pesar de que, cuando, entonces, ni, o, para que, pero, sino, y,* etc.
(1) The following conjunctions take the subjunctive:
    (a) *A fin de que* = "So that."
        E.g.: *Estudiaremos mucho a fin de que el profesor esté satisfecho.*
        We shall study hard so that the teacher will be pleased.
    (b) *A menos que* = "Unless."
        E.g.: *Iré al campo a menos que haga frío.*
        I shall go to the country unless it is cold.
    (c) *Antes de que* = "Before."
        E.g.: *Llegará antes de que salgas.*
        He will arrive before you leave.
    (d) *Con tal que* = "Provided that."
        E.g.: *Iré a Salamanca con tal que me acompañes.*
        I shall go to Salamanca provided that you accompany me.
    (e) *En caso de que* = "In case."
        E.g.: *Se llevó el paraguas en caso de que llueva.*
        He took his umbrella in case it might rain.
    (f) *Para que* = "So that."
        E.g.: *Vendrán mañana para que hablemos.*
        They will come tomorrow so that we might talk.
    (g) *Sin que* = "Without."
        E.g.: *Salen sin que su padre les vea.*
        They go out without their father seeing them.
(2) The following conjunctions are followed by the subjunctive only if they introduce a statement containing doubt, uncertainty, indefiniteness, or some anticipation:
    (a) *Así que* = "As soon as."
        E.g.: *Así que entraron, se sentaron.*
        As soon as they entered they sat down.
        BUT: *Te escribiré así que reciba tu carta.*
        I shall write you as soon as I receive your letter.

(b) *Aunque* = "Although, even though."
   E.g.: *Aunque tengo veinte años no sé conducir.*
   Although I am twenty years old, I do not know how to drive.
   BUT: *Aunque cueste mucho dinero, quiero comprar este coche.*
   Even though it might cost a lot of money, I want to buy that car.

(c) *Cuando* = "When."
   E.g.: *Cuando estoy de vacaciones no contesto el teléfono.*
   When I am on vacation, I don't answer the telephone.
   BUT: *Mi padre volverá cuando se termine el congreso.*
   My father will return when the conference ends.

(d) *De manera que* = "So that, in such a way that."
   E.g.: *Es demasiado grande de manera que no cabe en esta caja.*
   It is too big, so it doesn't fit in this box.
   BUT: *Compraré una caja grande de manera que esto quepa dentro.*
   I shall buy a large box so that this might fit in it.

(e) *De modo que* = "So that, in such a way that."
   E.g.: *Tengo mucho que hacer de modo que no puedo salir contigo.*
   I have a lot to do so (that) I cannot go out with you.
   BUT: *Saldré de la oficina temprano de modo que no tengas que esperar mucho tiempo.*
   I shall leave the office early so that you don't have to wait a long time.

(f) *Después de que* = "After."
   E.g.: *Fuimos al teatro después de que se cerraron los almacenes.*
   We went to the theater after the department stores closed.
   BUT: *Mis primos vendrán después de que terminen los cursos.*
   My cousins will come after classes are over.

(g) *En cuanto* = "As soon as."
   E.g.: *Siempre me levanto en cuanto suena el despertador.*
   I always get up as soon as the alarm clock rings.
   BUT: *Te llamaré en cuanto reciba noticias.*
   I shall call you as soon as I receive news.

(h) *Hasta que* = "Until."
   E.g.: *Siempre me quedo en la oficina hasta que he terminado mi trabajo.*
   I always stay in the office until I have finished my work.
   BUT: *Esta noche me quedaré en la oficina hasta que termine mi trabajo.*
   Tonight I shall stay in the office until I finish my work.

(l) *Luego que* = "As soon as."
   E.g.: *Salgo de casa luego que termino de desayunar.*
   I leave the house as soon as I have eaten breakfast.
   BUT: *Saldré de casa luego que me llames.*
   I shall leave the house as soon as you call me.

(j) *Mientras* = "While."
   E.g.: *No puedo escuchar la radio mientras estudio.*
   I cannot listen to the radio while I study.
   BUT: *Me quedaré en este hotel de lujo mientras tenga dinero.*
   I shall stay in this luxury hotel while I have money.

(k) *Tan pronto como* = "As soon as."
   E.g.: *Salieron de la casa tan pronto como oyeron el ruido.*
   They left the house as soon as they heard the noise.
   BUT: *Vendré tan pronto como termine de leer el libro.*
   I shall come as soon as I finish reading the book.

CONJUNCTIONS

+ SUBJUNCTIVE (always)	+ SUBJUNCTIVE (if anticipation, doubt, indefiniteness, uncertainty)	+ PAST TENSE if actions are not simultaneous
A fin de que	Así que	Cuando
A menos que	Aunque	Después de que
Antes de que	Cuando	Tan pronto como
Con tal que	De manera que	
En caso que	De modo que	
Para que	Después (de) que	
Sin que	En cuanto	
	Luego que	
	Mientras	
	Tan pronto como	

CONMIGO, CONTIGO, CONSIGO

See **CON**

CONOCER

(Transitive verb) = "To know, to be acquainted with."
PRES.: conozco, conoc-es, -e, -emos, -éis, -en.
IMPERF.: conocía, -ías, -ía, -íamos, -íais, -ían.
PRETER.: conoc-í, -iste, -ió, -imos, -isteis, -ieron.
FUT.: conocer-é, -ás, -á, -emos, -éis, -án.
CONDIT.: conocer-ía, -ías, -ía, -íamos, -íais, -ían.
SUBJ. PRES.: conozc-a, -as, -a, -amos, -áis, -an.
SUBJ. IMPERF. 1: conoci-era, -eras, -era, -éramos, -erais, -eran.
SUBJ. IMPERF. 2: conoci-ese, -eses, -ese, -ésemos, -eseis, -esen.
INFORMAL IMPERAT.: conoce (tú), no conozcas (tú); conoced (vosotros), no conozcáis (vosotros).
FORMAL IMPERAT.: conozca (Vd.); conozcamos; conozcan (Vds.).
PRES. PARTIC.: conociendo.
PAST PARTIC.: conocido.
NOTES:
(1) In the preterite, *conocer* means "To meet."
    E.g.: *La conocí el año pasado.*
        I met her last year.
(2) Do not confuse *conocer* with *saber*. See below.

CONOCER vs. *SABER*

Both verbs are translated as "To know," but BEWARE of the difference in meaning:
(1) *Conocer* = "To know, to be acquainted with (a person or a place)."
    E.g.: *Conozco a Carlos.*
        I know Charles.
        Conocen bien el museo del Prado.
        They know the Prado Museum well.
(2) *Saber* = "To know a fact, something one has learned, to know how."
    E.g.: *Mi abuelo no sabe manejar.*
        My grandfather does not know how to drive.
See **SABER vs. CONOCER vs. PODER**

CONSEGUIR

(Transitive verb) = "To get, to succeed in."
Conjugated like *SEGUIR.*
E.g.: *No consiguieron encontrar el libro.*
    They didn't succeed in finding the book.

CONSENTIR EN (QUE)

(Intransitive verb) = "To agree to, to consent to."
(1) *Consentir en* + infinitive.
    E.g.: *Mi padre consintió en prestarme el coche.*
        My father agreed to lend me the car.
(2) *Consentir en que* + subjunctive.
    E.g.: *Mi padre consintió en que yo tomara el coche.*
        My father agreed that I might take the car.

CONSISTIR

(Intransitive verb) = "To consist of." It is followed by the preposition *en.*
E.g.: *El trabajo consiste en arreglar las piezas de la máquina.*
    The work consists of repairing the parts of the machine.

CONSONANT

A consonant *(una consonante)* is a letter other than *a, e, i, o, u, y.* Consonants represent sounds produced by obstructing the flow of air partially or completely during speech.

CONSTRUIR

(Transitive verb) = "To construct, to build."
PRES.: *construy-o, -es, -e, construimos, construís, construyen.*
IMPERF.: *constru-ía, -ías, -ía, -íamos, -íais, -ían.*
PRETER.: *construí, construiste, construyó, construimos, construisteis, construyeron.*
FUT.: *construir-é, -ás, -á, -emos, -éis, -án.*
CONDIT.: *construir-ía, -ías, -ía, -íamos, -íais, -ían.*
SUBJ. PRES.: *construy-a, -as, -a, -amos, -áis, -an.*
SUBJ. IMPERF. 1: *construy-era, -eras, -era, -éramos, -erais, -eran.*
SUBJ. IMPERF. 2: *construy-ese, -eses, -ese, -ésemos, -eseis, -esen.*
INFORMAL IMPERAT.: *construye (tú), no construyas (tú); construid (vosotros), no construyáis (vosotros).*
FORMAL IMPERAT.: *construya (Vd.); construyamos; construyan (Vds.).*
PRES. PARTIC.: *construyendo.*
PAST PARTIC.: *construído.*

CONTAR

(Transitive verb) = "To count, to tell, to relate."
PRES.: *cuent-o, -as, -a, contamos, contáis, cuentan.*
IMPERF.: *cont-aba, -abas, -aba, -ábamos, -abais, -aban.*
PRETER.: *cont-é, -aste, -ó, -amos, -asteis, -aron.*
FUT.: *contar-é, -ás, -á, -emos, -éis, -án.*
CONDIT.: *contar-ía, -ías, -ía, -íamos, -íais, -ían.*
SUBJ. PRES.: *cuent-e, -es, -e, contemos, contéis, cuenten.*
SUBJ. IMPERF. 1: *cont-ara, -aras, -ara, -áramos, -arais, -aran.*
SUBJ. IMPERF. 2: *cont-ase, -ases, -ase, -ásemos, -aseis, -asen.*
INFORMAL IMPERAT.: *cuenta (tú), no cuentes (tú); contad (vosotros), no contéis (vosotros).*
FORMAL IMPERAT.: *cuente (Vd.); contemos; cuenten (Vds.).*
PRES. PARTIC.: *contando.*
PAST PARTIC.: *contado.*

CONTAR CON

(Idiomatic expression) = "To count on, to rely on."
E.g.: *Cuento contigo para que me ayudes.*
    I'm counting on you to help me.

CONTINUAR

(Transitive verb) = "To continue."
PRES.: *continú-o, -as, -a, continuamos, continuáis, continúan.*
IMPERF.: *continu-aba, -abas, -aba, -ábamos, -abais, -aban.*
PRETER.: *continu-é, -aste, -ó, -amos, -asteis, -aron.*
FUT.: *continuar-é, -ás, -á, -emos, -éis, -án.*
CONDIT.: *continuar-ía, -ías, -ía, -íamos, -íais, -ían.*
SUBJ. PRES.: *continú-e, -es, -e, continuemos, continuéis, continúen.*
SUBJ. IMPERF. 1: *continu-ara, -aras, -ara, -áramos, -arais, -aran.*
SUBJ. IMPERF. 2: *continu-ase, -ases, -ase, -ásemos, -aseis, -asen.*
INFORMAL IMPERAT.: *continúa (tú), no continúes (tú); continuad (vosotros), no continuéis (vosotros).*
FORMAL IMPERAT.: *continúe (Vd.); continuemos; continúen (Vds.).*
PRES. PARTIC.: *continuando.*
PAST PARTIC.: *continuado.*

to CONTINUE + VERB (-ing)

(Transitive verb) = *Seguir* or *continuar* + present participle.
E.g.: *Sigue leyendo.*
    Continue reading.
    Siguieron hablando durante toda la conferencia.
    They continued talking throughout the lecture.

CONTRA

(Preposition) = "Against."
E.g.: *Yo voto contra el partido radical.*
    I vote against the radical party.

CONTRACTION: *A* + *EL*

When the preposition *a* is followed by the definite article *el*, the two words contract to *al*.
E.g.: *Vamos al hotel.*
    We are going to the hotel.
NOTE:
There is no contraction when *a* is followed by *la, los* or *las.*
E.g.: *Vamos a las tiendas.*
    We are going to the stores.

CONTRACTION: *DE* + *EL*

When the preposition *de* is followed by the article *el*, the two words contract to *del*.
E.g.: *Las noticias del día.*
    The news of the day.
NOTE:
There is no contraction when *de* is followed by *la, los* or *las.*
E.g.: *La casa de los Jiménez.*
    The Jiménez' house.

CONTRARY-TO-FACT STATEMENTS

Contrary-to-fact statements are conveyed by the *si* + imperfect subjunctive or *si* + pluperfect subjunctive construction.

E.g.: *Si yo fuera rico, compraría una casa nueva.*

If I were rich, I would buy a new house.

Si ella hubiera comprado el coche, lo conduciría por la ciudad.

If she had bought the car, she would drive it around town.

See *"SI"* CLAUSES

CONVENIR EN

(Intransitive verb) = "To agree on, to agree to."

E.g.: *Convinieron en ir a la playa.*

They agreed to go to the beach.

COULD

(1) When "could" = "was (were) able to" (past tense of "can"), it is conveyed by *Poder* in the imperfect or preterite, depending on the context.

E.g.: *Podía tocar el piano durante horas.*

She could play the piano for hours on end.

Pude obtener el permiso sin dificultad.

I was able to obtain the permit without difficulty.

(2) When "could" is the conditional tense of "can," it is conveyed by the conditional tense of *Poder.*

E.g.: *Podrías viajar a Panamá si quisieras.*

You could travel to Panama if you wanted to.

See **CONDITIONAL MOOD**

CRECER

(Intransitive verb) = "To grow."

PRES.: *crezco, creces, crece, crecemos, crecéis, crecen.*

IMPERF.: *crec-ía, -ías, -ía, -íamos, -íais, -ían.*

PRETER.: *crec-í, -iste, -ió, -imos, -isteis, -ieron.*

FUT.: *crecer-é, -ás, -á, -emos, -éis, -án.*

CONDIT.: *crecer-ía, -ías, -ía, -íamos, -íais, -ían.*

SUBJ. PRES.: *crezc-a, -as, -a, -amos, -áis, -an.*

SUBJ. IMPERF. 1: *creci-era, -eras, -era, -éramos, -erais, -eran.*

SUBJ. IMPERF. 2: *creci-ese, -eses, -ese, -ésemos, -eseis, -esen.*

INFORMAL IMPERAT.: *crece (tú), no crezcas (tú); creced (vosotros), no crezcáis (vosotros).*

FORMAL IMPERAT.: *crezca (Vd.); crezcamos; crezcan (Vds.).*

PRES. PARTIC.: *creciendo.*

PAST PARTIC.: *crecido.*

CREER

(Transitive verb) = "To think, to believe."

PRES.: *cre-o, -es, -e, -emos, -éis, -en.*

IMPERF.: *cre-ía, -ías, -ía, -íamos, -íais, -ían.*

PRETER.: *creí, creíste, creyó, creímos, creísteis, creyeron.*

FUT.: *creer-é, -ás, -á, -emos, -éis, -án.*

CONDIT.: *creer-ía, -ías, -ía, -íamos, -íais, -ían.*

SUBJ. PRES.: *cre-a, -as, -a, -amos, -áis, -an.*

SUBJ. IMPERF. 1: *crey-era, -eras, -era, -éramos, -erais, -eran.*

SUBJ. IMPERF. 2: *crey-ese, -eses, -ese, -ésemos, -eseis, -esen.*

INFORMAL IMPERAT.: *cree (tú), no creas (tú); creed (vosotros), no creáis (vosotros).*

FORMAL IMPERAT.: *crea (Vd.); creamos; crean (Vds.).*

PRES. PARTIC.: *creyendo.*

PAST PARTIC.: *creído.*

NOTE:
In the affirmative, *creer* indicates a belief or opinion and is normally followed by the indicative in the subordinate clause.
E.g.: *Creo que tienes razón.*
  I think you are right.
In the negative, *no creer* frequently indicates doubt or uncertainty and is normally followed by the subjunctive in the subordinate clause.
E.g.: *No creo que vengan mañana.*
  I don't think they will come tomorrow.

CRUZAR

(Transitive verb) = "To cross."
PRES.: *cruz-o, -as, -a, -amos, -áis, -an.*
IMPERF.: *cruz-aba, -abas, -aba, -ábamos, -abais, -aban.*
PRETER.: *crucé, cruz-aste, -ó, -amos, -asteis, -aron.*
FUT.: *cruzar-é, -ás, -á, -emos, -éis, -án.*
CONDIT.: *cruzar-ía, -ías, -ía, -íamos, -íais, -ían.*
SUBJ. PRES.: *cruc-e, -es, -e, -emos, -éis, -en.*
SUBJ. IMPERF. 1: *cruz-ara, -aras, -ara, -áramos, -arais, -aran.*
SUBJ. IMPERF. 2: *cruz-ase, -ases, -ase, -ásemos, -aseis, -asen.*
INFORMAL IMPERAT.: *cruza (tú), no cruces (tú); cruzad (vosotros), no crucéis (vosotros).*
FORMAL IMPERAT.: *cruce (Vd.); crucemos; crucen (Vds.).*
PRES. PARTIC.: *cruzando.*
PAST PARTIC.: *cruzado.*

CUAL vs. CUÁL

(1) The relative pronoun *Cual* (plural: *Cuales*) is masculine and feminine = "Which, who, whom." It is usually preceded by the definite article: *el cual, la cual, lo cual, los cuales, las cuales,* and is used to indicate the more distant of two antecedents.
  E.g.: *La madre de Pedro, la cual está enferma, no podrá acompañarnos.*
    Peter's mother, who is ill, will not be able to accompany us.

NOTE:
Lo cual (neuter) = "Which (fact or idea)."
E.g.: *Destruyeron hasta la iglesia, lo cual me sorprende.*
  They destroyed even the church, which (fact) surprises me.

(2) The interrogative pronoun *Cuál* (plural *Cuáles*) is masculine and feminine = "Which one(s)."
  E.g.: *¿Cuál de estas pinturas prefiere Vd.?*
    Which one of these paintings do you prefer?

NOTE:
When used before the verb *ser, cuál(es)* asks for identification. It translates as "which" or "what."
E.g.: *¿Cuáles son sus libros predilectos?*
  What (or which) are your favorite books?

CUALQUIER(A), CUALESQUIERA

(1) Indefinite pronoun = "Anyone, anybody." It is both masculine and feminine.
  E.g.: *Cualquiera puede entenderlo.*
    Anyone can understand it.
(2) Indefinite adjective = "Any, whichever." The final *a* is dropped when it is followed by a noun or adjective.
  E.g.: *Cualquier otro hombre o cualquier otra mujer puede entenderlo.*
    Any other man or any other woman can understand it.

CUANDO

(Conjunction) = "When." It is followed by:
(a) the indicative:
    E.g.: *Voy al teatro cuando no tengo que trabajar.*
        I go to the theater when I don't have to work.
(b) the subjunctive (if it refers to a future action):
    E.g.: *Iremos al teatro cuando tengamos menos trabajo que hacer.*
        We shall go to the theater when we have less work to do.
See **AUN CUANDO**

CUÁNDO

(Interrogative adverb) = "When." Like all interrogatives it has a written accent.
E.g.: *¿Cuándo llega el avión?*
     When does the plane arrive?

CUANTO (-A, -OS, -AS)

(1) (Indefinite adjective) = "As many as, as much as, whatever."
    E.g.: *Te daré cuantas fotografías quieres* (if the number is known: indicative mood).
        I shall give you as many photographs as you want.

        Te daré cuantas fotografías quieras (if the number is not known: subjunctive mood).
        I shall give you as many photographs as you want.
(2) (Relative pronoun) = "As many as, as much as, all (that which), everything (which), whatever."
    E.g.: *Iba fotográfiando cuanto veía.*
        He went about photographing everything he saw.
(3) (Adverb of quantity) = "As much as."
    E.g.: *Trabajan cuanto pueden.*
        They work as much as they can.

CUÁNTO (-A, -OS, -AS)

(Interrogative adjective) = "How many, how much"
E.g.: *¿Cuántas revistas tienes?*
     How many magazines do you have?

     ¿Cuánto dinero?
     How much money?
It is also used as an exclamative adjective meaning "How, how much, how many."
E.g.: *¡Cuánto ha crecido!*
     How he has grown!

CUANTO ANTES

(Idiomatic expression) = "As soon as possible."
E.g.: *¡Llame Vd. al médico cuanto antes!*
     Call the doctor as soon as possible!

CUANTO MÁS . . . (TANTO) MÁS

(Adverbial construction) = "The more . . . the more."
E.g.: *Cuanto más comes (tanto) más te engordas.*
     The more you eat, the more you gain weight.

CUANTO MENOS . . . TANTO MENOS

(Adverbial construction) = "The less . . . the less."
E.g.: *Cuanto menos estudias tanto menos aprendes.*
     The less you study, the less you learn.

CUBRIR

(Transitive verb) = "To cover."
PRES.: *cubr-o, -es, -e, -imos, -ís, -en.*
IMPERF.: *cubr-ía, -ías, -ía, -íamos, -íais, -ían.*
PRETER.: *cubr-í, -iste, -ió, -imos, -isteis, -ieron.*
FUT.: *cubrir-é, -ás, -á, -emos, -éis, -án.*
CONDIT.: *cubrir-ía, -ías, -ía, -íamos, -íais, -ían.*
SUBJ. PRES.: *cubr-a, -as, -a, -amos, -áis, -an.*
SUBJ. IMPERF. 1: *cubri-era, -eras, -era, -éramos, -erais, -eran.*
SUBJ. IMPERF. 2: *cubri-ese, -eses, -ese, -ésemos, -eseis, -esen.*
INFORMAL IMPERAT.: *cubre (tú), no cubras (tú); cubrid (vosotros), no cubráis (vosotros).*
FORMAL IMPERAT.: *cubra (Vd.); cubramos; cubran (Vds.).*
PRES. PARTIC.: *cubriendo.*
PAST PARTIC.: *cubierto.*

CUIDAR

(1) *Cuidar a* (Transitive verb) = "To take care of, to look after."
    E.g.: *Una madre cuida a sus hijos.*
         A mother takes care of her children.
(2) *Cuidar de* (Intransitive verb) = "To take care of, to look after."
    E.g.: *Tengo que cuidar de mi hermanito.*
         I have to look after my little brother.
NOTE:
The reflexive verb = "To look after oneself."
E.g.: *Ese viejo no se cuida.*
       That old man doesn't look after himself.

CUMPLIR (CON)

(Transitive verb) = "To fulfill, to keep (one's promise)."
E.g.: *Ese traidor no cumplió con su palabra.*
       That traitor did not keep his word.
NOTES:
(1) *Cumplir* without the preposition *con* means "To complete."
    E.g.: *Cumplimos la tarea ayer.*
         We completed the assignment yesterday.
(2) The expression *Cumplir . . . años* = "To have a birthday."
    E.g.: *Guillermo cumplió cuatro años ayer.*
         William had his fourth birthday (reached the age of four) yesterday.

CUYO (-A, -OS, -AS)

(Relative pronoun indicating possession) = "Whose."
NOTE:
It functions as an adjective and must agree with the noun it modifies, not with the noun it refers to.
E.g.: *La película cuyo título he olvidado.*
       The film whose title I have forgotten.

D

DAR

(Transitive verb) = "To give."
PRES.: doy, das, da, damos, dáis, dan.
IMPERF.: d-aba, -abas, -aba, -ábamos, -abais, -aban.
PRETER.: di, diste, dio, dimos, disteis, dieron.
FUT.: dar-é, -ás, -á, -emos, -éis, -án.
CONDIT.: dar-ía, -ías, -ía, -íamos, -íais, -ían.
SUBJ. PRES.: dé, des, dé, demos, deis, den.
SUBJ. IMPERF. 1: di-era, -eras, -era, -éramos, -erais, -eran.
SUBJ. IMPERF. 2: di-ese, -eses, -ese, -ésemos, -eseis, -esen.
INFORMAL IMPERAT.: da (tú), no des (tú); dad (vosotros), no deis (vosotros).
FORMAL IMPERAT.: dé (Vd.); demos; den (Vds.).
PRES. PARTIC.: dando.
PAST PARTIC.: dado.

DAR A + noun or pronoun

(Transitive verb) = "To face, to look out upon."
E.g.: *Mi cuarto da a la calle.*
   My room faces the street.

DAR A CONOCER

(Verbal idiom) = "To make known."
E.g.: *Me dio a conocer el nombre de la nueva cantante.*
   He made known to me the name of the new singer.

DAR CON + noun or pronoun

(Verbal idiom) = "To stumble upon, to find, to run into."
E.g.: *Di con el señor Duarte ayer.*
   I ran into Mr. Duarte last night.
See **TROPEZAR CON**

DAR GANAS DE + infinitive

(Verbal idiom) = "To make (one) feel like + verb."
E.g.: *Esto me da ganas de llorar.*
   That makes me feel like crying.

DAR LA HORA

(Verbal idiom) = "To strike (the time)."
E.g.: *Ya dan las ocho.*
   It's already striking eight o'clock.

DAR LA VUELTA

(Verbal idiom).
(1) *Dar la vuelta al mundo* = To go around the world.
(2) *Dar la vuelta a una página* = To turn a page.
(3) *Dar la vuelta* = To change right around, to alter completely.
See **DAR UNA VUELTA**

DAR LAS GRACIAS (A)

(Verbal idiom) = "To thank, to give thanks to."
E.g.: *Hay que darles las gracias a tus padres.*
    You have to thank your parents.

DAR POR

(Verbal idiom) = "To consider as."
E.g.: *Yo doy por cierto que vamos a ganar.*
    I consider it certain that we are going to win.

DAR PRESTADO

(Verbal idiom) = "To lend."
E.g.: *¿Me puedes dar prestado tu lápiz?*
    Can you lend me your pencil?
See **PEDIR PRESTADO**

DAR RECUERDOS

(Verbal idiom) = "To give regards (to)."
E.g.: *Dale mis recuerdos a Juan.*
    Give my regards to John.

DAR UN PASEO

(Verbal idiom) = "To take a walk."
E.g.: *Mis padres dan un paseo todos los días.*
    My parents take a walk every day.
NOTE:
Dar un paseo en coche = "To go for a drive."
E.g.: *Dimos un paseo en el coche de Arturo.*
    We went for a drive in Arthur's car.

DAR UNA VUELTA

(Idiomatic expression) = "To take a walk, a stroll."
E.g.: *¿Quieres dar una vuelta conmigo?*
    Do you want to go for a walk with me?
See **DAR LA VUELTA**

DARSE CUENTA DE (QUE)

(Verbal idiom) = "To realize."
(1) When introducing a noun or pronoun: *Darse cuenta de.*
    E.g.: *Cuando leyeron el periódico se dieron cuenta de la situación.*
        When they read the newspaper they realized the situation.
(2) When introducing a clause: *Darse cuenta de que* + indicative.
    E.g.: *Al leer el periódico se dieron cuenta de que la situación estaba grave.*
        On reading the newspaper they realized that the situation was serious.

DARSE LA MANO

(Reciprocal construction) = "To shake hands."
E.g.: *Al encontrarse en la calle se dieron la mano.*
    Upon meeting in the street they shook hands.

DARSE PRISA

(Verbal idiom) = "To hurry."
E.g.: *¡Démonos prisa! Ya son las ocho y media.*
Let's hurry! It's already half past eight.

DATES

For the first day of the month use the ordinal number.
E.g.: *El primero de julio.*
The first of July.
All other days of the month are expressed in cardinal numbers.
E.g.: *El dos de julio.*
The second of July.

El veinticinco de abril.
The twenty-fifth of April.

NOTES:

(1) Always use the definite article *el* before the date.
(2) Names of months are not capitalized in Spanish: *enero, febrero, marzo, abril, mayo, junio, julio, agosto, se(p)tiembre, octubre, noviembre, diciembre.*
(3) To ask the date:
E.g.: *¿A cuántos estamos?*
What is the date?
or: *¿Cuál es la fecha de hoy?*
What is today's date?
(4) Do *not* use a preposition to say "On . . ." with a date.
E.g.: On April 23rd = *el 23 de abril.*
(5) The years are said as follows:
1492 = *mil cuatrocientos noventa y dos.*
1776 = *mil setecientos setenta y seis.*
(6) Remember to use the preposition *de* between the day and the month.
E.g.: *El tres de octubre.*
The third of October.
(7) A date, meaning an appointment = *Una cita.*

DAYS OF THE WEEK

Days of the week are masculine:

Monday = *el lunes*	Friday = *el viernes*
Tuesday = *el martes*	Saturday = *el sábado*
Wednesday = *el miércoles*	Sunday = *el domingo*
Thursday = *el jueves*	

NOTES:

(1) The definite article is always used with days of the week except after the verb *ser.*
E.g.: *Vendré el martes.*
I shall come on Tuesday.
BUT: *Hoy es jueves.*
Today is Thursday.
(2) Days of the week are not capitalized in Spanish. No preposition is used to convey the English "on."
E.g.: *No voy a clase los martes.*
I don't go to class on Tuesdays.
Iré a verte el viernes.
I shall go see you on Friday.
(3) The plural form for the days of the week is the same as the singular. When used in the plural, a repeated occurrence is indicated.
E.g.: *Voy a clase los lunes y los miércoles.*
I go to class on Mondays and Wednesdays.

DE

(Preposition). Its translation depends on the context:

(a) expressing possession = "of" (or conveyed by the possessive apostrophe in English).

E.g.: *El coche de María.*

Mary's car (the car of Mary).

(b) after a superlative = "in."

E.g.: *El edificio más alto de la ciudad.*

The tallest building in the city.

(c) indicating distance or origin = "from."

E.g.: *Toledo no está muy lejos de Madrid.*

Toledo is not very far from Madrid.

Mis abuelos son de Aranjuez.

My grandparents are from Aranjuez.

(d) indicating the subject or topic = "about" (or indicated by apposition in English).

E.g.: *Mi libro de matemáticas.*

My mathematics book.

Un curso de inglés.

An English course.

(e) indicating material = "of" (or indicated by an adjective in English).

E.g.: *Una mesa de madera.*

A wooden table.

(f) indicating content = "of."

E.g.: *Una botella de cerveza.*

A bottle of beer.

(g) indicating authorship = "by."

E.g.: *Una obra de Cortázar.*

A work by Cortázar.

(h) expressing purpose of an object = (expressed by apposition in English).

E.g.: *Una máquina de coser.*

A sewing machine.

(i) expressing manner or style = "in."

E.g.: *Estaba vestida de seda.*

She was dressed in silk.

(j) expressing cause = "with, for."

E.g.: *Está enfermo de pulmonía.*

He is ill with pneumonia.

(k) describing a person = "with."

E.g.: *El muchacho de pelo rubio.*

The boy with blond hair.

NOTES:

(1) *De* is used before a numeral to mean "than."

E.g.: *Tengo más de dos mil pesetas.*

I have more than two thousand pesetas.

(2) *De* is used in time expressions when a specific hour and a specific portion of the day are indicated, to mean "in."

E.g.: *Son las tres de la tarde.*

It is three o'clock in the afternoon.

BUT: When no specific hour is stated, "in" is translated as *por.*

E.g.: *No hay clases por la tarde.*

There are no classes in the afternoon.

(3) *De* is used after the numeral *millón, millones.*

E.g.: *Tres millones de dólares.*

Three million dollars.

DE + infinitive

See **PREPOSITIONS + infinitive**

DE + nouns

In English nouns are often used as adjectives (e.g.: A Spanish teacher, the bus schedule). In Spanish this is not possible. The qualifying noun must be preceded by the preposition *de:*
E.g.: *Un profesor de español.*
> A Spanish teacher (i.e. a teacher of Spanish.)
> *El horario del autobús.*
> The bus schedule.

DE ACUERDO

(Adverbial idiom) = "In agreement."
E.g.: *Estamos de acuerdo.*
> We are in agreement.

DE BUEN HUMOR

(Adverbal idiom) = "In a good mood."
E.g.: *Carolina siempre está de buen humor.*
> Caroline is always in a good mood.

See *DE MAL HUMOR.*

DE BUENA GANA

(Adverbal idiom) = "Willingly."
E.g.: *Te ayudaré de buena gana.*
> I shall help you willingly.

See *DE MALA GANA*

DE CUANDO EN CUANDO

(Adverbial idiom) = "From time to time."
E.g.: *Vamos al teatro de cuando en cuando.*
> We go to the theatre from time to time.

DE DÍA, DE NOCHE

(Idiomatic expressions) = "By day, during the day; By night, during the night."
E.g.: *Mi padre trabaja de noche y duerme de día.*
> My father works at night and sleeps during the day.

DE ESTA MANERA

(Adverbal idiom) = "In this manner, in this way."
E.g.: *Salieron temprano y de esta manera evitaron el tránsito.*
> They left early and in this way they avoided the traffic.

DE HOY EN ADELANTE

(Adverbial idiom) = "Henceforth, from now on."
E.g.: *De hoy en adelante no podrás conducir mi coche.*
> From now on you will not be allowed to drive my car.

DE MAL HUMOR

(Adverbal idiom) = "In a bad mood."
E.g.: *Cuando me levanto temprano siempre estoy de mal humor.*
> When I get up early I am always in a bad mood.

See *DE BUEN HUMOR*

DE MALA GANA

(Adverbal idiom) = "Unwillingly, against one's will."
E.g.: *Consintió en venir, pero de mala gana.*
     He agreed to come, but unwillingly.
See **DE BUENA GANA**

DE MANERA QUE

(Conjunctional construction) = "So that, in such a way that." It is followed by:
(a) the indicative
     E.g.: *Hace mucho ruido de manera que nadie puede dormir.*
          He makes a lot of noise so that (= as a result) nobody can sleep.
(b) the subjunctive (if there is intention or purpose).
     E.g.: *Habla en voz muy baja de manera que nadie le entienda.*
          He speaks in low voice so that nobody can (= might be able to) hear him.

DE MEMORIA

(Adverbial idiom) = "By heart."
E.g.: *Aprendieron el poema de memoria.*
     They learned the poem by heart.

DE MENOS

See **ECHAR DE MENOS**

DE MODA

(Adverbial idiom) = "In style, fashionable."
E.g.: *Josefina está vestida muy de moda.*
     Josephine is very fashionably dressed.

DE MODO QUE

(Conjunctional construction) = "So that, in such a way that." It is followed by:
(a) the indicative
     E.g.: *La silla es demasiado alta de modo que el niño no puede subirla.*
          The chair is too high so (as a result) the child cannot climb onto it.
(b) the subjunctive (if there is intention or purpose).
     E.g.: *Subió en una silla, de modo que todos le pudieran ver.*
          He climbed on a chair so that everyone might be able to see him.

DE NADA

(Idiomatic expression) = "Don't mention it, you're welcome."
E.g.: *- Gracias por ayudarme. - De nada.*
     "Thanks for helping me." "Don't mention it."

DE NINGÚN MODO

(Adverbial expression) = "By no means."
E.g.: *De ningún modo puedes salir esta noche.*
     By no means may you go out tonight.

DE NUEVO

(Adverbial idiom) = "Again, anew."
E.g.: *Tuvimos que hacer el trabajo de nuevo.*
     We had to do the work anew.

DE or *A* (with verbs)

(a) The following verbs require the preposition *a* before an infinitive:

acercarse a, to approach
acertar a, to happen (by chance) to
acostumbrarse a, to become accustomed to
aprender a, to learn to
apresurarse a, to hasten to
aspirar a, to aspire to
atreverse a, to dare to
ayudar (a alguien) a, to help (someone) to
comenzar a, to begin to
convidar (a alguien)a, to invite (someone) to
correr a, to run to
decidirse a, to decide to
dedicarse a, to devote oneself to
disponerse a, to get ready to

empezar a, to begin to
enseñar (a alguien) a, to teach (someone) to
invitar (a alguien) a, to invite (someone) to
ir a, to go to
llegar a, to succeed in
negarse a, to refuse to
obligar (a alguien) a, to force (someone) to
ponerse a, to begin to
principiar a, to begin to
regresar a, to return to (to . . . again)
resignarse a, to resign oneself to
salir a, to go out to
venir a, to come to
volver a, to return to (to . . . again)

(b) The following verbs require the preposition *de* before an infinitive:

acabar de, to have just
acordarse de, to remember to
alegrarse de, to be glad to
cesar de, to stop

dejar de, to fail to, to stop
encargarse de, to take charge of
olvidarse de, to forget to
tratar de, to try to

NOTES:

(1) Some verbs require the preposition *en* before an infinitive:

consentir en, to agree to
consistir en, to consist of
convenir en, to agree to

empeñarse en, to insist on
insistir en, to insist on
tardar en, to be long in, to delay in

(2) some verbs require the preposition *con* before an infinitive:

amenazar con, to threaten to
contar con, to count on

soñar con, to dream of

See **VERBS + (*A, CON, DE, EN,* or no preposition) + infinitive**
See also **PREPOSITIONS + infinitive**

DE OTRA MANERA

(Adverbial expression) = "In another way."
E.g.: *Tenemos que hacerlo de otra manera.*
We have to do it another way.

DE OTRO MODO

(Adverbal idiom) = "Otherwise, or else."
E.g.: *Haz tu tarea, de otro modo no podrás ir al cine.*
Do you homework or else you will not be able to go to the movies.

DE PAR EN PAR

(Adverbal idiom) = "From side to side (wide)."
E.g.: *Abrió la ventana de par en par.*
He opened the window wide.

DE PIE

(Adverbial idiom) = "Standing on one's feet."
E.g.: *Me quedé de pie el día entero.*
I stood on my feet all day.

DE PRISA

(Adverbial idiom) = "Hurriedly, in a hurry."
E.g.: *No hay mucho tiempo. Tenemos que hacerlo de prisa.*
    There is not much time. We have to do it in a hurry.

DE PRONTO

(Adverbial idiom) = "Suddenly, all of a sudden."
E.g.: *De pronto se levantaron y salieron.*
    Suddenly they stood up and left.

DE REOJO

(Adverbial idiom) = "Askance, out of the corner of one's eye."
E.g.: *Ella lo miró de reojo cuando dijo eso.*
    She looked at him from the corner of her eye when he said that.

DE REPENTE

(Adverbal idiom) = "Suddenly, all of a sudden."
E.g.: *De repente apareció un tigre.*
    Suddenly a tiger appeared.

DE RODILLAS

(Adverbal idiom) = "On one's knees."
Ponerse de rodillas = "To kneel."
E.g.: *Me pongo de rodillas cuando rezo.*
    I kneel when I pray.

DE SUERTE QUE

(Conjunctional construction) = "So (that), with the result that."
E.g.: *Me levanté tarde de suerte que perdí el autobús.*
    I got up late so (that) I missed the bus.

DE TODOS MODOS

(Adverbal idiom) = "At any rate, anyway."
E.g.: *No vinieron, o de todos modos no los vi.*
    They didn't come, or at any rate I didn't see them.

DE VERAS

(Adverbial idiom) = "Really, truly, honestly."
E.g.: *¿De veras que viste a la famosa estrella de cine?*
    Is it true that you saw the famous movie star?

DE VEZ EN CUANDO

(Adverbial idiom) = "From time to time."
E.g.: *Vamos al teatro de vez en cuando.*
    We go to the theater from time to time.

DE, verbs followed by

See **DE or A (with verbs)**

DEBAJO vs. DEBAJO DE

(1) *Debajo* (Adverb) = "Below, underneath."
    E.g.: *Las alcobas están en el segundo piso; la cocina está debajo.*
        The bedrooms are on the first floor; the kitchen is below.

(2) *Debajo de* (Prepositional construction) = "Below, beneath, under."
    E.g.: *El sótano está debajo de la cocina.*
        The cellar is underneath the kitchen.
See **ABAJO DE**

DEBER

(Transitive and intransitive verb) = "To owe, to have to, must, ought," *Deber* is used idiomatically to mean "Must, should, ought to," indicating obligation or duty.
E.g.: *Debo ir al centro mañana.*
    I have to go downtown tomorrow.
    Deberás trabajar todo el día.
    You will have to work all day.
    Deberíamos salir ahora.
    We ought to go out now.
NOTES:
(1) Do not confuse "should" and "would." "Should" is conveyed by using the conditional of *deber* + infinitive.
    E.g.: *Deberían pagar.*
        They should (ought to) pay.
    BUT: "Would" is conveyed by using the conditional of the verb.
    E.g.: *Pagarían si pudieran.*
        They would pay if they could.
(2) When "would" is used in English to indicate a repeated action, it must be conveyed in Spanish by the imperfect tense of the verb.
    E.g.: They would often go to the beach last year.
        Iban a menudo a la playa el año pasado.
(3) The imperfect subjunctive *debiera* is frequently used as an equivalent of the conditional *debería.*
    E.g.: *Debieras descansar un rato.*
        You ought to rest a while.

DECIMALS

The decimal point is a decimal comma *(la coma de decimales)* in Spanish.
E.g.: In English: $\pi = 3.141592\ldots$
    In Spanish: $\pi = 3,141592\ldots$
NOTE:
Conversely, the use of commas to separate numerals in English is replaced by the use of periods in spanish.
E.g.: In English: 1,234,567
    In Spanish: *1.234.567*

DECIR

(Transitive verb) = "To say, to tell."
PRES.: *digo, dices, dice, decimos, decís, dicen.*
IMPERF.: *dec-ía, -ías, -ía, -íamos, -íais, -ían.*
PRETER.: *dij-e, -iste, -o, -imos, -isteis, -eron.*
FUT.: *dir-é, -ás, -á, -emos, -éis, -án.*
CONDIT.: *dir-ía, -ías, -ía, -íamos, -íais, -ían.*
SUBJ. PRES.: *dig-a, -as, -a, -amos, -áis, -an.*
SUBJ. IMPERF. 1: *dij-era, -eras, -era, -éramos, -erais, -eran.*
SUBJ. IMPERF. 2: *dij-ese, -eses, -ese, -ésemos, -eseis, -esen.*
INFORMAL IMPERAT.: *di (tú), no digas (tú); decid (vosotros), no digáis (vosotros).*
FORMAL IMPERAT.: *diga (Vd.); digamos; digan (Vds.).*
PRES. PARTIC.: *diciendo.*
PAST PARTIC.: *dicho.*

NOTES:
(1) The person to whom one speaks is the indirect object.
   E.g.: *Yo le digo la verdad a mi padre.*
      I tell my father the truth.
(2) *Decir* is followed by the subjunctive if it used to give a command, i.e., "To tell someone to + verb."
   E.g.: *La diré a Manuela que vaya a la universidad.*
      I shall tell Manuela to go to the university.
   When *decir* is used negatively to convey uncertainty, it also takes the subjunctive.
   E.g.: *No dicen que seamos tontos.*
      They don't say that we are fools.
(3) If *decir* indicates a statement of fact it is followed by the indicative.
   E.g.: *Digo que Manuela va a la universidad.*
      I am saying that Manuela is going to the university.

DECLARATIVE SENTENCES

A declarative sentence is one that makes a statement. The normal word order in a declarative sentence is: Subject—verb—object.
E.g.: *Rafael estudia la lección.*
   Rafael studies the lesson.

DEFINITE ARTICLES
See ARTICLES, DEFINITE

DEJAR

(Transitive verb) =
(1) "To leave (behind)."
   E.g.: *Dejé mi libro en mi cuarto.*
      I left my book in my room.
(2) "To let, to allow." In this case it is followed by the subjunctive.
   E.g.: *El jefe no dejó que se marcharan antes de las siete.*
      The boss did not let them leave until seven o'clock.
It may also be followed by the infinitive even if there is a change of subject.
E.g.: *El jefe no les dejó salir antes de las siete.*
   The boss did not let them leave until seven o'clock.
See SUBJUNCTIVE vs. INFINITIVE
Do not confuse *dejar* with *salir*, which means "to leave, to go (out of a place)."
NOTE:
Although the normal rule is that a clause is required when there is change of subject between the main clause and the subordinate clause, *dejar* may take the infinitive, especially when the object of the verb is a pronoun.
E.g.: *No me dejaron hablar.*
   They didn't let me speak.
The normal construction "*Dejar* + subjunctive" may also be used.
E.g.: *Su padre no deja que salga de casa.*
   His father does not let him leave the house.

DEJAR CAER

(Verbal idiom) = "To drop."
E.g.: *Dejaron caer la caja.*
   They dropped the box.

DEJAR DE + infinitive

(Verbal construction). It has two quite different meanings:
(1) "To stop + present participle."
    E.g.: *Dejé de estudiar a las diez.*
        I stopped studying at ten o'clock.
(2) "To fail to, to neglect to + infinitive."
    E.g.: *Ella dejó de visitar a su abuela.*
        She neglected to visit her grandmother.
        No deje de llamar a sus padres.
        Don't fail to call your parents.

DEJAR vs. SALIR vs. IRSE vs. PARTIR vs. QUEDAR

(1) *Dejar* (Transitive) = "To leave, to abandon."
    E.g.: *El hombre dejó a sus niños.*
        The man abandoned his children.
See **DEJAR**
(2) *Salir* (Intransitive) = "To leave, to go out."
    E.g.: *El hombre salió a la calle.*
        The man went out into the street.
(3) *Irse* (Reflexive) = "To leave, to depart."
    E.g.: *El hombre se va a las nueve.*
        The man leaves at nine o'clock.
(4) *Partir* (Intransitive) = "To leave, to set out, to depart."
    E.g.: *Vamos a partir en diez minutos.*
        We are going to depart in ten minutes.
(5) *Quedar* (Intransitive) = "To be left over, to remain."
    E.g.: *Me quedan cincuenta pesetas.*
        I have fifty pesetas left.

DEL

(Preposition + article). This is the contraction of *de* + *el*.
E.g.: *Hablo del libro.*
    I talk about the book.
See **CONTRACTION: DE + EL**

DELANTE DE. vs. ANTES DE

Both are prepositional constructions.
(1) *Delante de* refers to spatial relationships.
    E.g.: *El coche está delante del garage.*
        The car is in front of the garage.
(2) *Antes de* refers to temporal relationships.
    E.g.: *Compré el coche antes de Navidades.*
        I bought the car before Christmas.

DEMÁS

(Invariable adjective) = "The rest of, the other." It is always used with the definite article.
E.g.: *Los demás boletos cuestan más.*
    The rest of the tickets cost more.

DEMASIADO

(1) The adjective *demasiado (-a, -os, -as)* = "Too much, too many."
E.g.: *Tengo demasiado trabajo.*
I have too much work.
Hay demasiadas sillas.
There are too many chairs.
(2) The adverb *demasiado* = "Too much."
E.g.: *Bebes demasiado.*
You drink too much.

DEMONSTRATIVE ADJECTIVES
See **ADJECTIVES, DEMONSTRATIVE**

DEMONSTRATIVE PRONOUNS
See **PRONOUNS, DEMONSTRATIVE**

DENTRO DE POCO

(Idiomatic expression) = "Shortly, soon."
E.g.: *Va a llegar dentro de poco.*
He will arrive shortly.

DENTRO vs. DENTRO DE vs. EN

(1) *Dentro* (Adverb) = "Inside."
E.g.: *El gato está dentro.*
The cat is inside.
(2) *Dentro de* (Prepositional construction) = "Inside, within."
E.g.: *El lápiz está dentro de la caja.*
The pencil is inside the box.
(3) *En* (Preposition) = "In."
E.g.: *Hay un lápiz en la caja.*
There is a pencil in the box.

DEPENDER DE

(Intransitive verb) = "To depend (on)."
E.g.: *El resultado depende de su trabajo.*
The result depends on his work.

DERECHA

(Feminine noun) = "Right hand, right side."
A la derecha = "To the right, at the right."
E.g.: *Mi casa está a la derecha del museo.*
My house is to the right of the museum.
NOTE:
Its opposite is *la izquierda.*
E.g.: *El restaurante está a la izquierda.*
The restaurant is on the left.

DERECHO (-A, -OS, -AS)

(1) The adjective *derecho (-a, os, -as)* = "Straight, upright."
E.g.: *Unos árboles derechos.*
Straight trees.

(2) The noun *derecho* = "The law, the right."

E.g.: *He estudiado el derecho constitucional.*

I have studied constitutional law.

No tienes el derecho de entrar.

You do not have the right to enter.

(3) The adverb *derecho* = "Directly, straight."

E.g.: *Vamos derecho a la oficina.*

We go straight to the office.

DESDE

(Preposition) = "From, all the way from." It is used for both time and space.

E.g.: *Desde el veinte de junio.*

From the twentieth of June.

Desde mi casa a la escuela.

From my house to the school.

DESDE HACE

(Idiomatic construction). The construction "Present tense + *desde hace* + time expression" conveys a past action or a situation continuing in the present.

E.g.: *Estudio el español desde hace dos años.*

I have been studying Spanish for two years.

In a past context, *hace* is in the imperfect tense: *hacía.*

E.g.: *Estábamos allí desde hacía diez minutos cuando llamaron.*

We had been there ten minutes when they called.

See **SINCE + time expression**

DESDE LUEGO

(Adverbial idiom) = "Of course."

E.g.: *Desde luego, no pudo obtener el empleo porque no tenía diploma.*

Of course, he could not get the job because he had no diploma.

DESDE QUE

(Conjunction) = "Since, inasmuch as." It is followed by the indicative.

E.g.: *Nunca hablo inglés desde que me mudé de Nueva York a Madrid.*

I never speak English anymore since I moved from New York to Madrid.

Desde que me operaron por úlceras, ya no bebo nada.

Since I was operated on for ulcers I no longer drink.

DESPEDIR

Conjugated like **pedir.**

(1) (Transitive verb) = "To see off."

E.g.: *Le despedimos en el aeropuerto.*

We saw him (her) off in the airport.

(2) (Reflexive verb) = "To take leave (of)."

E.g.: *Se despidieron de sus amigos.*

They took leave of their friends.

DESPITE (THE FACT THAT)

(1) *A pesar de* (Preposition) = "Despite."

E.g.: *Siguieron viajando a pesar del mal tiempo.*

They continued to travel despite the bad weather.

(2) *A pesar de que* (Conjunctional construction) = "Despite the fact that."

It is normally followed by the indicative.

E.g.: *Siguieron viajando a pesar de que hacía mal tiempo.*

They continued to travel despite the fact that the weather was bad.

DESPUÉS vs. *DESPUÉS DE* vs. *DESPUÉS DE QU*

(1) *Después* (Adverb) = "After(wards)."
  E.g.: *¿Qué vas a hacer después?*
    What are you going to do afterwards?
(2) *Después de* (Prepositional construction) = "After." It is used before (a) a noun, (b) a pronoun, (c) an infinitive.
  E.g.: (a) *Después de la guerra.*
      After the war.
    (b) *Después de ellos.*
      After them.
    (c) *Después de comer.*
      After eating.
(3) *Después de que* (Conjunctional construction) = "After." It is followed by the:
  (a) indicative.
      E.g.: *Ella se durmió después de que su madre le dio la píldora.*
        She fell asleep after her mother gave her the pill.
  (b) subjunctive (if it refers to a future action).
      E.g.: *Iremos a México después de que ellos vuelvan de Guatemala.*
        We shall go to Mexico after they return from Guatemala.

DEVOLVER

(Transitive verb) = "To return, give back; to throw up."
Conjugated like **volver**.
E.g.: *Tengo que devolver este libro a la biblioteca.*
    I have to return this book to the library.

  Comió demasiado y lo devolvió todo.
    He ate too much and threw it all up.

DIACRITICAL MARKS

A diacritical mark *(un signo diacrítico)* is a mark added to a letter to modify its value or pronunciation. The diacritical marks used in Spanish are:
(1) the accent *(el acento)* [´]
(2) the tilde *(la tilde)* [˜]
(3) The diaeresis *(la diéresis)* [¨]
See **ACCENT**
See also **DIAERESIS**
See also **TILDE**

DIAERESIS

The diaeresis *(la diéresis)* [¨] is a diacritical mark placed over the letter *u* in the syllables *güe* and *güi* to indicate that the sound *u* must be pronounced.
E.g.: *Bilingüe.*
    Bilingual.

  Bilingüismo.
    Bilingualism.

DIMENSIONS
See **SIZES AND MEASUREMENTS**

DIMINUTIVE ENDINGS

Diminutive endings are added to nouns to indicate small size or a pleasant or lovable nature. The most common diminutive suffixes are:
(a) *-ito (-a, -os, -as).*
  E.g.: *¡Mira este perrito!*
    Look at that little dog!

(b) *-llo (-a, -os, -as)*.
    E.g.: *Vive en una casilla muy bonita.*
        He lives in a pretty little house.
(c) *-uelo (-a, -os, -as)* (pejorative).
    E.g.: *Es un jovenzuelo.*
        He is an insignificant young man.

DIPHTHONG

A diphthong *(un diptongo)* is a combination of two or more vowels to form a single syllable. The weak vowels *i, y,* and *u* combine with the strong vowels *a, e,* and *o*.
E.g.: *Baile; hay; béisbol; cuerda; Dios; reunión.*

DIRECT OBJECT vs. INDIRECT OBJECT

(1) The direct object follows the verb directly (but is preceded by the personal *a* if it is a specific person or a personalized thing) to indicate who or what receives the action of the verb.
    E.g.: *Pedro compra las flores.*
        Peter buys the flowers.

        Encontré a Margarita.
        I met Margaret.
(2) The indirect object follows the verb by means of the preposition *a* to indicate to or for whom, to or for what the action of the verb is done.
    E.g.: *Pedro le escribe a María.*
        Peter writes to Mary.
REMEMBER: Some verbs which take an indirect object in English take a direct object in Spanish and vice-versa.
Buscar, escuchar, esperar, mirar, pagar are transitive:
E.g.: *Espero el autobús.*
       I am waiting for the bus.

       Busco un libro.
       I am looking for a book.

       Ella pide un helado.
       She asks for ice cream.

       Escucho la radio.
       I listen to the radio.

       Pagué mis compras.
       I paid for my purchases.

       Miro la pintura.
       I look at the painting.

DIRECT OBJECT PRONOUNS
See **PRONOUNS, OBJECT OF VERB**

DIRIGIR

(Transitive verb) = "To direct."
PRES.: *dirijo, diriges, dirige, dirigimos, dirigís, dirigen.*
IMPERF.: *dirig-ía, -ías, -ía, -íamos, -íais, -ían.*
PRETER.: *dirig-í, -iste, -ió, -imos, -isteis, -ieron.*
FUT.: *dirigir-é, -ás, -á, -emos, -éis, -án.*
CONDIT.: *dirigir-ía, -ías, -ía, -íamos, -íais, -ían.*
SUBJ. PRES.: *dirij-a, -as, -a, -amos, -áis, -an.*
SUBJ. IMPERF. 1: *dirigi-era, -eras, -era, -éramos, -erais, -eran.*
SUBJ. IMPERF. 2: *dirigi-ese, -eses, -ese, -ésemos, -eseis, -esen.*
INFORMAL IMPERAT.: *dirige (tú), no dirijas (tú); dirigid (vosotros), no dirijáis (vosotros).*
FORMAL IMPERAT.: *dirija (Vd.); dirijamos; dirijan (Vds.).*
PRES. PARTIC.: *dirigiendo.*
PAST PARTIC.: *dirigido.*

DISCURSO INDIRECTO (INDIRECT DISCOURSE)
See **INDIRECT DISCOURSE**

DISPONERSE A + **infinitive**
(Idiomatic expression) = "To prepare to, to get ready to."
E.g.: *Mi madre se dispone a salir para la tienda.*
   My mother is getting ready to go to the store.

DISTINGUIR
(Transitive verb) = "To distinguish."
PRES.: *distingo, distingu-es, -e, -imos, -ís, -en.*
IMPERF.: *distingu-ía, -ías, -ía, -íamos, -íais, -ían.*
PRETER.: *distingu-í, -iste, -ió, -imos, -isteis, -ieron.*
FUT.: *distinguir-é, -ás, -á, -emos, -éis, -án.*
CONDIT.: *distinguir-ía, -ías, -ía, -íamos, -íais, -ían.*
SUBJ. PRES.: *disting-a, -as, -a, -amos, -áis, -an.*
SUBJ. IMPERF. 1: *distingui-era, -eras, -era, -éramos, -erais, -eran.*
SUBJ. IMPERF. 2: *distingui-ese, -eses, -ese, -ésemos, -eseis, -esen.*
INFORMAL IMPERAT.: *distingue (tú), no distingas (tú); distinguid (vosotros), no distingáis (vosotros).*
FORMAL IMPERAT.: *distinga (Vd.); distingamos; distingan (Vds.).*
PRES PARTIC.: *distinguiendo.*
PAST PARTIC.: *distinguido.*

DIVERTIRSE
(Reflexive verb) = "To amuse oneself, to enjoy oneself."
Conjugated like *sentir*.
E.g.: *Nos divertimos mucho ayer en tu casa.*
   We enjoyed ourselves very much last night at your house.

to **DO**
"To do" = *Hacer.*
NOTE:
In English "to do" is used as an auxiliary verb to form interrogative and negative sentences. This is not possible in Spanish.
(a) To form a question in Spanish use the interrogative construction "Verb + subject + direct object."
   E.g.: *¿Habla Ud. japonés?*
      Do you speak Japanese?
(b) To form negative statements use the negative *no* before the verb.
   E.g.: *No hablo japonés.*
      I do not speak Japanese.
See **WORD ORDER IN QUESTIONS**
See also the idiomatic expressions with *HACER*

to **DO WITHOUT**
(Idiomatic expression) = *Pasar sin.*
E.g.: *No puedo pasar sin mi medicina.*
   I can't do without my medicine.

DOLER

(Intransitive verb) = "To ache, to grieve."
PRES.: *duel-o, -es, -e, dolemos, doléis, duelen.*
IMPERF.: *dol-ía, -ías, -ía, -íamos, -íais, -ían.*
PRETER.: *dol-í, -iste, -ió, -imos, -isteis, -ieron.*
FUT.: *doler-é, -ás, -á, -emos, -éis, -án.*
CONDIT.: *doler-ía, -ías, -ía, -íamos, -íais, -ían.*
SUBJ. PRES.: *duel-a, -as, -a, dolamos, doláis, duelan.*
SUBJ. IMPERF. 1: *doli-era, -eras, -era, -éramos, -erais, -eran.*
SUBJ. IMPERF. 2: *doli-ese, -eses, -ese, -ésemos, -eseis, -esen.*
INFORMAL IMPERAT.: *duele (tú), no duelas (tú); doled (vosotros), no doláis (vosotros).*
FORMAL IMPERAT.: *duela (Vd.); dolamos; duelan (Vds.).*
PRES. PARTIC.: *doliendo.*
PAST PARTIC.: *dolido.*
USAGE:
The part of the body which hurts is the subject and the person is the indirect object.
E.g.: *Le duelen los dientes.*
    My teeth hurt.

    Le duele todavía la muerte de su madre.
    He still grieves the death of his mother.

DONDE vs. DÓNDE

(1) *Donde* (Adverb) = "Where."
    E.g.: *Iremos donde hace sol.*
        We shall go where it is sunny.
(2) *Dónde* (Interrogative adverb) = "Where?"
    E.g.: *¿Dónde vamos a comer?*
        Where are we going to eat?

DONDEQUIERA

(Indefinite Adverb) = "Anywhere."
E.g.: *Puedes viajar dondequiera.*
    You may travel anywhere.
NOTE:
The idiomatic construction *Dondequiera que* (= "Wherever") is followed by the subjunctive.
E.g.: *No quiero verle dondequiera que esté.*
    I don't want to see him wherever he may be.

DORMIR

(Intransitive verb) = "To sleep."
PRES.: *duerm-o, duermes, duerme, dormimos, dormís, duermen.*
IMPERF.: *dorm-ía, -ías, -ía, -íamos, -íais, -ían.*
PRETER.: *dorm-í, -iste, durmió, dorm-imos, -isteis, durmieron.*
FUT.: *dormir-é, -ás, -á, -emos, -éis, -án.*
CONDIT.: *dormir-ía, -ías, -ía, -íamos, -ías, -ían.*
SUBJ. PRES.: *duerm-a, -as, -a, durmamos, durmáis, duerman.*
SUBJ. IMPERF. 1: *durmi-era, -eras, -era, -éramos, -erais, -eran.*
SUBJ. IMPERF. 2: *durmi-ese, -eses, -ese, -ésemos, -eseis, -esen.*
INFORMAL IMPERAT.: *duerme (tú), no duermas (tú); dormid (vosotros), no durmáis (vosotros).*
FORMAL IMPERAT.: *duerma (Vd.); durmamos; duerman (Vds.).*
PRES. PARTIC.: *durmiendo.*
PAST PARTIC.: *dormido.*

NOTE:
The transitive *Dormir* = "To put to sleep."
E.g.: *Este predicador me duerme.*
>   This preacher puts me to sleep.

DORMIR vs. *DORMIRSE*

(1) *Dormir* (intransitive) = "To sleep."
>   E.g.: *Duermen ocho horas.*
>>   They sleep eight hours.

(2) *Dormirse* (reflexive) = "To fall asleep."
>   E.g.: *Se durmieron a las once.*
>>   They fell asleep at eleven o'clock.

DOUBLE NEGATIVE

The use of the double negative is correct and quite frequent in Spanish.
E.g.: *No hay nadie.*
>   There is nobody.

>   *Salieron sin abrigo ni suéter.*
>   They left without overcoat or sweater.

DOUBLE OBJECT PRONOUNS
See **PRONOUN PAIRS**

DOUBT

The concept of doubt or uncertainty is conveyed by *Dudar que* + subjunctive or *No creer que* + subjunctive.
E.g.: *Dudo que vengan con nosotros.*
>   I doubt that they will come with us.
See **SUBJUNCTIVE MOOD**

to DROP

There is no direct equivalent for the verb "To drop" in Spanish. It must be translated by the idiom *Dejar caer.*
E.g.: *Dejó caer su libro.*
>   He dropped (let fall) his book.

NOTE:
The idiomatic English expression "To drop a course, a class, etc." = *Abandonar* or *dejar.*
E.g.: *Abandoné* (or *dejé*) *el curso de álgebra.*
>   I dropped the algebra course.
See *DEJAR CAER*

DURATION OF TIME constructions

(1) To express actions or situations which began in the past and are continuing in the present, use:
>   (a) *Hace* + time expression + *que* + present tense.
>>   E.g.: *Hace dos horas que estoy aquí.*
>>>   I have been here for two hours.

>   (b) Present tense + *desde hace* + time expression.
>>   E.g.: *Estoy aquí desde hace dos horas.*
>>>   I have been here for two hours.

(2) To express actions or situations which began in the past and which were still going on at a certain point in time in the past, use:
>   (a) *Hacía* + time expression + *que* + imperfect.
>>   E.g.: *Hacía dos horas que estaba aquí (cuando llegaste).*
>>>   I had been here for two hours (when you arrived).

(b) Imperfect + *desde hacía* + time expression.

E.g.: *Estaba aquí desde hacía dos horas (cuando llegaste).*

I had been here for two hours (when you arrived).

(3) To express the concept that an action or situation has *not* occurred for a certain period of time, use *Llevar* + time expression + *sin* + infinitive.

E.g.: *Lleva dos horas aquí sin hacer nada.*

He has been here for two hours without doing anything.

DURING

(Preposition) = *Durante*.

E.g.: *Durante la guerra.*

During the war.

NOTE:

During the day = *De día*.

BUT: "During the night, the morning, the afternoon" = *Por la noche, por la mañana, por la tarde.*

E

E

(Conjunction). *E* is used instead of *y* before words beginning with *i-* or *hi-*.

E.g.: *Somos libres e independientes.*

We are free and independent.

Madre e hijo han llegado.

Mother and child have arrived.

EACH OTHER

(Reciprocal pronouns).

(1) If the context is clear use the reciprocal pronouns: *nos, os, se*.

E.g.: *Pedro y María se quieren.*

Peter and Mary love each other.

(2) If further clarification is needed add: *el uno al otro, la una a la otra, los unos a los otros, las unas a las otras,* or the adverb *mutuamente*.

E.g.: *Estos estudiantes se ayudan los unos a los otros.*

These students help each other.

Estos estudiantes se ayudan mutuamente.

These students help each other.

NOTE:

If a preposition is used it must be placed between *uno (-a, -os, -as)* and *otro (-a, -os, -as)*.

E.g.: *Lo hacen los unos para los otros.*

They do it for each other.

See **VERBS, RECIPROCAL**

ECHAR

(Transitive verb) = "To throw, to toss."

E.g.: *Echó la pelota al perro.*

He threw the ball to the dog.

ECHAR AL CORREO

(Verbal idiom) = "To mail."

E.g.: *Eché la carta al correo ayer.*

I mailed the letter yesterday.

ECHAR DE MENOS

(Verbal idiom) = "To miss."
E.g.: *Cuando se fue a la escuela, el niño echó de menos a su madre.*
When the child went to school he missed his mother.

ECHAR LA CULPA

(Verbal idiom) = "To blame."
E.g.: *Carolina siempre echa la culpa a su hermanita.*
Caroline always blames her little sister.

ECHARSE A + infinitive

(Reflexive verb) = "To start to."
E.g.: *La muchacha se echó a llorar.*
The girl began to cry.

ELEGIR

(Transitive verb) = "To elect, to choose."
PRES.: *elijo, elig-es, -e, elegimos, elegís, eligen.*
IMPERF.: *elig-ía, -ías, -ía, -íamos, -íais, -ían.*
PRETER.: *eleg-í, -iste, eligió, elegimes, elegisteis, eligieron.*
FUT.: *eligir-é, -ás, -á, -emos, -éis, -án.*
CONDIT.: *eligir-ía, -ías, -ía, -íamos, -íais, -ían.*
SUBJ. PRES.: *elij-a, -as, -a, -amos, -áis, -an.*
SUBJ. IMPERF. 1: *eligi-era, -eras, -era, -éramos, -erais, -eran.*
SUBJ. IMPERF. 2: *eligi-ese, -eses, -ese, -ésemos, -eseis, -esen.*
INFORMAL IMPERAT.: *elige (tú), no elijas (tú); elegid (vosotros), no elijáis (vosotros).*
FORMAL IMPERAT.: *elija (Vd.); elijamos; elijan (Vds.).*
PRES. PARTIC.: *eligiendo.*
PAST PARTIC.: *elegido.*

ELLO

(Neuter pronoun) = "It, this business, this whole affair." It refers to a previously expressed idea, concept, or situation.
E.g.: *Quiero viajar por la América del Sur; para ello se necesita mucho dinero.*
I want to travel around South America; for this you need a lot of money.

EMPEZAR

(Transitive verb) = "To begin."
PRES.: *empiez-o, -as, -a, empezamos, empezáis, empiezan.*
IMPERF.: *empez-aba, -abas, -aba, -ábamos, -abais, -aban.*
PRETER.: *empec-é, empez-aste, -ó, -amos, -asteis, -aron.*
FUT.: *empezar-é, -ás, -á, -emos, -éis, -án.*
CONDIT.: *empezar-ía, -ías, -ía, -íamos, -íais, -ían.*
SUBJ. PRES.: *empiec-e, -es, -e, empecemos, empecéis, empiecen.*
SUBJ. IMPERF. 1: *empez-ara, -aras, -ara, -áramos, -arais, -aran.*
SUBJ. IMPERF. 2: *empez-ase, -ases, -ase, -ásemos, -aseis, -asen.*
INFORMAL IMPERAT.: *empieza (tú), no empieces (tú); empezad (vosotros), no empecéis (vosotros).*
FORMAL IMPERAT.: *empiece (Vd.); empecemos; empiecen (Vds.).*
PRES. PARTIC.: *empezando.*
PAST PARTIC.: *empezado.*
NOTE:
Empezar takes the preposition *a* before an infinitive.

EN

(Preposition). It is used to indicate:
(a) place = "at, in, into."
    E.g.: *Están en casa.*
           They are at home.
           Puso el dinero en la caja.
           He put the money in the box.
           Entraron en la ciudad.
           They went into the city.
(b) time = "in."
    E.g.: *En el siglo XVI.*
           In the 16th century.
           En 1492.
           In 1492.

NOTE:
Do not confuse *en* with *a*, which means "To, at."
E.g.: *Vendré a las diez.*
      I shall come at ten o'clock.
      Vamos a la tienda.
      We go to the shop.
See **A (preposition)**

EN (verbs followed by)

See **VERBS + (A, CON, DE, EN or no prep.) + infinitive**

EN BROMA

(Idiomatic expression) = "In jest."
E.g.: *¡No te enfades! Lo dije en broma.*
      Don't get angry. I said it in jest.

EN CAMBIO

(Idiomatic expression) = "On the other hand."
E.g.: *No trabajo el lunes; en cambio tengo que trabajar el domingo.*
      I don't work on Monday; on the other hand, I have to work on Sunday.

EN CASA

(Idiomatic expression) = "At home."
E.g.: *Mis padres están en casa todos los sábados.*
      My parents are at home every Saturday.

EN CASO DE

(Prepositional construction) = "In case of."
E.g.: *En caso de incendio.*
      In case of fire.

EN CUANTO

(Conjunctional construction) = "As soon as."
E.g.: *En cuanto lo vi lo reconocí.*
      As soon as I saw him I recognized him.
NOTE:
If there is doubt, anticipation, or uncertainty, *en cuanto* is followed by the subjunctive.
E.g.: *En cuanto vengas podremos charlar de eso.*
      As soon as you arrive we will be able to chat about that.

EN CUANTO A

(Prepositional construction) = "As for, in regard to, with respect to."
E.g.: *En cuanto a Miguel, no lo quiero ver.*
    As for Michael, I don't want to see him.

EN EFECTO

(Idiomatic expression) = "Indeed, in fact, really."
E.g.: *En efecto, lo compramos.*
    Indeed, we bought it.

EN LUGAR DE

(Prepositional construction) = "In place of, instead of."
E.g.: *Compraron flores en lugar de un regalo.*
    They bought flowers instead of a present.

EN MEDIO DE

(Prepositional construction) = "In the middle of."
E.g.: *Me dormí en medio de la clase.*
    I fell asleep in the middle of class.

EN OCHO DÍAS

(Idiomatic expression) = "In a week, a week from today."
E.g.: *Los cursos terminarán en ocho días.*
    Courses will end a week from today.

EN PUNTO

(Idiomatic expression) = "Sharp, on the dot."
E.g.: *La clase empieza a las nueve en punto.*
    Class begins at nine o'clock sharp.

EN QUINCE DÍAS

(Idiomatic expression) = "In two weeks, two weeks from today."
E.g.: *Saldré para México en quince días.*
    I shall leave for Mexico in two weeks.

EN SEGUIDA

(Idiomatic expression) = "Immediately, at once."
E.g.: *Voy a ayudarte en seguida.*
    I am going to help you immediately.

EN SERIO

(Idiomatic expression) = "Seriously."
E.g.: *Ella nunca habla en serio.*
    She never speaks seriously.

EN VEZ DE

(Prepositional construction) = "Instead of, in place of."
E.g.: *Volví a casa en vez de continuar mi viaje.*
    I returned home instead of continuing my trip.

ENCONTRAR vs. ENCONTRARSE

(1) *Encontrar* (Transitive verb) = "To find, to meet, to run into."
E.g.: *Encontré a Roberto en el parque.*
I met Robert in the park.
See **TROPEZAR CON**
(2) *Encontrarse* = "To meet, to be located."
E.g.: *Carolina y yo nos encontramos en el parque.*
Caroline and I met in the park.

La estación se encuentra cerca de mi oficina.
The station is located near my office.

ENTRE

(Preposition) = "Between, among(st), in the midst of."
E.g.: *Terminaremos entre las tres y las cuatro.*
We shall finish between three and four o'clock.

Vivieron un año entre los pigmeos.
They lived for a year among the pygmies.
NOTE:
When pronouns follow *entre* they must be subject pronouns (not object pronouns as one would expect).
E.g.: *Entre tú y yo, no voy a hacer nada.*
Between you and me, I am not going to do anything.

ENVIAR

(Transitive verb) = "To send."
PRES.: *envío, envías, envía, enviamos, enviáis, envían.*
IMPERF.: *envi-aba, -abas, -aba, -ábamos, -abais, -aban.*
PRETER.: *envi-é, -aste, -ó, -amos, -asteis, -aron.*
FUT.: *enviar-é, -ás, -á, -emos, -éis, -án.*
CONDIT.: *enviar-ía, -ías, -ía, -íamos, -íais, -ían.*
SUBJ. PRES.: *enví-e, -es, -e, enviemos, enviéis, envíen.*
SUBJ. IMPERF. 1: *envi-ara, -aras, -ara, -áramos, -arais, -aran.*
SUBJ. IMPERF. 2: *envi-ase, -ases, -ase, -ásemos, -aseis, -asen.*
INFORMAL IMPERAT.: *envía (tú), no envíes (tú); enviad (vosotros), no enviéis (vosotros).*
FORMAL IMPERAT.: *envíe (Vd.); enviemos; envíen (Vds.).*
PRES. PARTIC.: *enviando.*
PAST PARTIC.: *enviado.*

ERGUIR

(Transitive verb) = "To erect."
PRES.: *yergo, yergues, yergue, erguimos, erguís, yerguen. or: irgo, irgues, irgue, erguimos, erguís, irguen.*
IMPERF.: *ergu-ía, -ías, -ía, -íamos, -íais, -ían.*
PRETER.: *erguí, erguiste, irguió, erguimos, erguisteis, irguieron.*
FUT.: *erguir-é, -ás, -á, -emos, -éis, -án.*
CONDIT.: *erguir-ía, -ías, -ía, -íamos, -íais, -ían.*
SUBJ. PRES.: *yerga, yergas, yerga, irgamos, irgáis, yergan. or: irg-a, -as, -a, -amos, -áis, -an.*
SUBJ. IMPERF. 1: *irgui-era, -eras, -era, -éramos, -erais, -eran.*
SUBJ. IMPERF. 2: *irgui-ese, -eses, -ese, -ésemos, -eseis, -esen.*
INFORMAL IMPERAT.: *yergue (tú) or: irgue (tú), no yergas (tú) or: no irgas (tú); erguid (vosotros), no yergáis (vosotros) or: no irgáis (vosotros).*
FORMAL IMPERAT.: *yerga (Vd.) or: irga (Vd.); yergamos or: irgamos; yergan (Vds.) or: irgan (Vds.).*
PRES. PARTIC.: *irguiendo.*
PAST PARTIC.: *erguido.*

ERRAR

(Transitive verb) = "To err."
PRES.: *yerro, yerras, yerra, erramos, erráis, yerran.*
IMPERF.: *err-aba, -abas, -aba, -ábamos, -abais, -aban.*
PRETER.: *err-é, -aste, -ó, -amos, -asteis, -aron.*
FUT.: *errar-é, -ás, -á, -emos, -éis, -án.*
CONDIT.: *errar-ía, -ías, -ía, -íamos, -íais, -ían.*
SUBJ. PRES.: *yerre, yerres, yerre, erremos, erréis, yerren.*
SUBJ. IMPERF. 1: *err-ara, -aras, -ara, -áramos, -arais, -aran.*
SUBJ. IMPERF. 2: *err-ase, -ases, -ase, -ásemos, -aseis, -asen.*
INFORMAL IMPERAT.: *yerra (tú) no yerres (tú); errad (vosotros), no erréis (vosotros).*
FORMAL IMPERAT.: *yerre (Vd.); erremos; yerren (Vds.).*
PRES. PARTIC.: *errando.*
PAST PARTIC.: *errado.*

ESCOGER

(Transitive verb) = "To choose."
PRES.: *escojo, escog-es, -e, -emos, -éis, -en.*
IMPERF.: *escog-ía, -ías, -ía, -íamos, -íais, -ían.*
PRETER.: *escog-í, -iste, -ió, -imos, -isteis, -ieron.*
FUT.: *escoger-é, -ás, -á, -emos, -éis, -án.*
CONDIT.: *escoger-ía, -ías, -ía, -íamos, -íais, -ían.*
SUBJ. PRES.: *escoj-a, -as, -a, -amos, -áis, -an.*
SUBJ. IMPERF. 1: *escogi-era, -eras, -era, -éramos, -erais, -eran.*
SUBJ. IMPERF. 2: *escogi-ese, -eses, -ese, -ésemos, -eseis, -esen.*
INFORMAL IMPERAT.: *escoge (tú), no escojas (tú); escoged (vosotros), no escojáis (vosotros).*
FORMAL IMPERAT.: *escoja (Vd.); escojamos; escojan (Vds.).*
PRES. PARTIC.: *escogiendo.*
PAST PARTIC.: *escogido.*

ESCRIBIR

(Transitive verb) = "To write."
PRES.: *escrib-o, -es, -e, -imos, -ís, -en.*
IMPERF.: *escrib-ía, -ías, -ía, -íamos, -íais, -ían.*
PRETER.: *escrib-í, -iste, -ió, -imos, -ís, -ieron.*
FUT.: *escribir-é, -ás, -á, -emos, -éis, -án.*
CONDIT.: *escribir-ía, -ías, -ía, -íamos, -íais, -ían.*
SUBJ. PRES.: *escrib-a, -as, -a, -amos, -áis, -an.*
SUBJ. IMPERF. 1: *escribi-era, -eras, -era, -éramos, -erais, -eran.*
SUBJ. IMPERF. 2: *escribi-ese, -eses, -ese, -ésemos, -eseis, -esen.*
INFORMAL IMPERAT.: *escribe (tú), no escribas (tú); escribid (vosotros), no escribáis (vosotros).*
FORMAL IMPERAT.: *escriba (Vd.); escribamos; escriban (Vds.).*
PRES. PARTIC.: *escribiendo.*
PAST PARTIC.: *escrito.*

ESCUCHAR

(Transitive verb of perception) = "To listen to."
The preposition "to" is included in the verb.
E.g.: *Escuchamos la radio.*
　　　　We listen to the radio.

NOTE:

When *escuchar* is followed by a verb ("To listen to + direct object + present participle"), the corresponding Spanish construction is: "*Escuchar* + direct object + infinitive."

E.g.: *Escucho a María tocar el piano.*

I listen to Mary playing the piano.

ESO

(Neuter demonstrative pronoun) = "That, that matter, that thing." It is used to refer to abstract ideas or general concepts.

E.g.: *No quiero hablar de eso.*

I don't want to talk about that.

See **AQUELLO**

See also **ESTO**

ESPERAR

(1) (Transitive verb) = "To wait for, to await."

The preposition "for" is included in the verb.

E.g.: *Espero a mi esposa.*

I am waiting for my wife.

(2) (Intransitive verb) = "To hope, to expect."

E.g.: *Espero verte mañana.*

I hope to see you tomorrow.

ESQUIAR

(Intransitive verb) = "To ski."

PRES.: *esqu-ío, -ías, -ía, -iamos, -iáis, -ían.*

IMPERF.: *esqui-aba, -abas, -aba, -ábamos, -abais, -aban.*

PRETER.: *esqui-é, -aste, -ó, -amos, -asteis, -aron.*

FUT.: *esquiar-é, -ás, -á, -emos, -éis, -án.*

CONDIT.: *esquiar-ía, -ías, -ía, -íamos, -íais, -ían.*

SUBJ. PRES.: *esqu-íe, -íes, -íe, -iemos, -iéis, -íen.*

SUBJ. IMPERF. 1: *esqui-ara, -aras, -ara, -áramos, -arais, -aran.*

SUBJ. IMPERF. 2: *esqui-ase, -ases, -ase, -ásemos, -aseis, -asen.*

INFORMAL IMPERAT.: *esquía (tú), no esquíes (tú); esquiad (vosotros), no esquiéis (vosotros).*

FORMAL IMPERAT.: *esquíe (Vd.); esquiemos; esquíen (Vds.).*

PRES. PARTIC.: *esquiando.*

PAST PARTIC.: *esquiado.*

ESTAR

(Intransitive verb) = "To be."

PRES.: *estoy, estás, está, estamos, estáis, están.*

IMPERF.: *est-aba, -abas, -aba, -ábamos, -abais, -aban.*

PRETER.: *estuv-e, -iste, -o, -imos, -isteis, -ieron.*

FUT.: *estar-é, -ás, -á, -emos, -éis, -án.*

CONDIT.: *estar-ía, -ías, -ía, -íamos, -íais, -ían.*

SUBJ. PRES.: *esté, estés, esté, estemos, estéis, estén*

SUBJ. IMPERF. 1: *estuvi-era, -eras, -era, -éramos, -erais, -eran.*

SUBJ. IMPERF. 2: *estuvi-ese, -eses, -ese, -ésemos, -eseis, -esen.*

INFORMAL IMPERAT.: *está (tú), no estés (tú); estad (vosotros), no estéis (vosotros).*

FORMAL IMPERAT.: *esté (Vd.); estemos; estén (Vds.).*

PRES. PARTIC.: *estando.*

PAST PARTIC.: *estado.*

See *ESTAR* **vs.** *SER*

ESTAR PARA vs. ESTAR POR

(1) *Estar para* = "To be about to + infinitive."

    E.g.: *Estaba para salir cuando llamé.*

        He was about to leave when I called.

(2) *Estar por* = "To be half inclined to + infinitive."

    E.g.: *Estoy por buscar otro empleo.*

        I am half inclined to seek another job.

ESTAR vs. SER

Both verbs mean "To be" but their usages are very different.

(1) **Estar** is used:

  (a) to express the location, situation, or position of the subject.

      E.g.: *Mi padre está en Toledo.*

          My father is in Toledo.

          Los coches están delante de la casa.

          The cars are in front of the house.

  (b) with adjectives to express the condition or state that the subject is in.

      E.g.: *Estoy contento.*

          I am glad.

          El autobús estaba lleno.

          The bus was full.

          Las ventanas están abiertas.

          The windows are open.

          María está sentada.

          Mary is seated.

  (c) with the gerund to form progressive tenses.

      E.g.: *Estaba leyendo cuando sonó el teléfono.*

          I was reading when the telephone rang.

  (d) with certain expressions, such as:

      Estar de jefe = to be the acting head.

      Estar de vacaciones = to be on vacation.

      Estar de acuerdo = to agree.

(2) **Ser** is used:

  (a) to express an inherent characteristic or quality of the subject.

      E.g.: *Mi casa es de ladrillo.*

          My house is (made) of brick.

          La electrónica es difícil.

          Electronics is difficult.

  (b) with adjectives to describe an inherent quality of the subject.

      E.g.: *Pedro es alto.*

          Peter is tall.

          Mi abuelo es viejo.

          My grandfather is old.

  (c) to express the origin or the ownership of the subject.

      E.g.: *Mi abuelo es de Guatemala.*

          My grandfather is from Guatemala.

          El coche es de mi hermana.

          The car is my sister's.

  (d) to express the material of which the subject is made.

      E.g.: *La cuchara es de plata.*

          The spoon is made of silver.

(e) to express the time, the date, or the location of an event.

E.g.:   *Son las cuatro.*

It is four o'clock.

Es el diez de octubre.

It is the tenth of October.

La exposición es en el Prado.

The exhibit is in the Prado.

(f) with many impersonal expressions.

E.g.   *Es posible que venga.*

It is possible that he may come.

Es difícil de comprender eso.

It is difficult to understand that.

EXCEPTION: *Está claro* = It is obvious.

(g) to construct the passive voice (with the past participle).

E.g.:   *El soldado fue matado.*

The soldier was killed.

Sus poemas fueron publicados el año pasado.

His poems were published last year.

ESTO

(Neuter demonstrative pronoun) = "This, this matter, this affair." It is used to refer to abstract ideas or general concepts.

E.g.:   *Esto de la visita de tus padres.*

This business about your parents' visit.

See **AQUELLO**

See also **ESO**

EVERYTHING

= *Todo* (Adjective).

E.g.:   *Todo está en orden.*

Everything is in order.

NOTE:

When it is direct object *todo* is preceded by the neuter article *lo.*

E.g.:   *Lo comió todo.*

He ate everything.

EXCLAMATIONS

Exclamations are preceded by an inverted exclamation mark (¡).

E.g.:   *¡No lo creo!*

I don't believe it!

NOTES:

(1) When used in exclamations, *Qué* means "What a, what . . . !"

E.g.:   *¡Qué historia increíble!*

What an incredible story!

If an adjective follows the noun, the adjective can be preceded by *más* or *tan.*

E.g.:   *¡Qué día más fantástico!*

What an incredible day!

(2) *Qué* means "How" when it modifies an adjective or an adverb.

E.g.:   *¡Qué grandes son!*

How big they are!

¡Qué bien cantan!

How well they sing!

F

FALTAR

(Intransitive verb) = "To lack, to be missing, to be absent."
E.g.: *¿Cuánto dinero te falta?*
    How much money do you lack?
¿Quién falta?
    Who is absent?

FAMILIAR vs. FORMAL FORMS

See *TÚ* vs. *USTED*

FAST

(1) Adjective = *Rápido (-a, -os, -as).*
    E.g.: *Es un coche rápido.*
        It's a fast car.
(2) Adverb = *Rápidamente* or *rápido.*
    E.g.: *Ella habla muy rápidamente* or *rápido.*
        She speaks very fast.

to FEEL SORRY

(Idiomatic construction) = "*Sentir que* + subjunctive."
E.g.: *Siento que estés enfermo.*
    I feel sorry that you are sick.

FEMININE NOUNS, identified by the ending

Nouns ending in: *-a, -d, -umbre, -ción* and *-sión* are feminine.

E.g.: *La carta.*	*La universidad.*	*La virtud.*
The letter.	The university.	The virtue.
La muchedumbre.	*La lección.*	*La decisión.*
The crowd.	The lesson.	The decision.

EXCEPTION:
El día.
The day.
NOTE:
A few nouns ending in *-ma, -pa, -ta* are masculine.

E.g.: *El dilema.*	*El mapa.*	*El poeta.*
The dilemma.	The map.	The poet.

EXCEPTION:
La trama.
The plot.
See **GENDER**

FEMININE OF ADJECTIVES

See **ADJECTIVES, FEMININE OF**

FEW

(Adjective) = *Pocos (-as)*.
E.g.: *Hay pocas flores este año.*
There are few flowers this year.
Pocos han llegado.
Few have arrived.

FEWER AND FEWER
See **LESS AND LESS, FEWER AND FEWER**

FIARSE DE

(Reflexive verb) = "To trust."
E.g.: *No me fío de ellos.*
I don't trust them.

FIJARSE EN

(Reflexive verb) = "To notice, to stare at."
E.g.: *Ellas se fijaron en la estatua de Miguel Ángel.*
They stared at Michelangelo's statue.

FIRST

(1) *Primero (-a)* (Adjective).
E.g.: *Mi primera clase empieza a las nueve.*
My first class begins at nine o'clock.
NOTE:
Primero drops the final -*o* before a masculine noun.
E.g.: *El primer día de la semana.*
The first day of the week.
(2) *Primeramente* or *primero* (Adverb) = "First of all, firstly."
E.g.: *Primero, quiero felicitarle.*
First, I want to congratulate you.

FOR

(Preposition). Its translation depends on the context:
(a) indicating destination or purpose = *para*.
E.g.: *Tengo una sorpresa para ti.*
I have a surprise for you.

Esta máquina es para pelar las manzanas.
This machine is for peeling apples.
(b) meaning "in exchange for" = *por*.
E.g.: *Te lo vendo por dos mil pesetas.*
I'll sell it to you for two thousand pesetas.
(c) meaning "in favor of" = *por*.
E.g.: *Yo estoy por los demócratas.*
I am for the democrats.
(d) indicating reason or cause = *por, a causa de*.
E.g.: *México es famoso por sus pirámides.*
Mexico is famous for its pyramids.
(e) indicating time past = *for (duration)*.
E.g.: *Catalina se quedó en Madrid por ocho días.*
Catherine stayed in Madrid for a week.
See *PARA* **vs.** *POR*

FOR + time expressions

(1) To express duration use *por* (but it can be omitted altogether).
   E.g.: *Nos quedamos en Acapulco (por) dos semanas.*
       We stayed in Acapulco for two weeks.
(2) To emphasize the termination of a period of time use *para*.
   E.g.: *Obtuve un empleo para tres meses.*
       I got a job for three months.

FOR LACK OF

(Prepositional expression) = *Por falta de.*
E.g.: *No lo terminaron por falta de tiempo.*
   They didn't finish it for lack of time.

to FORGET

(Transitive verb) = *Olvidar.*
E.g.: *Olvidaron mi cumpleaños.*
   They forgot my birthday.
NOTES:
(1) The reflexive construction *Olvidarse de* is frequently used:
   E.g.: *Se olvidaron de mi cumpleaños.*
       They forgot my birthday.
(2) The idiomatic construction *Olvidarse a uno* is also frequently used.
   E.g.: *Se me olvidó el libro.*
       I forgot my book.
   In this construction the English direct object ("my book") is the subject in Spanish *(el libro).*
See **OLVIDAR vs. OLVIDARSE**

FORMAL vs. FAMILIAR FORMS
See **USTED(ES) vs. TÚ/VOSOTROS (-AS)**

FORMER . . . LATTER

(Idiomatic construction) = *Éste . . . aquél.*
This construction is the reverse of the English construction (*éste* = the latter, *aquél* = the former).
E.g.: *María y Juana estudian en la universidad. Ésta estudia la contabilidad, aquélla la literatura.*
   Mary and Joan study at the university. The former studies literature, the latter accounting.

FORZAR

(Transitive verb) = "To force."
PRES.: *fuerz-o, -as, -a, forzamos, forzáis, fuerzan.*
IMPERF.: *forz-aba, -abas, -aba, -ábamos, -abais, -aban.*
PRETER.: *forcé, forz-aste, -ó, -amos, -asteis, -aron.*
FUT.: *forzar-é, -ás, -á, -emos, -éis, -án.*
CONDIT.: *forzar-ía, -ías, -ía, -íamos, -íais, -ían.*
SUBJ. PRES.: *fuerc-e, -es, -e, forcemos, forcéis, fuercen.*
SUBJ. IMPERF. 1: *forz-ara, -aras, -ara, -áramos, -arais, -aran.*
SUBJ. IMPERF. 2: *forz-ase, -ases, -ase, -ásemos, -aseis, -asen.*
INFORMAL IMPERAT.: *fuerza (tú), no fuerces (tú); forzad (vosotros), no forcéis (vosotros).*
FORMAL IMPERAT.: *fuerce (Vd.); forcemos; fuercen (Vds.).*
PRES. PARTIC.: *forzando.*
PAST PARTIC.: *forzado.*

FRACTIONS

Use ordinal numbers, as in English.

E.g.: ⅕ = *un quinto.*

⅜ = *dos octavos.*

EXCEPTIONS:

⅓ = *un tercio.*

½ = *un medio.*

NOTE:

La mitad also means "half."

E.g.: *La mitad de la clase.*

Half the class.

La primera mitad del libro.

The first half of the book.

FROM . . . ON (= beginning on/at)

= *Desde* (Preposition).

E.g.: *El banco está abierto desde las nueve.*

The bank is open from nine o'clock on.

FROM . . . TO

= *De* (or *desde*) . . . *hasta* (Preposition).

E.g.: *Trabajamos de las nueve hasta las cinco.*

We work from nine to five.

Carmen fue de Barcelona hasta Santander.

Carmen went from Barcelona to Santander.

NOTE:

Desde stresses more emphatically than *de* the point of departure. It corresponds to the English "all the way from."

FUERA DE SÍ

(Idiomatic expression) = "Beside oneself."

E.g.: *Cuando se enteró de la noticia estaba fuera de sí.*

When he learned the news he was beside himself.

See *SACAR DE QUICIO*

FUERA (DE)

(1) *Fuera* (Adverb) = "Out, outside."

E.g.: *María está fuera.*

Mary is outside.

(2) *Fuera de* (Prepositional construction) = "Outside of, away from."

E.g.: *Pasan unos días fuera de Guadalajara.*

They are spending a few days outside Guadalajara.

FURTHERMORE

= *Además* (Adverb).

E.g.: *Está cansado y además tiene dolor de cabeza.*

He is tired and, furthermore, he has a headache.

FUTURE in a subordinate clause

A subordinate clause introduced by a verb in the present, future, present perfect, or imperative, or a conjunction such as *cuando, tan pronto como*, etc., and referring to a future action must be expressed in the subjunctive mood.

E.g.: *No creo que lleguen tarde.*
I don't think that they will arrive late.

Siento que no vengas conmigo.
I'm sorry that you will not come with me.

Diles que vayan al centro mañana.
Tell them to go downtown tomorrow.

See **SUBJUNCTIVE MOOD**

FUTURE in the past

If the main clause is in the past, the future is conveyed by using the conditional. This is exactly the same construction as in English.

E.g.: *Ella dijo que iría a Segovia.*
She said that she would go to Segovia.

See **INDIRECT DISCOURSE**

FUTURE PERFECT TENSE

This tense *(el futuro anterior)* describes an action which will take place in the future before a point in time (or another action) which is also in the future.

FORMATION:

Future of *haber* + past participle.

E.g.: *Ella habrá terminado antes de salir.*
She will have finished before going out.

USAGE:

(1) It is used as in English to indicate an action which will occur in the future before some point which is also in the future.

E.g.: *Habré terminado para el miércoles.*
I shall have finished by Wednesday.

(2) It is also used to express probability in the past.

E.g.: *¿No ha llegado? Habrá tenido un accidente.*
He has not arrived? He must (probably) have had an accident.

FUTURE TENSE

The future describes an action which is still to take place.

E.g.: *Saldremos mañana.*
We shall go out tomorrow.

FORMATION:

Infinitive + *-é, -ás, -á, -emos, -éis, -án.*

EXCEPTIONS:

The following verbs use a slightly irregular stem to form the future:

Decir → dir-é	To say
Haber → habr-é	To have
Hacer → har-é	To do, to make
Poder → podr-é	To be able
Poner → pondr-é	To put
Querer → querr-é	To want, to love
Saber → sabr-é	To know
Salir → saldr-é	To go out
Tener → tendr-é	To have
Venir → vendr-é	To come

USAGE:

This tense corresponds to the English "shall" or "will."

NOTES:
(1) When "will" means "To be willing," it must be translated by using the verb *querer*.
>   E.g.: *Pedro no quiere venir con nosotros.*
>   Peter is not willing to come with us.

(2) The future is sometimes used to express probability.
See **FUTURE to express probability**
(3) It can also be used to express commands.
>   E.g.: *Vds. leerán el capítulo cuatro para mañana.*
>   You will read chapter four for tomorrow.

See **PROXIMATE FUTURE**

FUTURE to express probability

The future tense can be used to express probability (i.e. "must be," "probably").
>   E.g.: *Hay alguien en la sala. ¿Quién será?*
>   There is somebody in the living room. Who could it be?
>
>   *Arturo estará enfermo.*
>   Arthur must be sick.

NOTE:
Likewise, the future perfect can be used to express probability in the past.
>   E.g.: *¿Dónde habrán encontrado eso?*
>   Where could they have (= Where have they probably) found that?

FUTURE WITH *IR A* + infinitive

This construction is called the proximate future. It corresponds to the English "going to + verb."
Its use generally implies that the action will take place in a relatively near future.
>   E.g.: *Voy a ir al teatro la semana próxima.*
>   I am going to go to the theater next week.

See **PROXIMATE FUTURE**

FUTURO ANTERIOR
See **FUTURE PERFECT TENSE**

G

GANA

(Feminine noun) = "Desire, will."
See *TENER GANAS (DE)*

GENDER

The gender *(el género)* is a grammatical property of nouns. In Spanish all nouns are either masculine or feminine. While the gender of each noun should be memorized, it is sometimes possible to tell the gender by looking at the ending of the noun.
GENERAL RULES:
(1) Nouns ending in *-o* are masculine.
>   E.g.: *El libro*   the book
>   *el muchacho*   the boy

(2) Nouns ending in *-a, -d, -ción, -sión, -umbre* are generally feminine.
>   E.g.: *La muchacha*   the girl
>   *la ciudad*   the city
>   *la virtud*   the virtue
>   *la confusión*   the confusion
>   *la muchedumbre*   the multitude

EXCEPTIONS:
(1) The following nouns ending in *-a* are masculine.

E.g.:	*El clima*	the climate
	el día	the day
	el drama	the drama
	el idioma	the language
	el mapa	the map
	el poeta	the poet
	el problema	the problem
	el programa	the program
	el telegrama	the telegram
	el tranvía	the streetcar

(2) The following nouns ending in *-o* are feminine:

la mano	the hand
la radio	the radio

See **FEMININE NOUNS, identified by the ending**
See also **MASCULINE NOUNS, identified by the ending**

GENTE

(Feminine noun) = "People, folks."
This is a singular noun although it refers to a plural concept.

E.g.: *La gente rica vive en palacios.*
Rich people live in palaces.

GEOGRAPHICAL NAMES

As all other nouns, names of countries, rivers, oceans, mountains, etc., are either masculine or feminine.

GENERAL RULES:
(1) Names of countries ending in *-a* are feminine. All others are masculine.

E.g.:	*la Argentina*	Argentina
	la Gran Bretaña	Great Britain
	el Japón	Japan
	el Uruguay	Uruguay

EXCEPTION:

el Canadá	Canada

NOTE:
Some countries, cities, and states are sometimes preceded by the definite article (but this usage is gradually becoming optional):

la Argentina	Argentina	*La Habana*	Havana
el Brasil	Brazil	*el Japón*	Japan
el Canadá	Canada	*el Paraguay*	Paraguay
la China	China	*el Perú*	Peru
los Estados Unidos	The United States	*El Salvador*	El Salvador
la Florida	Florida	*el Uruguay*	Uruguay
la Gran Bretaña	Great Britain		

(2) Names of rivers, oceans, seas and mountains are masculine.
E.g.: *el Ebro.* The Ebro River. *los Pirineos,* The Pyrenees. *el Pacífico.* The Pacific Ocean.
BUT if the word *montañas* or *sierra* is part of the name then it is feminine.
E.g.: *la Sierra Nevada.* The Sierra Nevada. *las Montañas Rocosas.* the Rocky Mountains.

NOTES:
(1) Countries are sometimes personified and therefore take the personal *a* (with no definite article).
E.g.: *Visitamos a Chile.*
We visited Chile.
(2) The definite article is used before geographical names which are modified.
E.g.: *la América del Sur.*
South America.

(3) The names of American states are the same as in English except the following:

la Carolina del Norte	North Carolina
la Carolina del Sur	South Carolina
la Luisiana	Louisiana
Nuevo México	New Mexico
Dakota del Norte	North Dakota
Dakota del Sur	South Dakota
Virginia del Oeste	West Virginia

GERUND

(El gerundio).
See **PARTICIPLE, PRESENT (GERUND)**

to GET

This verb may be translated in many different ways depending on the meaning. It is wise to think of an English synonym and then translate that synonym into Spanish.

E.g.:

I got this in Madrid.	= I bought this in Madrid.	= *Compré esto en Madrid.*
We got a letter.	= We received a letter.	= *Recibimos una carta.*
Go get your books!	= Go fetch your books!	= *¡Ve por tus libros!*
You must get ready.	= You must prepare yourself.	= *Debes prepararte.*
They got there at noon.	= They arrived at noon.	= *Llegaron a mediodía.*
He got sick last week.	= He became sick.	= *Se enfermó la semana pasada.*
I am getting fat.	= I am becoming fat.	= *Me engordo.*

See **HACERSE**

GOING TO + verb

This is the "proximate future" construction = "*Ir a* + infinitive."
E.g.: *Vamos a comprar una casa.*
  We are going to buy a house.
See **PROXIMATE FUTURE**

GOZAR DE

(Intransitive verb) = "To enjoy, to benefit from."
E.g.: *Mi hermano gozó mucho de sus vacaciones en la Costa Brava.*
  My brother enjoyed his vacation on the Costa Brava very much.

GRACIAS A

(Preposition construction) = "Thanks to."
E.g.: *Pude obtenerlo gracias a Miguel.*
  I was able to obtain it thanks to Michael.

GRAN(DE)

(Adjective) = "Great, big, large."
NOTE:
When *grande* is followed by a singular noun it drops the ending: *gran.*
E.g.: *Han construído un gran edificio.*
  They have built a great building.

GUARDAR CAMA

(Verbal idiom) = "To stay in bed."
E.g.: *La muchacha guardó cama durante un mes entero.*
  The girl stayed in bed for a whole month.

GUSTAR

(Transitive verb used with direct object) = "To please, to be pleasing."
This verb is used to express the English "To like" but BEWARE because it requires a special construction! An English sentence using "To like" must be changed to a sentence using "To be pleasing (to)" to approach the Spanish construction.

E.g.: I like the book.	= The book is pleasing to me.	= *Me gusta el libro.*
I like the books.	= The books are pleasing to me.	= *Me gustan los libros.*
We like the books.	= The books are pleasing to us.	= *Nos gustan los libros.*

NOTES:

(1) The word order is inverted: "To us-are pleasing-the books." The most frequently used forms of *gustar* are the third persons singular and plural *(gusta, gustan, gustaba, gustaban, gustó, gustaron,* etc.)

(2) The person who does the liking becomes the indirect object (or the "experiencer") in Spanish.

(3) When the indirect object of *gustar* is a noun, remember to also use the indirect object pronoun *(le, les)*.

E.g.: *A María no le gustan las uvas.*
Mary doesn't like grapes.

Remember that *gustar* must be conjugated to agree with the Spanish subject (or the "theme") of the verb, i.e., with the English direct object.

(4) The subject generally follows the verb *gustar*.

E.g.: *Me gusta tu camisa.*
I like your shirt.

Les gusta la novela.
They like the novel.

¿Os gustó la obra?
Did you like the play?

A Guillermo le gustaba nadar.
William used to like swimming.

Al profesor no le gustaron nuestros chistes.
The teacher did not like our jokes.

(5) The following verbs also take this construction:

(a)	*Agradar*	To be pleasing
(b)	*Agradecer*	To thank
(c)	*Bastar*	To suffice
(d)	*Doler*	To ache, to be painful
(e)	*Faltar*	To lack, to be missing or absent
(f)	*Hacer falta*	To be missing or absent, to need
(g)	*Importar*	To matter
(h)	*Interesar*	To interest
(i)	*Parecer*	To seem
(j)	*Placer*	To be pleasing, to like
(k)	*Quedar(le) (a alguien)*	To have left, to remain
(l)	*Sobrar*	To remain, to be left over
(m)	*Tocar*	to concern, to affect

E.g.: (a) *No me agrada este hombre.*
I don't like that man.

(b) *Te agradezco la ayuda.*
I thank you (am grateful) for your help.

(c) *Me bastan cinco horas para hacer esto.*
Five hours are enough (suffice) for me to finish this.

(d) *Me duelen los dientes.*
My teeth hurt. (I have a toothache.)

(e) *¿Cuánto dinero te falta?*
How much money do you need (lack)?

(f) *Les hacía falta el ánimo para combatir.*
They lacked the courage to fight.

(g) *A mí no me importa el precio.*
The price does not matter to me.
(h) *No nos interesa el béisbol.*
We are not interested in baseball.
(i) *Les parecerá difícil.*
It will seem difficult to them.
(j) *Nos place oír música moderna.*
We like to hear modern music.
(k) *¿Cuánto tiempo nos queda?*
How much time do we have left?
(l) *Les sobraban cinco minutos.*
They had five minutes left.
(m) *A tí te toca este problema.*
This problem concerns you.

HABER

(Auxiliary verb) = "To have, to get."
PRES.: *he, has, ha, hemos, habéis, han.* Impersonal form: *hay.*
IMPERF.: *había, habías, había, habíamos, habíais, habían.* Impersonal form: *había.*
PRETER.: *hube, hubiste, hubo, hubimos, hubisteis, hubieron.* Impersonal form: *hubo.*
FUT.: *habr-é, -ás, -á, -emos, -éis, -án.* Impersonal form: *habrá.*
CONDIT.: *habr-ía, -ías, -ía, -íamos, -íais, -ían.* Impersonal form: *habría.*
SUBJ. PRES.: *hay-a, -as, -a, -amos, -áis, -an.* Impersonal form: *haya.*
SUBJ. IMPERF. 1: *hubi-era, -eras, -era, -éramos, -erais, -eran.* Impersonal form: *hubierae*
SUBJ. IMPERF. 2: *hubi-ese, -eses, -ese, -ésemos, -eseis, -esen.* Impersonal form: *hubiese.*
INFORMAL IMPERAT.: *he (tú), no hayas (tú); habed (vosotros), no hayáis (vosotros).*
FORMAL IMPERAT.: *haya (Vd.); hayamos; hayan (Vds.).*
PRES. PARTIC.: *habiendo.*
PAST PARTIC.: *habido.*
Haber is an auxiliary verb used with the past participle to form all compound tenses of verbs:
(a) The present tense of *haber* + past participle = present perfect tense.
(b) The imperfect tense of *haber* + past participle = pluperfect tense.
(c) The future tense of *haber* + past participle = future perfect.
(d) The conditional tense of *haber* + past participle = conditional perfect.
(e) The subjunctive present of *haber* + past participle = past subjunctive (or present perfect subjunctive).
(f) The imperfect subjunctive of *haber* + past participle = pluperfect subjunctive.
NOTES:
(1) *Haber* is used impersonally to mean "There is, there are."
Do not confuse *hay* with *es* and *son* (= "It is, they are").
Haber is conjugated impersonally in all tenses:
PRES.: *hay* = there is, there are.
IMPERF.: *había* = there was, there were.
PRETER.: *hubo* = there was, there were.
FUT.: *habrá* = there will be.
CONDIT.: *habría* = there would be.
PRES. PERF.: *ha habido* = there has (or have) been.
PLUPERF.: *había habido* = there had been.
SUBJ. PRES.: *haya* = there be.
SUBJ. IMPERF. 1: *hubiera* = there be.
SUBJ. IMPERF. 2: *hubiese* = there be.

(2) *Haber que* + infinitive = "It is necessary to, one has to, you have to."
    E.g.: *Hay que estudiar más.*
        You have (one has) to study more.
(3) The past participle used with *haber* always has a masculine singular ending.
(4) Do not separate *haber* from the past participle. Pronoun objects must be placed before the form of *haber* or between the negative and the form of *haber*.
    E.g.: *Hemos comido la carne.*
        We have eaten the meat.

        Ellos no la habían comido.
        They had not eaten it.
(5) *Haber de* + infinitive = "to have to" (somewhat less emphatic than *haber que*).
See **HABER DE** + **infinitive**
(6) When "must" indicates a personal obligation, use *Tener que* + infinitive.
    E.g.: *Tenemos que ir a la escuela a las siete y media.*
        We have to go to school at half past seven.

HABER DE + infinitive

(Verbal idiom) = "To have to, to be supposed to."
E.g.: *Hemos de llegar antes de las siete.*
    We are supposed to arrive before seven.

HABER LUNA

(Verbal idiom) = "The moon is shining."
E.g.: *Hubo luna toda la noche.*
    The moon shone all night.

HABER QUE (HAY QUE)

See **HABER**

HABER SOL

(Verbal idiom) = "To be sunny."
E.g.: *En el verano hay mucho sol aquí.*
    It is very sunny here in the summer.

HABLAR

(Transitive verb) = "To speak."
PRES.: *habl-o, -as, -a, amos, -áis, -an.*
IMPERF.: *habl-aba, -abas, -aba, -ábamos, -abais, -aban.*
PRETER.: *habl-é, -aste, -ó, -amos, -asteis, -aron.*
FUT.: *hablar-é, -ás, -á, -emos, -éis, -án.*
CONDIT.: *hablar-ía, -ías, -ía, -íamos, -íais, -ían.*
SUBJ. PRES.: *habl-e, -es, -e, -emos, -éis, -en.*
SUBJ. IMPERF. 1: *habl-ara, -aras, -ara, -áramos, -arais, -aran.*
SUBJ. IMPERF. 2: *habl-ase, -ases, -ase, -ásemos, -aseis, -asen.*
INFORMAL IMPERAT.: *habla (tú), no hables (tú); hablad (vosotros), no habléis (vosotros).*
FORMAL IMPERAT.: *hable (Vd.); hablemos; hablen (Vds.).*
PRES. PARTIC.: *hablando.*
PAST PARTIC.: *hablado.*

HACER

(Transitive verb) = "To do, to make."
PRES.: *hago, haces, hace, hacemos, hacéis, hacen.*
IMPERF.: *hac-ía, -ías, -ía, -íamos, -íais, -ían.*
PRETER.: *hice, hiciste, hizo, hicimos, hicisteis, hicieron.*
FUT.: *har-é, -ás, -á, -emos, -éis, -án.*
CONDIT.: *har-ía, -ías, -ía, -íamos, -íais, -ían.*
SUBJ. PRES.: *hag-a, -as, -a, -amos, -áis, -an.*
SUBJ. IMPERF. 1: *hici-era, -eras, -era, -éramos, -erais, -eran.*
SUBJ. IMPERF. 2: *hici-ese, -eses, -ese, -ésemos, -eseis, -esen.*
INFORMAL IMPERAT.: *haz (tú), no hagas (tú); haced (vosotros), no hagáis (vosotros).*
FORMAL IMPERAT.: *haga (Vd.); hagamos; hagan (Vds.).*
PRES. PARTIC.: *haciendo.*
PAST PARTIC.: *hecho.*
See below the many idiomatic uses of *HACER*

HACER + **infinitive**

This is the causative construction. It corresponds to the English "To have + direct object + past participle (+ indirect object)."
E.g.: *Les hicimos construir una casa.*
   We had a house built for them.
See **CAUSATIVE CONSTRUCTIONS WITH *HACER***

HACER + **time expression**

(Verbal idioms)
(1) To indicate an action begun in the past and still going on:
   (a) *Hace* + time expression + *que* + present tense.
      E.g.: *Hace dos horas que miro la televisión.*
         I have been watching television for two hours.
or: (b) Present tense + *desde hace* + time expression.
      E.g.: *Miro la televisión desde hace dos horas.*
         I have been watching television for two hours.
(2) To indicate an action which had been going on for a certain length of time and was still going on when something else happened:
   (a) *Hacía* + time expression + *que* + imperfect tense.
      E.g.: *Hacía dos horas que miraba la televisión cuando ella entró.*
         It had been two hours that I was watching television when she entered.
or: (b) Imperfect tense of verb needed + *desde hacía* + time expression.
      E.g.: *Miraba la televisión desde hacía dos horas cuando ella entró.*
         I had been watching television for two hours when she entered.
(3) To express "ago," i.e.: an action that took place in the past in relation to the present time:
   (a) Past tense (preterite or present perfect) + *hace* + time expression.
      E.g.: *Compraron una televisión hace dos meses.*
         They bought a television set two months ago.
or: (b) *Hace* + time expression + *que* + past tense (preterite or present perfect).
      E.g.: *Hace dos meses que compramos esta televisión.*
         We bought this television set two months ago.

HACER + weather

(Verbal idioms) = "It is + weather expression."
E.g.: *Hace sol.*
    It is sunny.
    Hace frío.
    It is cold.
    Hace mucho calor.
    It is very hot.
    Hace mal tiempo.
    It is bad weather.
    Hace viento.
    It is windy.
Hacer is used impersonally (in any tense) to describe the weather or the temperature.
NOTE:
Calor, fresco, frío, viento and *sol* are nouns. Therefore they are modified by the adjective *mucho* (not the adverb *muy*).
E.g.: *Hace mucho frío.*
    Hace mucho sol.
See **WEATHER**

HACER(LE) CASO

(Verbal idiom) = "To heed, pay attention to."
E.g.: *Haz caso a lo que te digo.*
    Pay attention to what I am telling you.
NOTE:
It frequently occurs with an indirect object.
E.g.: *No le hagas caso a ella.*
    Don't pay attention to her.

HACER(LE) DAÑO A

(Verbal idiom) = "To damage, to harm."
E.g.: *El tabaco les hace daño a los pulmones.*
    Tobacco harms the lungs.
NOTE:
It frequently occurs with an indirect object.

HACER EL PAPEL DE

(Verbal idiom) = "To play the part of."
E.g.: *El actor hace el papel de Hamlet.*
    The actor plays the part of Hamlet.

HACER FALTA

(Verbal idiom) = "To need, to be lacking."
E.g.: *Nos hacen falta los documentos oficiales.*
    We need the official documents.
NOTE:
This construction is the same as that used with **GUSTAR**.

HACER in causative constructions
See **CAUSATIVE CONSTRUCTIONS WITH *HACER***

HACER PEDAZOS

(Verbal idiom) = "To break into pieces."
E.g.: *Hizo pedazos la ventana con una pelota.*
    He broke the window (in pieces) with a ball.

HACER SABER

(Verbal idiom) = "To inform, to let (somebody) know."
E.g.: *El gerente nos hizo saber que no vendría la semana próxima.*
    The manager informed us that he would not come next week.

HACER UN VIAJE

(Verbal idiom) = "To take a trip, to go on a trip."
E.g.: *Hicimos un viaje a Puerto Rico.*
    We went on a trip to Puerto Rico.

HACER UNA PREGUNTA

(Verbal idiom) = "To ask a question."
E.g.: *Mis padres nunca hacen preguntas.*
    My parents never ask questions.

HACER UNA VISITA

(Verbal idiom) = "To pay a visit."
E.g.: *Les hice una visita a mis abuelos.*
    I paid a visit to my grandparents.

HACERSE + noun

(Reflexive verb) = "To become [through one's efforts]."
E.g.: *Si trabajas mucho puedes hacerte médico.*
    If you work hard you can become a doctor.
See **to BECOME**

HACERSE TARDE

(Verbal idiom) = "To get late."
E.g.: *Vamos a irnos porque ya se hace muy tarde.*
    We're going to leave because it's already getting late.

HACIA

(Preposition) = "Toward(s), about."
E.g.: *Anduvimos hacia el río.*
    We walked toward the river.
    Te llamaré hacia las cuatro.
    I shall call you about four o'clock.

HALLARSE

(Reflexive verb) = "To find oneself, to be (located)."
E.g.: *¿Dónde se halla la iglesia?*
    Where is the church (located)?

to HAPPEN

= *Pasar* or *Ocurrir* (Intransitive verbs).
E.g.: *¿Qué pasa?*
    What's happening?
    ¿Qué le ocurrió a Juan?
    What happened to John?

HARDLY ANY

= *Apenas* (Adverb).
E.g.: *Apenas tiene dinero.*
    He has hardly any money.

HASTA

(1) Adverb = "Even."
    E.g.: *He leído hasta los anuncios.*
        I even read the advertisements.
(2) Preposition:
    (a) expressing time = "Until."
        E.g.: *Me voy hasta el martes.*
            I'm leaving until Tuesday.
    (b) expressing place = "As far as."
        E.g.: *Fuimos hasta la frontera.*
            We went as far as the border.

HASTA QUE

(Conjunctional construction) = "Until." It is followed by:
(a) the indicative
    E.g.: *El niño durmió hasta que su madre le despertó.*
        The child slept until his mother woke him.
(b) the subjunctive if it refers to a future action.
    E.g.: *Dormirán hasta que los despiertes.*
        They will sleep until you wake them up.

to HAVE + direct object + past participle

(Causative construction) = *Hacer* + infinitive, or *Mandar* + infinitive.
E.g.: *Hice reparar mi coche.*
    I had my car repaired.

    Mandé reparar mi coche.
    I had my car repaired.
See **CAUSATIVE CONSTRUCTIONS WITH *HACER***

to HAVE A GOOD TIME

= *Divertirse* (Reflexive verb) or *pasarlo bien* (Verbal idiom).
E.g.: *Nos divertimos mucho anoche.*
    We had a good time last night.

    Lo pasamos bien contigo.
    We had a good time with you.

to HAVE (a drink)

= *Tomar (una bebida)* (Verbal idiom).
E.g.: *Tomaron unas tazas de café anoche.*
    They had a few cups of coffee last night.

to HAVE JUST + past participle

This idiomatic construction is called the recent past. The Spanish equivalent is *Acabar de* + infinitive.
E.g.: *Acabamos de llegar.*
    We have just arrived.
See **ACABAR DE + infinitive**

to HAVE TO + verb

(Idiomatic construction) = *Tener que* + infinitive.
E.g.: *Tenemos que ir a casa.*
>   We have to go home.
See **TENER QUE**

HAY

(Impersonal verb *Haber*) = "There is, there are."
E.g.: *Hay mucha comida.*
>   There is a lot of food.
>   *Hay muchos libros.*
>   There are a lot of books.
NOTE:
Hay is used for both singular ("There is") and plural ("There are").
See **HABER**

HAY + noun + *QUE* + infinitive

(Impersonal construction) = "There is (are) + noun + infinitive."
E.g.: *¡Hay tantos libros que leer!*
>   There are so many books to read!

HAY QUE + infinitive

(Impersonal construction) = "To have to, to be necessary."
E.g.: *Hay que estudiar para sacar buenas notas.*
>   One has to study to get good grades.

to HEAR ABOUT vs. HEAR THAT

(1) "Hear about" = *Oír hablar de.*
>   E.g.: *¿Has oído hablar de ese hombre?*
>   Have you heard about that man?
(2) "Hear that" = *Oír decir que.*
>   E.g.: *He oído decir que es difícil.*
>   I have heard that it is difficult.

HELP (CAN'T)

(Idiomatic expressions)
(1) "Can't help + present participle" = *No poder menos de* + infinitive.
>   E.g.: *No puedo menos de reír.*
>   I can't help laughing.
(2) "It can't be helped" = *No hay remedio.*

HELPING VERBS
See **VERBS, AUXILIARY**

HOME

(1) The noun = *La casa* or *el hogar.*
>   E.g.: *Mi casa está cerca.*
>   My home is nearby.
(2) The adverb ("at home") = *En casa.*
>   E.g.: *Están en casa todas las tardes.*
>   They are at home every afternoon.

to HOPE + verb

= *Esperar* (Transitive verb).
E.g.: *Espero ganar el premio.*
   I hope to win the prize.

HORA vs. TIEMPO vs. VEZ (VECES)

(1) *La hora* = "The hour."
   E.g.: *¿Qué hora es?*
      What time is it?

   ¿A qué hora comienza la película?
      At what time does the movie begin?
(2) *El tiempo* = "The (length of) time."
   E.g.: *¿Cuánto tiempo dura la película?*
      How long (how much time) does the movie last?
(3) *Vez, veces* = "Time, times."
   E.g.: *He visto esta película tres veces.*
      I have seen this movie three times.

   Quiero ver la película otra vez.
      I want to see the movie again (another time).

See **TIME vs. HOUR vs. TIMES**

HOW

(1) Interrogative adverb = *¿Cómo?*
   E.g.: *¿Cómo estás?*
      How are you?
(2) Exclamative adverb = *¡Qué!*
   E.g.: *¡Qué bonita es Carmen!*
      How beautiful Carmen is!

HOW MANY, HOW MUCH

= *Cuánto (-a, -os, -as)* (Interrogative adjective).
E.g.: *¿Cuánto dinero hay?*
   How much money is there?

   ¿Cuántas hermanas tienes?
   How many sisters do you have?

HOY (EN) DÍA

(Adverbial idiom) = "Nowadays."
E.g.: *Hoy día un televisor no cuesta mucho.*
   Nowadays a television set is not expensive.

HOY MISMO

(Adverbial idiom) = "This very day."
E.g.: *Prometió hacerlo hoy mismo.*
   He promised to do it this very day.

HUBO

(Preterite of the impersonal verb *haber*) = "There was, there were."
E.g.: *Hubo un accidente.*
   There was an accident.
NOTE:
Hubo is used for both singular and plural.
See **HABER**

to be HUNGRY

= *Tener hambre* (Verbal idiom).
E.g.: *Arturo siempre tiene hambre.*
    Arthur is always hungry.

to HURT

(1) The transitive verb "To hurt" = *Hacer daño.*
    E.g.: *Me estás haciendo daño.*
        You're hurting me.
(2) The intransitive verb "To hurt" = *Doler.*
    E.g.: *Me duele la pierna.*
        My leg hurts.
NOTE:
The person is the indirect object.
(3) The transitive verb "To hurt (morally)" = *Ofender.*
    E.g.: *No quiero ofenderte, pero te equivocas.*
        I don't want to hurt you but you are wrong.

HYPOTHETICAL STATEMENTS

Hypothetical, or imaginary, statements are conveyed by the conditional mood.
E.g.: *Iría al cine si tuviera el tiempo.*
    I would go to the movies if I had the time.
See **CONDITIONAL TENSES**

I

IDIOMS

Idioms *(los modismos)* are expressions peculiar to one language which cannot be translated literally into another language. An example of idiom in English is "He doesn't have a leg to stand on." The Spanish equivalent is *"No tiene razón alguna."* An example of a Spanish idiom is *"Mudarse a cualquier aire,"* which means "To be fickle." Every language has a large number of idioms which must be learned through practice in context.

(1) Some common idioms with *dar* are *dar a, dar con, dar en, dar las gracias, dar la hora, dar un paseo, dar recuerdos, dar una vuelta, darse cuenta de, darse la mano, darse prisa.*
(2) Some common idioms with *echar* are *echarse a, echar al correo, echar la culpa, echar de menos.*
(3) Some common idioms with *haber* are *haber de, haber que, haber luna, haber sol.*
(4) Some common idioms with *hacer* are *hace poco, hacer buen (mal) tiempo, hacer viento, hacer caso, hacer daño, hacer el papel de, hacer pedazos, hacer una visita, hacer una pregunta, hacer un viaje, hacerse + noun, hacerse tarde.*
(5) Some common idioms with *tener* are *tener calor (frío), tener cuidado, tener dolor de (cabeza, dientes, etc.), tener éxito, tener ganas de, tener hambre (sed), tener la culpa de, tener lugar, tener miedo de, tener por, tener prisa, tener que ver con, tener razón, tener sueño, tener suerte, tener vergüenza.*

See the alphabetical listing for each of these idioms.

"IF" CLAUSES
See *"SI"* CLAUSES

IGNORE

(Transitive verb) = *No hacerle caso.*

E.g.: *Ella no me hizo caso toda la tarde.*
    She ignored me all afternoon.

See **HACER(LE) CASO**

Do not confuse with the verb *ignorar,* which means "not to know."

E.g.: *Ignoro su dirección.*
    I don't know his address.

IMAGINARY STATEMENTS
See **HYPOTHETICAL STATEMENTS**

IMPERATIVE MOOD

The imperative mood *(el imperativo)* presents the action of the verb as a command or exhortation.

FORMS:

FAMILIAR COMMANDS:

(a) <u>Singular Affirmative</u>: The singular form is the same as the third person singular of the present indicative, whether it is regular or not.

EXCEPTIONS:

decir → di
hacer → haz
ir → ve
poner → pon
salir → sal
ser → sé
tener → ten
valer → val
venir → ven

(b) <u>Plural Affirmative</u>: The plural is formed by dropping the final *-r* of the infinitive and replacing it with *-d.* It is always regular.

FORMAL COMMANDS:

Both affirmative and negative formal commands are expressed by the present subjunctive.

NOTES:

(1) The negative commands are rendered by the subjunctive forms:

For the purposes of comparison, here is a summary of all familiar command forms:

E.g.: Infinitive	Sing. Affirmative	Sing. Negative	Plur. Affirmative	Plur. Negative
Hablar	*¡Habla!*	*¡No hables!*	*¡Hablad!*	*¡No habléis!*
Comer	*¡Come!*	*¡No comas!*	*¡Comed!*	*¡No comáis!*
Escribir	*¡Escribe!*	*¡No escribas!*	*¡Escribid!*	*¡No escribáis!*

(2) Again, for purposes of comparison, here is a summary of all the formal command forms. They are conveyed by the subjunctive mood. For negative commands, simply use *no* before the verb.

E.g.: Infinitive	Sing. Affirmative	Sing. Negative	Plur. Affirmative	Plur. Negative
Hablar	*¡Hable Vd.!*	*¡No hable Vd.!*	*¡Hablen Vds.!*	*¡No hablen Vds.!*
Comer	*¡Coma Vd.!*	*¡No coma Vd.!*	*¡Coman Vds.!*	*¡No coman Vds.!*
Escribir	*¡Escriba Vd.!*	*¡No escriba Vd.!*	*¡Escriban Vds.!*	*¡No escriban Vds.!*

COMMANDS OF REFLEXIVE VERBS:

REMEMBER:

(1) Reflexive pronouns are placed after—and linked to—the verb in the affirmative commands but before the verb in the negative commands.

(2) In affirmative commands a written accent must be used to maintain the stress in its natural position.

FORMS:
FAMILIAR COMMANDS:

E.g.: Infinitive	Sing. Affirmative	Sing. Negative	Plur. Affirmative	Plur. Negative
Levantarse	¡Levántate!	¡No te levantes!	¡Levantaos!*	¡No os levantéis!
Ponerse	¡Pontel	¡No te pongas!	¡Pongaos!*	¡No os pongáis!
Irse	¡Vete!	¡No te vayas!	¡Idos!	¡No os vayáis!

*NOTE:
The final -d of the familiar plural command forms disappears when followed by the reflexive os.
E.g.: ¡Levantaos!
    Get up!

    ¡Sentaos!
    Sit down!

FORMAL COMMANDS:

E.g.: Infinitive	Sing. Affirmative	Sing. Negative	Plur. Affirmative	Plur. Negative
Levantarse	¡Levántese Vd.!	¡No se levante Vd.!	¡Levántense Vds.!	¡No se levanten Vds.!
Ponerse	¡Póngase Vd.!	¡No se ponga Vd.!	¡Pónganse Vds.!	¡No se pongan Vds.!
Irse	¡Váyase Vd.!	¡No se vaya Vd.!	¡Váyanse Vds.!	¡No se vayan Vds.!

OBJECT PRONOUNS WITH COMMANDS:
Object pronouns are placed after and linked to affirmative command forms.
NOTES
(1) If there are two pronouns, an accent mark must be placed on the verb to retain the original stress.
    E.g.: ¡Dámelo!
        Give it to me!

        ¡Dígasela!
        Tell it to him (to her, to them).
(2) In negative commands, the object pronouns precede the verb.
    E.g.: ¡No me los des!
        Don't give it to me!

        ¡No se la diga Vd.!
        Don't tell it to him (to her, to them).

IMPERATIVE, position of object pronouns with
See IMPERATIVE MOOD

IMPERFECT TENSE

(El imperfecto)
FORMATION:
(a) First conjugation verbs:
    The stem + aba, abas, aba, ábamos, abais, aban.
(b) Second conjugation (-er), and Third conjugation (-ir) verbs:
    The stem + ía, ías, ía, íamos, íais, ían.

E.g.: Yo hablaba	Tu comías	Ella viviá
I spoke (was speaking)	You ate (were eating)	She lived (was living)
Nosotros estudiábamos	Vosotros sabíais	Ellos escribían
We studied (were studying)	You knew	They wrote (were writing)

EXCEPTIONS:
Ir = iba, ibas, iba, íbamos, ibais, iban.
Ser = era, eras, era éramos, erais, eran.
Ver = veía, veías, veía, veíamos, veíais, veían.

USAGE:

The imperfect tense is used in four principal cases:

(1) To describe actions in the past which were going on (but not yet finished) when something else happened.

E.g.: *Leía cuando tú entraste.*

I was reading when you entered.

Ellos querían ir al teatro.

They wanted to go to the theater.

(2) To give a description or a state of affairs in the past.

E.g.: *Ella llevaba traje azul.*

She was wearing a blue dress.

Mis padres eran muy pobres.

My parents were very poor.

(3) To describe actions performed habitually or repeatedly in the past. This corresponds to the English "used to" or "would".

E.g.: *Me levantaba siempre muy temprano.*

I always used to get up early.

Ella siempre hablaba inglés con su hermana.

She always spoke (would speak, used to speak) English with her sister.

(4) To express the time of day in the past.

E.g.: *Eran las cinco y media.*

It was half past five.

NOTES:

(1) The interrupted or ongoing action goes in the imperfect, while the interrupting action goes in the preterite.

E.g.: *Dormía cuando el teléfono sonó.*

I was sleeping when the telephone rang.

E.g.: *Llovía cuando salí.*

It was raining when I went out.

(2) Do not use the conditional in Spanish for repeated actions. This must be rendered by the imperfect.

E.g.: *Iba a nadar frecuentemente cuando era niño.*

I would often go swimming when I was young.

See **IMPERFECT vs. PRETERITE**

IMPERFECT vs. PRETERITE

(1) The IMPERFECT tense is used:

(a) to describe ongoing or continuing actions or situations in the past.

E.g.: *Estudiábamos el ruso.*

We studied (were studying) Russian.

(b) to describe habitual or repeated actions or events in the past. In this sense it corresponds to the English "Used to + infinitive" or "Would + infinitive."

E.g.: *Iba a la piscina todos los días.*

I went (used to go, would go) to the swimming pool every day.

(c) to describe conditions, states of mind, people, etc.

E.g.: *Hacía frío.*

It was cold.

Estaban furiosos.

They were furious.

Era una muchacha muy inteligente.

She was a very intelligent girl.

In general terms, the IMPERFECT expresses what is incomplete, or an action, situation, etc., whose limits are not known. It describes an action, condition, or scene taking place in the past, but without giving any indication as to the beginning or end of this action. It describes an action under way but not finished. The imperfect tense is always used as the Spanish equivalent of the English "used to + infinitive." It is also generally used to convey the English "was (were) + present participle."

(2) The PRETERITE tense is used:
   (a) to express specific events or actions in the past.
       E.g.: *Fueron a Bilbao.*
             They went to Bilbao.
   (b) to express a series of actions which occurred in the past.
       E.g.: *Entraron, se sentaron y pidieron el menú.*
             They entered, sat down, and asked for the menu.

In general terms, the PRETERITE expresses what is complete, or an action or situation whose limits are (at least implicitly) known and definite.

IMPERSONAL EXPRESSIONS

Impersonal expressions are those which include a verb in the third person singular whose subject is not a person.

E.g.: *Es imposible* = It is impossible
      Es lástima = It is a pity (It's too bad)
      Es verdad = It's true
      Hay = There is, there are
      Llueve = It is raining

Impersonal expressions of doubt, uncertainty, probability, etc. take:
(a) *que* + subjunctive.
    E.g.: *Es imposible que María te acompañe.*
          It is impossible for Mary to accompany you.

See **SUBJUNCTIVE MOOD**

(b) The infinitive.
    E.g.: *Me es imposible acompañarte.*
          It is impossible for me to accompany you.

IMPERSONAL EXPRESSIONS

+ SUBJUNCTIVE	+ INDICATIVE
es dudoso que	es cierto que
es importante que	es claro que
es imposible que	es evidente que
es lástima que	es verdad que
es mejor que	no hay duda que
es menester que	
es necesario que	
es preciso que	
es posible que	
es preferible que	
es probable que	
importa	
más vale	

IMPERSONAL REFLEXIVE CONSTRUCTION

The impersonal reflexive construction is frequently used in Spanish instead of a passive construction when no agent is expressed. The English equivalent is frequently expressed by "they" or "one."

E.g.: *Se venden legumbres en el mercado.*

They sell vegetables at the market.

Se habla portugués en el Brasil

They speak Portuguese in Brazil.

REMEMBER that the reflexive verb must agree with the subject. In the first example above, *se venden* is plural because the subject is *legumbres.*

IMPORTAR

(Intransitive verb) = "To be important, to matter."

It is followed by:

(a) the subjunctive.

E.g.: *Nos importa que llegues temprano.*

It is important to us that you should arrive early.

(b) the infinitive if the indirect object is a pronoun.

E.g.: *Me importa comprender esto.*

It is important for me to understand this.

IN SPITE OF (THE FACT THAT)
See DESPITE (THE FACT THAT)

INCLUSO

(Irregular past participle of *incluir* used as adverb) = "Including."

E.g.: *Todo está bien, incluso los detalles.*

Everything is fine, including the details.

INDEFINITE ADJECTIVES
See ADJECTIVES, INDEFINITE

INDEFINITE ARTICLES
See ARTICLES, INDEFINITE

INDEFINITE EXPRESSIONS

(1) *Algo* = Something, anything
(2) *Alguien* = Someone, somebody, anyone, anybody
(3) *Nada* = Nothing
(4) *Nadie* = Nobody, no one
(5) *Nunca* = Never
(6) *Siempre* = Always

NOTES:

(1) *Nada, nadie*, and *nunca* may precede or follow the verb. When they follow the verb the negative *no* must be used before the verb. When they precede the verb or are used without any verb the *no* is not needed.

E.g.: *No veo a nadie.*

I do not see anybody.

BUT: *Nadie habla.*

Nobody speaks.

(2) *Alguien* and *nadie* require the personal *a* if they are used as direct object of the verb.

E.g.: *No encontré a nadie.*

I didn't meet anyone.

INDEFINITE PRONOUNS
see **PRONOUNS, INDEFINITE**

INDEFINITE SUBJECT

In English an indefinite subject is generally conveyed by "They, people, you." The Spanish equivalent is:

(a) the impersonal reflexive construction *Se* + third person singular of the verb.

E.g.: *¿Qué se construye en esa fábrica?*
What do they build in that factory?

See **IMPERSONAL REFLEXIVE CONSTRUCTION**

(b) the third person plural of the verb.

E.g.: *¿Qué construyen en esa fábrica?*
What do they build in that factory?

INDICATIVE MOOD

The indicative mood *(el modo indicativo)* reflects the attitude that the action of the verb should be regarded as factual.

E.g.: *Este hombre trabaja.*
This man is working.

There are ten tenses in the indicative:

(a) *PRESENTE* (Present)
E.g. *Ella come.*
She eats.

(b) *FUTURO* (Future)
E.g.: *Ella comerá.*
She will eat.

(c) *PRESENTE DE POTENCIAL* (Present conditional)
E.g.: *Ella comería.*
She would eat.

(d) *PASADO DE POTENCIAL* (Past conditional)
E.g.: *Ella habría comido.*
She would have eaten.

(e) *IMPERFECTO* (Imperfect)
E.g.: *Ella comía.*
She was eating.

(f) *PRETÉRITO* (Preterite)
E.g.: *Ella comió.*
She ate.

(g) *PRESENTE PERFECTO* (Present perfect)
E.g.: *Ella ha comido.*
She has eaten.

(h) *PLUSCUAMPERFECTO* (Pluperfect)
E.g.: *Ella había comido.*
She had eaten.

(i) *FUTURO ANTERIOR* (Future perfect)
E.g.: *Ella habrá comido.*
She will have eaten.

(j) *PRETÉRITO ANTERIOR* or *PRETÉRITO PERFECTO* (Past preterite)
(This tense is literary and rare. It is preceded by a conjunction of time (*cuando, en cuanto,* etc.) to indicate that an action has just taken place.
E.g.: *Cuando hubieron terminado, se pusieron a cantar.*
When they had finished, they began to sing.

See the entry for each of these tenses: **CONDITIONAL TENSES, FUTURE PERFECT TENSE, FUTURE TENSE, IMPERFECT TENSE, PAST PRETERITE, PLUPERFECT TENSE, PRESENT PERFECT TENSE, PRESENT TENSE, PRETERITE TENSE**

INDICATIVE vs. SUBJUNCTIVE

The rules governing the use of the subjunctive are complex. In very general terms one can say:

(1) If the main clause is a simple statement devoid of emotion, doubt, uncertainty, desire, or will, use the indicative in the subordinate clause.

E.g.: *Dice que está cansado.*
    He says that he is tired.

Creo que estás enfermo.
I think that you are ill (= It is my opinion that you are ill).

Sabemos que tienes razón.
We know that you are right.

Nos quedaremos aquí porque está lloviendo.
We shall stay here because it is raining.

Te acuestas temprano cuando estás cansado.
You go to bed early when you are tired.

(2) If the main clause contains an idea of emotion, doubt, uncertainty, desire, or will, use the subjunctive in the subordinate clause (unless the subject is the same as that of the main clause).

E.g.: *Temo que esté cansado.*
    I fear that he is tired.

Dudo que ella venga.
I doubt that she will come.

No estamos seguros de que tengas razón.
We are not certain that you are right.

No es cierto que ella conozca al hombre que viene.
It is not certain that she knows the man who is coming.

Ella quiere que nos quedemos aquí.
She wants us to stay here.

Es necesario que te acuestes temprano.
You have to go to bed early.

See **SUBJUNCTIVE MOOD**

INDIRECT COMMANDS

Indirect commands are expressed by a verb such as *decir, mandar,* or *ordenar + que +* subjunctive.

E.g.: *¡Dígaıes que salgan!*
    Tell them to go out.

See **INDIRECT DISCOURSE**
See also **COMMANDS**

INDIRECT DISCOURSE

As opposed to the direct discourse (or direct style), where statements or thoughts of another person are quoted directly (*Ella dice: «Estoy enferma.»* = She says: "I am ill."), in the indirect discourse (or indirect style) *(el discurso indirecto)*, these words or thoughts are conveyed by subordinating them to a main verb such as *decir, declarar, anunciar,* etc.

E.g.: *Ella dice que está enferma.*
    She says that she is ill.

Declaran que van a marcharse.
They declare that they will leave.

NOTE:

If the sentence conveys an indirect command, the subordinate clause must be in the subjunctive.

E.g.: *Ordena que nos levantemos.*
    He commands that we get up.

INDIRECT DISCOURSE IN THE PAST:

If the main verb is in a past tense (imperfect, preterite, present perfect, pluperfect, etc.), the verb in the indirect statement will be:

(1) in the imperfect, to indicate simultaneity with the main verb.

    E.g.: *Ellos dijeron que leían el libro.*

        They said that they were reading the book.

(2) the present conditional, to indicate a future in relation to the main verb.

    E.g.: *Ellos dijeron que leerían el libro.*

        They said that they would read the book.

(3) the pluperfect, to indicate a past in relation to the main verb.

    E.g.: *Ellos dijeron que habían leído el libro.*

        They said that they had read the book.

(4) the subjunctive, to convey a command.

    E.g.: *Me dicen que lea los libros.*

        They tell me to read the books.

        Me dijeron que leyera (or lea) los libros.

        They told me to read the books.

INDIRECT QUESTIONS:

Indirect questions use *si* instead of *que*.

E.g.: *Ella me preguntó si yo iba (iría, había ido) al teatro.*

        She asked me if I went (would go, had gone) to the theater.

INDIRECT OBJECT

See **DIRECT OBJECT vs. INDIRECT OBJECT**

INDIRECT OBJECT PRONOUNS

See **PRONOUNS, OBJECT OF VERB**

INDIRECT QUESTIONS

See **INDIRECT DISCOURSE**

INFINITIVE

The infinitive *(el infinitivo)* expresses the action of the verb. It is the noun form of the verb.

E.g.: *Quiero comer.*

    I want to eat.

    Beber tanto es malo para la salud.

    To drink so much is harmful to health.

FORMS: There are two tenses of the infinitive:

(a) PRESENT INFINITIVE:

    E.g.: *Levantarse.*   *Poder.*

        To get up.   To be able.

        Trabajar.   *Venir.*

        To work.   To come.

(b) PAST INFINITIVE (The infinitive of the auxiliary verb *haber* + the past participle):

    E.g.: *Haber trabajado.*   *Haber podido.*

        To have worked.   To have been able.

        Haber venido.   *Haberse levantado.*

        To have come.   To have gotten up.

NOTES:

(1) REMEMBER to agree the reflexive pronoun according to the context.

    E.g.: *Después de habernos levantado, fuimos al comedor.*

        After getting up, we went to the dining room.

(2) In English the noun form of the verb can be expressed by the present participle. The Spanish equivalent must always be the infinitive.

E.g.: I like <u>watching</u> movies = *Me gusta ver películas.*

(3) Although in English the preposition "to," which is part of the infinitive, can be given the value of "in order to," this is not the case in Spanish. A Spanish infinitive never contains the concept of purpose. The preposition *para* must be used with the infinitive to convey purpose or intention.

E.g.: We are going downtown <u>to</u> buy clothes = *Vamos al centro para comprar ropa.*

INFINITIVE AFTER IMPERSONAL EXPRESSIONS
See **IMPERSONAL EXPRESSIONS**

INFINITIVE AFTER PREPOSITIONS

While in English the gerund (or present participle) is frequently used after prepositions, in Spanish the infinitive is always used.

E.g.: *Antes de salir.*
Before leaving.

Sin hablar.
Without speaking.

INFINITIVE OF REFLEXIVE VERBS

The reflexive pronoun is placed after the infinitive and is connected to it.

E.g.: *Levantarse.*   *Irse.*
To get up.   To leave.

However, when a reflexive verb is introduced by an auxiliary verb, the reflexive pronoun may be placed immediately before the introductory verb.

E.g.: *No me quiero levantar.*
I don't want to get up.

Nos pudimos equivocar.
We could have made a mistake.

REMEMBER to agree the reflexive pronoun according to the context.

E.g.: *No querías despertarte.*
You did not want to wake up.

INFINITIVE WITH *HACER*
See ***HACER* + infinitive**

INFINITIVES PRECEDED BY *A, CON, DE,* or *EN*
See **VERBS + (*A, CON DE, EN,* or no preposition) + infinitive**

INSIDE

(1) The adjective "Inside" = *Interior(es)* or *interno (-a, -os, -as).*

E.g.: *Es un cuarto interior.*
It is an inside room.

(2) The adverb "Inside" = *Adentro.*

E.g.: *Pusimos la maleta adentro.*
We put the suitcase inside.

(3) The preposition "Inside" = *Dentro de.*

E.g.: *La maleta está dentro del armario.*
The suitcase is inside the wardrobe.

INSIDE OUT

(Idiomatic construction) = *Al revés.*
E.g.: *Te pusiste el suéter al revés.*
   You put your sweater on inside out.

INSISTIR EN (QUE)

(Intransitive verb) = "To insist on."
It is followed by:
(a) the subjunctive if the subjects of the two clauses are different.
   E.g.: *El profesor insiste en que hablemos español.*
      The teacher insists that we speak Spanish.
(b) the infinitive if the subject of the two clauses is the same.
   E.g.: *El profesor insiste en hablar español.*
      The teacher insists on speaking Spanish.

to be INTERESTED in

(a) *Interesarse en (or por)* (Reflexive verb).
   E.g.: *El jefe se interesa en (por) la política.*
      The boss is interested in politics.
(b) *Interesar* (Intransitive verb) + indirect object.
   E.g.: *Me interesa la historia mexicana.*
      I am interested in Mexican history.

INTERJECTIONS

Interjections *(las interjecciones)* are expressions of surprise, fear, or another emotion which do not have any true grammatical meaning but are more like cries or shouts.
E.g.: *¡Ay!* = Gosh! Wow!
   ¡Qué barbaridad! = How awful!
   ¡Caramba! = Gee!
   ¡Caray! = Gosh!
   ¡Vamos! = Come now!
   ¡Vaya! = Whew!

INTERROGATIVE ADJECTIVES
See **ADJECTIVES, INTERROGATIVE**

INTERROGATIVE ADVERBS
See **ADVERBS, INTERROGATIVE**

INTERROGATIVE EXPRESSIONS

(1) *¿Por qué?* = Why? (= "Because of what?").
   E.g.: *¿Por qué no quieres ir al cine?*
      Why (= for what reason) don't you want to go to the movies?
(2) *¿Para qué?* = Why? (= "For what purpose?").
   E.g.: *¿Para qué quieres comprar este libro?*
      Why (= for what purpose) do you want to buy this book?
NOTE:
The answer to a *¿Por qué?* question begins with *Porque.*
The answer to a *¿Para qué?* question begins with *Para.*

E.g.: *¿Por qué fuiste a España?*
Why (for what reason) did you go to Spain?

Porque mis padres viven allá.
Because my parents live there.

¿Para qué fuiste a España?
Why (for what purpose) did you go to Spain?

Para estudiar la lengua.
To study the language.

REMEMBER that all interrogative words have a written accent.

INTERROGATIVE PRONOUNS

See **PRONOUNS, INTERROGATIVE**

INTERROGATIVE SENTENCES

In an interrogative sentence (i.e., a question), a subject pronoun is sometimes placed immediately after the verb to avoid ambiguity. At other times it is simply omitted.

E.g.: *¿Viene Vd. conmigo?*
Are you coming with me?

If the subject is very long it is placed at the end of the question.

E.g.: *¿Viene con nosotros el sobrino del señor Sánchez?*
Is Mr. Sánchez' nephew coming with us?

An interrogative word is generally placed at the beginning of the sentence.

E.g.: *¿Cuándo llegaste?*
When did you arrive?

¿Por qué dices esto?
Why do you say that?

REMEMBER that questions always begin with an inverted question mark (¿).

E.g.: *Pedro, ¿dónde estás?*
Peter, where are you?

INTRANSITIVE VERBS

See **VERBS, INTRANSITIVE**

INVERSION

Inversion *(la inversión)* is the reversing of the normal word order. Inversion of the subject and the verb is the normal construction of an interrogative sentence in Spanish.

E.g.: *¿Vienen tus amigos?*
Are your friends coming?

IR

(Intransitive verb) = "To go."
PRES.: *voy, vas, va, vamos, váis, van.*
IMPERF.: *iba, ibas, iba, íbamos, ibais, iban.*
PRETER.: *fui, fuiste, fue, fuimos, fuisteis, fueron.*
FUT.: *ir-é, -ás, -á, -emos, -éis, -án.*
CONDIT.: *ir-ía, -ías, -ía, -íamos, -íais, -ían.*
SUBJ. PRES.: *vay-a, -as, -a, -amos, -áis, -an.*
SUBJ. IMPERF. 1: *fu-era, -eras, -era, -éramos, -erais, -eran.*
SUBJ. IMPERF. 2: *fu-ese, -eses, -ese, -ésemos, -eseis, -esen.*
INFORMAL IMPERAT.: *ve (tú), no vayas (tú), id (vosotros), no vayáis (vosotros).*
FORMAL IMPERAT.: *vaya (Vd.); vamos, no vayamos; vayan (Vds.).*
PRES. PARTIC.: *yendo.*
PAST PARTIC.: *ido.*

IR A + infinitive
See **PROXIMATE FUTURE**

IRREGULAR VERBS
See the heading for each verb

IRSE
(Reflexive verb) = "To go away, to leave."
E.g.: *Me voy porque tengo prisa.*
      I am leaving because I am in a hurry.

IT
(Neuter personal pronoun)
(1) When part of an impersonal expression, "it" is not literally translated.
    E.g.: *Llueve.*
        It is raining.

        Es interesante viajar a un país extranjero.
        It is interesting to travel to a foreign country.
(2) When "it" is a direct object, it is translated as *lo.*
    E.g.: *No lo comprendo.*
        I don't understand it.

J

to JOIN
(1) Transitive verb meaning "To join together" = *Unir* or *Juntar.*
    E.g.: *Las dos compañías se unieron para fabricar el producto a menor precio.*
      The two firms joined to manufacture the product more cheaply.
(2) Reflexive verb meaning "To become a member of" = *Hacerse socio (-a) de.*
    E.g.: *Me hice socio del club de deportes.*
      I joined the sports club.

JUGAR
(Transitive verb) = "To play (a game or sport)."
PRES.: *jueg-o, -as, -a, jugamos, jugáis, juegan.*
IMPERF.: *jug-aba, -abas, -aba, -ábamos, -abais, -aban.*
PRETER.: *jugué, jug-aste, -ó, -amos, -asteis, -aron.*
FUT.: *jugar-é, -ás, -á, -emos, -éis, -án.*
CONDIT.: *jugar-ía, -ías, -ía, -íamos, -íais, -ían.*
SUBJ. PRES.: *jueg-ue, -ues, -ue, juguemos, juguéis, jueguen.*
SUBJ. IMPERF. 1: *jug-ara, -aras, -ara, -áramos, -arais, -aran.*
SUBJ. IMPERF. 2: *jug-ase, -ases, -ase, -ásemos, -aseis, -asen.*
INFORMAL IMPERAT.: *juega (tú), no juegues (tú); jugad (vosotros), no juguéis (vosotros).*
FORMAL IMPERAT.: *juegue (Vd.); juguemos; jueguen (Vds.).*
PRES. PARTIC.: *jugando.*
PAST PARTIC.: *jugado.*

JUGAR vs. *TOCAR*
See *TOCAR* vs. *JUGAR*

JUNTO A

(Prepositional construction) = "Next to."
E.g.: *La tienda está junto al restaurante.*
The shop is next to the restaurant.

JUST (to have just)

See **to HAVE JUST + past participle**

L

to LACK

(1) The transitive verb "To lack" = *Carecer de* or *necesitar.*
E.g.: *Carecemos de empleados.*
We lack employees.
(2) The construction "To lack (to be lacking)" = *Faltar.*
E.g.: *Al investigador le faltan los detalles para descubrir la solución.*
The investigator lacks the details to find the solution.
NOTE:
The person is the indirect object.
See **HACER FALTA**

LACK (for lack of)

= *Por falta de* (Prepositional construction).
E.g.: *No pude hacerlo por falta de tiempo.*
I could not finish it for lack of time.

LANGUAGES, names of

The names of languages *(los idiomas)* are the same as the masculine singular form of the adjective of nationality and are preceded by the definite article *el* (except after the verbs *hablar* and *estudiar*). Names of languages are not capitalized.
E.g.: *El ruso.*   Russian.
El japonés.   Japanese.

LAST NIGHT

= *Anoche* (Adverb).
E.g.: *Miré la televisión anoche.*
I watched television last night.

LAST vs. LASTLY vs. to LAST

(1) The adjective "last:"
(a) meaning "final" = *último.*
E.g.: *El último día del año.*
The last day of the year.
(b) meaning "most recent" = *pasado.*
E.g.: Last month.
El mes pasado.
(2) The adverb "last" meaning "lastly, last of all" = *por último.*
E.g.: *Visitaron Chile, el Brasil y por último México.*
They visited Chile, Brazil, and, last of all, Mexico.
(3) The verb "to last" = *durar* (Intransitive verb).
E.g.: *La película duró dos horas.*
The film lasted two hours.

LATTER . . . FORMER
See **FORMER . . . LATTER**

LE

(Personal pronoun)
(1) Indirect object:
Third person singular = "To him, to her, to it; to you *(Usted)*.
E.g.: *Le di el cuaderno (a Pedro).*
    I gave the book (to Peter).

   Le di el cuaderno (a Carolina).
    I gave the notebook (to Caroline).
(2) Direct object (not acceptable usage in Latin America):
(a) Third person singular (for male persons only) = "Him."
    E.g.: *Le veo ahora.*
      I see him now.
(b) Relating to *Usted* = "You."
    E.g.: *No le he visto ayer, Sr. Galdós.*
      I didn't see you yesterday, Mr. Galdós.

See **LES (plural)**

to LEAVE

(1) Meaning "To go away" (Intransitive) = *Salir, Irse* or *Marcharse.*
E.g.: *Salieron a las dos.*
    They left at two o'clock.

   Me voy.
    I'm leaving.

   Se marcharán a las seis y media.
    They will leave at six thirty.

NOTE:
Both *salir* and *irse* take the preposition *de* before an object.
E.g.: *Salgo (or me voy) de la univesidad.*
    I leave the university.
See **SALIR vs. IRSE vs. MARCHARSE**
(2) Meaning "To leave behind" (Transitive) = *Dejar.*
E.g.: *Dejé mi paraguas en casa.*
    I left my umbrella at home.
See **PARTIR vs. DEJAR vs. SALIR**

LEER

(Transitive verb) = "To read."
PRES.: *le-o, -es, -e, -emos, -éis, -en.*
IMPERF.: *le-ía, -ías, -ía, -íamos, -íais, -ían.*
PRETER.: *le-í, -iste, leyó, le-ímos, -isteis, leyeron.*
FUT.: *leer-é, -ás, -á, -emos, -éis, -án.*
CONDIT.: *leer-ía, -ías, -ía, -íamos, -íais, -ían.*
SUBJ. IMPERF.: *le-a, -as, -a, -amos, -áis, -an.*
SUBJ. IMPERF. 1: *ley-era, -eras, -era, -éramos, -erais, -eran.*
SUBJ. IMPERF. 2: *ley-ese, -eses, -ese, -ésemos, -eseis, -esen.*
INFORMAL IMPERAT.: *lee (tú), no leas (tú); leed (vosotros), no leáis (vosotros).*
FORMAL IMPERAT.: *lea (Vd.); leamos; no lean (Vds.).*
PRES. PARTIC.: *leyendo.*
PAST PARTICL.: *leído.*

LES (plural)

(Personal pronoun).
(1) Indirect object:
    (a) "To them."
        E.g.: *Les hablamos la semana pasada.*
            We spoke to them last week.
    (b) Relating to *Ustedes* = "To you."
        E.g.: *Les enviaremos un regalo, Sres. Durán.*
            We shall send you a gift, Mr. and Mrs. Durán.
(2) Direct object (not acceptable usage in Latin America):
    (a) Third person plural (for male persons only) = "Them."
        E.g.: *Les veo ahora.*
            I see them now.
    (b) Relating to *Ustedes* = "You."
        E.g.: *No les he visto ayer, Sres. Galdós.*
            I didn't see you yesterday, Mr. and Mrs. Galdós.
See **LE**

LESS AND LESS, FEWER AND FEWER

(Adverbial expressions)
Both are translated by *Cada vez menos.*
E.g.: *Tengo cada vez menos energía.*
    I have less and less energy.

    Hay cada vez menos turistas.
    There are fewer and fewer tourists.
See **MORE AND MORE, LESS AND LESS**

LEST

(Conjunction)
(1) If the two clauses have the same subject: *Por miedo de* + infinitive.
    E.g.: *Te pago ahora por miedo de olvidarlo.*
        I pay you now lest I forget it.
(2) If the two clauses have a different subject: *En caso de que* + subjunctive.
    E.g.: *Te pago ahora en caso de que no vengas mañana.*
        I pay you now lest you should not come tomorrow.

to LET

(Transitive verb) = *Dejar* or *Permitir.*
These verbs are followed by either:
(a) the infinitive construction:
    E.g.: *El profesor no nos deja* (or *permite*) *fumar.*
        The professor doesn't let us smoke.
(b) the subjunctive:
    E.g.: *El profesor no permite que fumemos.*
        The teacher doesn't let us smoke.

LET'S

This is the English first person plural of the imperative mood. The equivalent in Spanish is the first person plural of the imperative.
E.g.: *¡Comamos una paella!*
    Let's eat a paella.

    ¡Vamos a la playa!
    Let's go to the beach!

LEVANTARSE

(Reflexive verb) = "To get up [from bed], to stand up [from a chair]."
E.g.: *Nos levantamos a las seis.*
     We get up at six o'clock.
     Me levanto cuando entra una mujer.
     I stand up when a woman enters.
NOTE:
The transitive verb *Levantar* = "To raise, to lift."
E.g.: *Los alumnos levantan la mano.*
     The students raise their hands.

to LIKE

See *GUSTAR*

to LISTEN

(Transitive verb) = *Escuchar.*
Note:
The preposition "to" is included in the verb.
E.g.: *Escucho la música.*
     I listen to the music.

LITTLE

In English, "little" can be an adjective or an adverb. The two are different in Spanish.
(1) Adjective = *Pequeño (-a, -os, -as).*
     E.g.: *Una casa pequeña.*
          A little house.
          Unos niños pequeños.
          Some little children.
(2) Adverb = *Poco.*
     E.g.: *Ella come poco.*
          She eats little.

LL

This is a single letter in the Spanish alphabet. It is listed separately in Spanish dictionaries between the letters *L* and *M*. It is pronounced like a "y."

LLEGAR

(Intransitive verb) = "To arrive."
PRES.: *lleg-o, -as, -a, -amos, -áis, -an.*
IMPERF.: *lleg-aba, -abas, -aba, -ábamos, -abais, -aban.*
PRETER.: *llegu-é, -aste, -ó, -amos, -asteis, -aron.*
FUT.: *llegar-é, -ás, -á, -emos, -éis, -án.*
CONDIT.: *llegar-ía, -ías, -ía, -íamos, -íais, -ían.*
SUBJ. PRES.: *llegu-e, -es, -e, -emos, -éis, -en.*
SUBJ. IMPERF. 1: *lleg-ara, -aras, -ara, -áramos, -arais, -aran.*
SUBJ. IMPERF. 2: *lleg-ase, -ases, -ase, -ásemos, -aseis, -asen.*
INFORMAL IMPERAT.: *llegue (tú), no llegues; llegad (vosotros), no lleguéis (vosotros).*
FORMAL IMPERAT.: *llegue (Vd.); lleguemos; lleguen (Vds.).*
PRES. PARTIC.: *llegando.*
PAST PARTIC.: *llegado.*

LLEGAR A SER

(Verbal idiom) = "To become, to get to be."

E.g.: *Si estudias mucho, llegarás a ser abogado.*

If you study a lot, you will get to be a lawyer.

NOTE:

This is only one of several translations of "to become." *Llegar a ser* implies "To become by promotion or by studying."

See **to BECOME**

See also **PONERSE + adjective**

See also **HACERSE**

LLEVAR

(Transitive verb).

(1) "To carry, to take, to transport, to lead."

E.g.: *Este autobús lo llevará al centro.*

This bus will transport you downtown.

Beatriz lleva su libro a clase.

Beatrice takes her book to school.

Yo lo llevaré hasta el banco.

I shall lead (take) you to the bank.

(2) "To wear."

E.g.: *Ella siempre lleva ropa muy elegante.*

She always wears very elegant clothes.

LLEVAR A CABO

(Verbal idiom) = "To carry out, to accomplish, to finish."

E.g.: *Llevaron a cabo su misión.*

They accomplished their mission.

LLEVARSE

(Reflexive verb) = "To carry off, to remove."

E.g.: *El ladrón se llevó mi computadora.*

The thief carried off my computer.

NOTE:

The idiom *Yo me lo llevo* = "I'll take (or buy) it."

LO

(1) Masculine direct object pronoun = "Him."

E.g.: *En cuanto a Pedro, lo vi ayer.*

As for Peter, I saw him yesterday.

(2) *Lo* is used with adverbs in expressions of possibility.

E.g.: *Llegarán lo más pronto posible.*

They will arrive as soon as possible.

(3) Neuter article: *Lo* is also used with the neuter form of adjectives (which is identical to the masculine singular form) to express abstract statements.

E.g.: *Lo malo de eso es que perdimos mucho tiempo.*

The bad thing about that is that we lost much time.

(4) *Lo* is also used to complete a sentence with such verbs as *creer, decir, pedir, preguntar, saber* when no direct object is expressed.

E.g.: *¡Ya lo creo!*

I should think so!

(5) *Lo de* + noun = "This business of . . ." or "That business about . . ." or "What happened."

E.g.: *Lo del año pasado fue un susto terrible.*

That business of last year was a terrible fright.

LO CUAL

(Neuter relative pronoun with neuter antecedent) = "Which [fact, situation]."
It is used to sum up a previous idea, situation, or statement.
E.g.: *No estudiaron la gramática, lo cual les hizo perder muchos puntos en el examen.*
They didn't study the grammar, which (fact) made them lose a lot of points on the exam.

LO QUE

(Neuter relative pronoun with neuter antecedent) = "(That) which, what."
It is used when there is no stated antecedent to the relative pronoun *que.*
E.g.: *Nunca comprendo lo que dice el profesor.*
I never understand what (= that which) the teacher says.

LOGRAR

(Transitive verb) = "To achieve, to attain, to succeed in."
E.g.: *Logró gran éxito.*
He attained great success.

Lograron terminar el trabajo en dos días.
They succeeded in finishing the work in two days.

to LOOK at

(Transitive verb) *Mirar.*
NOTE:
The preposition "at" is included in the verb.
E.g.: *Estoy mirando la estatua.*
I am looking at the statue.

to LOOK for

(Transitive verb) *Buscar.*
NOTE:
The preposition "for" is included in the verb.
E.g.: *Patricia busca un empleo.*
Patricia is looking for a job.

to LOOK FORWARD to

(1) = . . . *me hace ilusión* + infinitive (Verbal idiom).
(2) I look forward to seeing you = *Me alegro de antemano de verte.*
I rejoice in advance to see you.
(3) I look forward to the party = *Pienso en la fiesta con mucha ilusión.*
I think of the party with much excitement.
(4) I am looking forward to going to Spain = *Anticipo con mucho gusto ir a España.*
I anticipate with much pleasure going to Spain.

a LOT

= *Mucho* (Adverb).
E.g.: *Usted trabaja mucho.*
You work a lot.
NOTE:
The adjectival construction "A lot of + noun" = *Mucho (-a, -os, -as).*
E.g.: *Tengo muchas amigas.*
I have a lot of girl friends.

LUEGO QUE

(Conjunctional construction) = "As soon as."
It is followed by:
(a) the indicative:
   E.g.: *Se levanta luego que suena su despertador.*
      He gets up as soon as his alarm clock rings.
(b) the subjunctive if it refers to a future action:
   E.g.: *Me marcharé luego que me llames.*
      I shall depart as soon as you call me.

M

MAÑANA

(1) *La mañana* (Noun) = "The morning."
   E.g.: *Trabajo por la mañana.*
      I work during the morning.
(2) *Mañana* (Adverb) = "Tomorrow."
   E.g.: *Mi sobrina vendrá mañana.*
      My cousin will come tomorrow.

to MARRY

(1) Meaning "To take in marriage" = *Casarse con* (Reflexive verb).
   E.g.: *Carolina se casó con Pedro.*
      Caroline married Peter.
(2) Meaning "To give away in marriage" = *Casar* (Transitive verb).
   E.g.: *El sacerdote casó a Luis y María en la iglesia de Santa Ana.*
      The priest married Louis and Mary in St. Ann's church.

MÁS

(1) *Más* (Adverb) = "More."
   E.g.: *Ella es más trabajadora que yo.*
      She is more industrious than I.
NOTE:
Más is also used before an adjective in exclamations.
E.g.: *¡Qué hombre más alto!*
      What a tall man!
See **EXCLAMATIONS**
(2) *Más* (Adjective) = "More."
   E.g.: *Tú tienes más dinero que nosotros.*
      You have more money than we.
See **ADJECTIVES, COMPARISON OF**
See also **ADVERBS, COMPARATIVE AND SUPERLATIVE OF**
NOTE:
Do not confuse *más* with the conjunction *mas*, an archaic synonym of *pero*.
See **MÁS. vs. MAS**

MÁS DE vs. MÁS QUE vs. MÁS DE LO QUE

(1) *Más de* (Comparative construction used before a numeral) = "More than."
   E.g.: *Ganaron más de dos mil pesetas.*
      They won more than two thousand pesetas.

NOTE:

In a negative sentence *No más que* (meaning "only") is used.

E.g.: *No ganaron más que dos mil pesetas.*

They won only two thousand pesetas.

(2) *Más que* (Adverbial construction) = "More than." This construction is used in comparisons of inequality.

E.g.: *Ella estudia más que yo.*

She studies more than I.

Carlos es más alto que Jorge.

Charles is taller than George.

(3) *Más de lo que* (Conjunctional construction) = "More than." It is used when the second term of the comparison is a clause.

E.g.: *Cuesta más de lo que pensaba.*

It costs more than I thought.

See **ADJECTIVES, COMPARISON OF**

See also **ADVERBS, COMPARATIVE AND SUPERLATIVE OF**

MÁS VALE (QUE)

(Verbal idiom) = "It is better (than)."

E.g.: *Más vale tarde que nunca.*

It is better late than never.

See **it is BETTER to**

MÁS vs *MAS*

(1) The adverb or adjective *Más* (with an accent) = "More."

E.g.: *Tiene más dinero.*

He has more money.

(2) The archaic conjunction *Mas* (without accent) = "But."

E.g.: *Estoy cansado mas trabajo.*

I am tired but I work.

See **MÁS**

MASCULINE NOUNS, identified by the ending

The following are masculine:

(1) Most nouns ending in *-o*.

E.g.: *El libro.*   The book.

El gobierno.   The government.

EXCEPTIONS:

La mano.   The hand.

La radio.   The radio.

(2) Nouns ending in *-e, -i, -j, -l, -n* (but not *-ión*), *-r, -s* and *-u*.

E.g.: *El cohete.*   The rocket.

El colibrí.   The hummingbird.

El reloj.   The clock.

El papel.   The paper.

El huracán.   The hurricane.

El sur.   The south.

El país.   The country.

El espíritu.   The spirit.

BUT: *La nación.*   The nation.

See **GENDER**

to MATTER

(1) "It doesn't matter." = *No importa.*
(2) "What does it matter if . . . ?" = *¿ Qué importa si . . . ?*
(3) "What's the matter?" = *¿Qué hay?* or *¿Qué pasa?*
(4) "What's the matter with you?" = *¿Qué tiene Ud.?* or *¿Qué le pasa?*

MAY

(1) Indicating possibility: Use the adverb *Quizá(s)* or *Tal vez.*
    E.g.: *Tal vez vendrá mañana.*
         He may come tomorrow.
         Quizá se ha perdido.
         He may have gotten lost.

See **UNCERTAINTY**

(2) Indicating permission: Use *Poder* + infinitive.
    E.g.: *¿Puedo marcharme temprano?*
         May I leave early?
         Podéis ir a casa.
         You may go home.

MAYOR

(Comparative form of the adjective *grande*):
(a) "Larger:"
    E.g.: *Barcelona es mayor que Salamanca.*
         Barcelona is larger than Salamanca.
(b) "Older (when applied to persons):"
    E.g.: *Gerardo es mayor que Juan.*
         Gerard is older than John.

to MEAN

(Transitive verb) = *Significar* or *Querer decir.* The most frequently used expression is *querer decir.*
E.g.: *¿Qué quiere decir esto?*
      What does this mean?

MEASUREMENTS

See **SIZES AND MEASUREMENTS**

MEDIO (-A, -OS, -AS) vs. *MITAD*

(1) The adjective *Medio (-a, -os, -as)* = "Half."
    E.g.: *Media manzana.*
         Half an apple.
(2) The adverb *Medio* is invariable.
    E.g.: *Estoy medio muerto de hambre.*
         I am half dead of hunger.
(3) The noun *La mitad* = "The half."
    E.g.: *La mitad de la clase.*
         Half (of) the class.

MEJOR

(1) Comparative form of the adjective *Bueno* = "Better."
 E.g.: *Esta comida es mejor que aquélla.*
  This food is better than that one.
(2) Comparative form of the adverb *Bien* = "Better."
 E.g.: *Sara cocina mejor que Marta.*
  Sarah cooks better than Martha.

MENOR

(Comparative form of the adjective *pequeño*):
(a) "Smaller:"
 E.g.: *Portugal es menor que España.*
  Portugal is smaller than Spain.
(b) "Younger (when applied to persons):"
 E.g.: *Alberto es menor que Margarita.*
  Albert is younger than Margaret.

MENOS

(1) *Menos* (Adverb) = "Less."
 E.g.: *Estudiamos menos que Carmen.*
  We study less than Carmen.
(2) *Menos* (Adjective) = "Fewer, less."
 E.g.: *Ella tiene menos libros que tú.*
  She has fewer books than you.

   Tengo menos dinero que tú.
   I have less money than you.

See **ADJECTIVES, COMPARISON OF**
See also **ADVERBS, COMPARATIVE AND SUPERLATIVE OF**

MENOS DE vs. *MENOS QUE* vs. *MENOS DE LO QUE*

(1) *Menos de* (Comparative construction before numerals) = "Less (fewer) than."
 E.g.: *Tengo menos de cien dólares.*
  I have less than a hundred dollars.
(2) *Menos que* (Adverbial construction) = "Less than." This construction is used in comparisons of inequality.
 E.g.: *Juan trabaja menos que Carmen.*
  John works less than Carmen.

   Pedro es menos inteligente que Gloria.
   Peter is less intelligent than Gloria.
(3) *Menos de lo que* (Conjunctional construction) = More than." It is used when the second term of the comparison is a clause.
 E.g.: *Ella ha cambiado menos de lo que pensaba.*
  She has changed less than I thought.

See **ADJECTIVES, COMPARISON OF**
See also **ADVERBS, COMPARATIVE AND SUPERLATIVE OF**

METRIC SYSTEM

The metric system *(el sistema métrico)*, used in most countries, is based on the number 10.
MEASURES OF LENGTH

		EQUIVALENCE
1 metro	= *10 decímetros*	1 m. = 1.0936 yards
1 decímetro	= *10 centímetros*	
1 centímetro	= *10 milímetros*	
10 metros	= *1 decámetro*	
100 metros	= *1 kilómetro*	1km. = 0.214 mi.

LIQUID MEASURES

1 litro   *= 10 decilitros*
1 decilitro   *= 10 centilitros*
1 centilitro   *= 10 mililitros*

1 l. = 0.2642 US gal.
     0.2200 Imp. gal.

SURFACE MEASURES

1 área   *= 10^2 metros (10 metros cuadrados)*
1 hectárea   *= 10^4 metros (1000 metros cuadrados)*

1 hect. = 2.4711 acres

100 hectáreas   *= 1 kilómetro cuadrado*

1 sq. km. = 0.3861 sq. mi.

WEIGHT MEASURES

1 kilo   *= 1000 gramos*
1 tonelada   *= 1000 kilos*

1 k. = 2.2046 lb.
1 T. = 1.1023 short ton
     0.9842 long ton

MIEDO

See *TENER MIEDO (DE)*

MIENTRAS

(1) Conjunction = "While, as long as." It is followed by:
  (a) the indicative when referring to a past situation:
    E.g.: *Mientras vivíamos en Sudamérica no hablábamos inglés.*
        As long as we lived in South America we did not speak English.
  (b) the subjunctive when referring to a future situation:
    E.g.: *Mientras vivamos en Chile nunca hablaremos inglés.*
        As long as we live in Chile we shall never speak English.
(2) Adverb = "While."
  E.g.: *Ella cose mientras yo lavo los platos.*
      She sews while I wash the dishes.

MIENTRAS TANTO

(Adverbial idiom) = "Meanwhile."
E.g.: *Ellos estudiaban. Mientras tanto, yo escribía cartas.*
    They were studying. Meanwhile, I was writing letters.

MIGHT

(1) to indicate suggestion: Use *Poder* in the present conditional or in the imperfect subjunctive.
  E.g.: *Podrías venir conmigo.*
      You might come with me.

      Pudieras ir al campo.
      You could go to the country.
(2) To express a wish: Use *Ojalá* + subjunctive.
  E.g.: *Ojalá tengan éxito!*
      Might they succeed!

MIL

(Invariable numerical adjective) = "Thousand."
The indefinite article is not used with *mil.*
E.g.: *Mil libras.* (not: *Un mil*)
    One thousand pounds.
Mil does not vary in the plural.
E.g.: *Cinco mil edificios.*
    Five thousand buildings.

MILLÓN

(Masculine noun). It takes the preposition *de* before a noun.

E.g.: *Cuatro millones de habitantes.*
   Four million inhabitants.

MÍO(-A, -OS, -AS)

(1) Emphatic possessive adjective = "Of mine."

E.g.: *Es una amiga mía.*
   She is a friend of mine.

See **ADJECTIVES, POSSESSIVE**

(2) Possessive pronoun = "Mine."

E.g.: *Su hermana es ingeniera. La mía es profesora.*
   His sister is an engineer. Mine is a professor.

See **PRONOUNS, POSSESSIVE**

MIRAR vs. VER

(1) *Mirar* (Transitive verb) = "To look at, to watch."

E.g.: *Miramos el panorama.*
   We look at the panorama.

   Nunca miro la televisión.
   I never watch television.

(2) *Ver* (Transitive verb) = "To see."

E.g.: *Vieron el accidente.*
   They saw the accident.

See **PERCEPTION, VERBS OF**

MISMO (-A, -OS, -AS)

(Adjective). Its meaning depends on its position:

(a) Before the noun = "Same."

E.g.: *El mismo día.*
   The same day.

(b) After the noun it indicates emphasis = "Very."

E.g.: *La casa misma fue destruída.*
   The very house (the house itself) was destroyed.

(c) Used with personal pronouns = "Self."

E.g.: *Lo hice yo mismo.*
   I did it myself.

to MISS

(Transitive verb)

(1) Meaning "Not to catch (e.g., a train)" = *Perder.*

E.g.: *Perdió el tren de las once.*
   He missed the eleven o'clock train.

(2) Meaning "To long for (someone or something)" = *Echar de menos.*

E.g.: *Echo de menos a mi novio.*
   I miss my fiancé.

MISS

Srta. (= *Señorita;* plural, *Srtas.*). This abbreviation is preceded by the definite article unless one is addressing the person directly.

E.g.: *La Srta. Dianderas está en casa.*
   Miss Dianderas is at home.

BUT: *Buenas tardes, Srta. Rubio.*
   Good afternoon, Miss Rubio.

MITAD vs. MEDIO (-A, -OS, -AS)
See **MEDIO (-A, -OS, -AS) vs. MITAD**

MONTHS

The names of the months are masculine.
enero, febrero, marzo, abril, mayo, junio, julio, agosto, septiembre, octubre, noviembre, diciembre.
NOTES:
(1) Names of months are not capitalized.
(2) The preposition *en* is used to say "in."
    E.g.: *Ella nació en julio.*
        She was born in July.

MOOD

The mood *(el modo)* is the form of a verb which conveys whether the action or state is a fact, a wish, a command, etc.
There are four moods in Spanish:
(1) The infinitive *(el infinitivo)*, expresses no number, person or tense.
(2) The indicative *(el indicativo)* contains 10 tenses: the present, the imperfect, the preterite, the future, the present conditional, the past conditional, the present perfect, the pluperfect, the future perfect, and the past preterite.
    E.g.: *Hablo.*   I speak.
          Hablaba.   I was speaking.
          Hablé.   I spoke.
(3) The imperative *(el imperativo)*.
    E.g.: *¡Habla!*   Speak!
(4) The subjunctive *(el subjuntivo)* contains 4 tenses: the present, the imperfect, the past, and the pluperfect.
    E.g.: *Hable.*   (That) I (should) speak.
          Hablara.   (That) I (should) speak.
See the entry for each of these moods: **IMPERATIVE MOOD, INDICATIVE MOOD, INFINITIVE, SUBJUNCTIVE MOOD**

MORE AND MORE, LESS AND LESS

    = *Cada vez más, Cada vez menos* (Adverbial idioms).
E.g.: *Los días son cada vez más cortos.*
    The days are shorter and shorter.

    Ella trabaja cada vez menos.
    She works less and less.
See **LESS AND LESS, FEWER AND FEWER**

MOST

(1) "Most of + singular noun" = *La mayor parte de.*
    E.g.: *La mayor parte del tiempo.*
        Most of the time.
(2) "Most of + plural noun" = *La mayoría de.*
    E.g.: *La mayoría de los estudiantes.*
        Most of the students.

MOST + adjective or adverb

This is the superlative construction.
E.g.: *Es el problema más difícil.*
> It is the most difficult problem.

> *Ella corre lo más rápidamente de todas.*
> She runs the fastest of all.

See **ADJECTIVES, SUPERLATIVE OF**
See also **ADVERBS, COMPARATIVE AND SUPERLATIVE OF**

MR. (MISTER)

Sr. (= *Señor;* plural, *Sres.*).
This abbreviation is preceded by the definite article unless one is addressing the person directly.
E.g.: *El Sr Muñoz ha llegado.*
> Mr. Muñoz has arrived.

> *Los Sres. Durán y Borges están aquí.*
> Messrs. Durán and Borges are here.

BUT: *Buenos días, Sr. Galdós.*
> Hello, Mr. Galdós.

NOTE:
Before a first name use *Don.*
E.g.: *Don Roberto Pidal.*
> Mr. Robert Pidal.

MRS. (MISTRESS)

Sra. (= *Señora;* plural, *Sras.*).
This abbreviation is preceded by the definite article unless one is addressing the person directly.
E.g.: *La Sra. Vidal está en casa.*
> Mrs. Vidal is at home.

BUT: *Buenas tardes, Sra. Campo.*
> Good afternoon, Mrs. Campo.

NOTE:
Before a first name use *Doña.*
E.g.: *Doña María Pidal.*
> Mrs. Mary Pidal.

MUCHO vs. *MUY*

(1) The adjective *Mucho (-a, -os, -as)* = "Much, many, a lot of."
> E.g.: *Hay muchas fotografías en esta revista.*
> There are many photographs in this magazine.

(2) The adverb *Mucho* = "Much, a lot."
> E.g.: *Ella trabaja mucho.*
> She works a lot.

NOTE:
Mucho does not take a modifier. To translate "very much" use *muchísimo.*
E.g.: I love you very much.
> *Te quiero muchísimo.*

(3) The adverb *Muy* = "Very." (As its English equivalent, it can modify adjectives and adverbs but not verbs.)
> E.g.: *Ellos son muy inteligentes.*
> They are very intelligent.

> *Ellas hablan muy rápidamente.*
> They speak very fast.

MULTIPLE OBJECT PRONOUNS
See **PRONOUN PAIRS**

MUST

(Auxiliary verb)

(1) To indicate obligation: *Deber* + infinitive, or *Tener que* + infinitive.

    E.g.: *Debo ir a la oficina (*or *Tengo que ir a la oficina).*

        I must go to the office.

NOTE:

For a general statement which does not apply to a particular person, use the impersonal construction *Hay que* + infinitive.

E.g.: *Hay que pensar en los otros.*

    One must think of others.

    Habrá que trabajar mucho.

    It will be necessary to work hard.

(2) To indicate probability:

    (a) *Deber de* + infinitive:

        E.g.: *Deben de tener mucho dinero.*

            They must (probably) have a lot of money.

    (b) Future tense of the verb.

        E.g.: *Tendrán mucho dinero.*

            They must (probably) have a lot of money.

See **PROBABILITY**

MUY vs. *MUCHO*
See *MUCHO* vs. *MUY*

N

Ñ

The seventeenth letter of the Spanish alphabet, called *eñe*. In Spanish dictionaries it is listed separately after the letter *N*.

NACER

(Intransitive verb) = "To be born."

Remember that when used in the past it refers to a completed action, hence it is in the preterite or present perfect (not the imperfect).

E.g.: *Nací en Zaragoza.*

    I was born in Saragossa.

NADA

(Indefinite pronoun) = "Nothing." When it follows the verb there must be a *no* or another negative word before the verb.

E.g.: *No hice nada.*

    I didn't do anything.

    Nunca dicen nada.

    They never say anything.

NADIE

(Indefinite pronoun) = "Nobody." When it follows the verb there must be a *no* or another negative word before the verb.

E.g.: *Nadie vino ayer.*
    Nobody came yesterday.

No vino nadie ayer.
    Nobody came yesterday.

Ella nunca ve a nadie.
    She never sees anybody.

NOTE:

The personal *a* is needed when *nadie* is the direct object.

NAMES, FAMILY

Family names *(los apellidos)* often include both the names of father and mother (father's name first followed by mother's name).

E.g.: *Laura Rodríguez López.*
    Rafael Fuster y Calleja.

NOTE:

(1) The second *apellido* is frequently omitted except for formal occasions. Thus, in the above examples, the persons would be referred to (and indexed as): *Laura Rodríguez* and *Rafael Fuster.*

(2) Contrary to the English practice, family names do not take a plural ending when referring to the entire family.

    E.g.: *Los Dávila.*
        The Dávilas.

NAMES, GEOGRAPHICAL
See **GEOGRAPHICAL NAMES**

NECESSITY

The concept of necessity can be rendered by:

(1) *Deber* + infinitive.
    E.g.: *Debemos trabajar.*
        We have to work.

(2) *Tener que* + infinitive.
    E.g.: *Tenemos que trabajar.*
        We have to work.

(3) *Es necesario* + infinitive.
    E.g.: *Es necesario trabajar.*
        It is necessary to work.

If the expression refers to a specific person use "*Es necesario que* + subjunctive."

E.g.: *Es necesario que (nosotros) trabajemos.*
    It is necessary that we work.

(4) *Hacer falta.*
    E.g.: *El dinero me hace falta.*
        I need money.

NEGAR

(Transitive verb) = "To deny, to refuse."
PRES.: *nieg-o, -as, -a, negamos, negáis, niegan.*
IMPERF.: *neg-aba, -abas, -aba, -ábamos, -abais, -aban.*
PRETER.: *negu-é, negaste, -ó, -amos, -asteis, -aron.*
FUT.: *negar-é, -ás, -á, -emos, -éis, -án.*
CONDIT.: *negar-ía, -ías, -ía, -íamos, -íais, -ían.*
SUBJ. PRES.: *niegu-e, -es, -e, neguemos, neguéis, nieguen.*
SUBJ. IMPERF. 1: *neg-ara, -aras, -ara, -áramos, -arais, -aran.*
SUBJ. IMPERF. 2: *neg-ase, -ases, -ase, -ásemos, -aseis, -asen.*
INFORMAL IMPERAT.: *niega (tú), no niegues (tú); negad (vosotros), no neguéis (vosotros).*
FORMAL IMPERAT.: *niegue (Vd.); neguemos; nieguen (Vds.).*
PRES. PARTIC.: *negando.*
PAST PARTIC.: *negado.*

NEGARSE A + infinitive

(Reflexive verb) = "To refuse to + infinitive."
E.g.: *Yo me niego a decir tales mentiras.*
   I refuse to tell such lies.

NEGATION

In negative sentences there must always be a negative word before the verb. What appears to be double negation is in fact perfectly correct Spanish.
E.g.: *No comieron nada.*
   They didn't eat anything.

   Nunca hablan con nadie.
   They never speak with anyone.

NEGATIVE EXPRESSIONS

The most common negative expressions are:
(1) *Apenas* = "Scarcely."
   E.g.: *Apenas viene.*
      He scarcely comes.
(2) *Jamás* = "Never."
   E.g.: *Jamás he oído tal cosa.*
      I have never heard such a thing.
   REMEMBER: If *jamás* comes after the verb a negative word must be used before the verb.
   E.g.: *No he visto jamás tal cosa.*
      I have never seen such a thing.
(3) *Nada* = "Nothing."
   .E.g.: *Nada me interesa.*
      Nothing interests me.
   REMEMBER: If *nada* comes after the verb a negative word must be used before the verb.
   E.g.: *No comprendo nada.*
      I understand nothing. (I do not understand anything.)
(4) *Nadie* = "Nobody."
   E.g.: *Nadie comprende.*
      Nobody understands.
   REMEMBER: If *nadie* comes after the verb a negative word must be used before the verb.
   E.g.: *No veo a nadie.*
      I see nobody. (I don't see anybody.)
(5) *Ni . . . ni* = "Neither . . . nor."
   E.g.: *No tenemos ni perro ni gato.*
      We have neither dog nor cat.

(6) *Ni siquiera* = "Not even."
E.g.: *No tiene ni siquiera una bicicleta.*
He doesn't even have a bicycle.

(7) *Ni . . . tampoco* = "Nor . . . either."
E.g.: *María no vino ni Margarita tampoco.*
Mary didn't come, nor Margaret either.

(8) *No* = "Not"
E.g.: *Ellos no hablan.*
They do not speak.

(9) *No . . . ninguno(a)* = "Not any at all."
E.g.: *No tengo diccionario ninguno.*
I have no dictionary (at all).

(10) *No más que . . .* = "No more than, only."
E.g.: *No tengo más que un hermano.*
I have only one brother.

(11) *No . . . ni* = "Neither . . . nor."
E.g.: *No llama ni escribe.*
He neither calls nor writes.

(12) *Nunca* = "Never."
E.g.: *Nunca viene.*
He never comes.

(13) *Sin* = "Without."
E.g.: *Ha venido sin su esposa.*
He came without his wife.

(14) *Todavía no* = "Not yet."
E.g.: *Todavía no he terminado.*
I have not finished yet.

(15) *Ya no* = "No longer."
E.g.: *Ya no trabaja.*
He no longer works.

NEGATIVE IMPERATIVE

(a) The negative imperative informal forms are the same as the second person singular and the second person plural of the present subjunctive.
E.g.: *¡No hables (tú)!*
Don't speak!
¡No vengáis (vosotros)!
Don't come!

(b) The negative formal command forms are the same as the third person singular and third person plural of the present subjunctive.
E.g.: *¡No diga (Ud.)!*
Don't say!
¡No hablen (Uds.)!
Don't talk!

See **IMPERATIVE MOOD**

NEITHER . . . NOR

(Conjunction) = *No . . . ni.*
E.g.: *No tengo ni hermanos ni hermanas.*
I have neither brothers nor sisters.

NOTE:

If the expression precedes the verb *no* is not needed.
E.g.: *Ni Pedro ni Arturo han llegado.*
Neither Peter nor Arthur has arrived.

See **NO . . . NI**

NEUTER

The neuter gender *(el neutro)* does not exist for nouns in Spanish. It is used only for the definite article *lo* and the demonstrative pronouns *esto, eso,* and *aquello* to refer to an abstract concept or idea.

E.g.: *Lo difícil del problema es la fórmula.*

The difficult (thing or part) of the problem is the formula.

Eso es increíble.

That (thing, idea, event) is incredible.

NEXT

(1) The adjective "Next":

    (a) Meaning "Forthcoming" = *Próximo (-a, -os, -as).*

        E.g.: *Iré a Costa Rica el próximo mes.*

           I shall go to Costa Rica next month.

    (b) Meaning "Following" = *Siguiente(s).*

        E.g.: *Iré a Gran Bretaña el mes siguiente.*

           I shall go to Great Britain the following month.

(2) The adverb "Next" (expressing an order of events) = *Después.*

        E.g.: *Nos levantamos, nos vestimos y después comimos.*

           We got up, we got dressed, and next we ate.

NEXT TO

See *JUNTO A*

NI . . . TAMPOCO

(Negative construction) = "Nor . . . either."

E.g.: *Mi padre no habla inglés ni mi madre tampoco.*

My father doesn't speak English, nor my mother either.

NI SIQUIERA

(Adverbial idiom) = "Not even"

E.g.: *Guillermo ni siquiera abrió su libro.*

William didn't even open his book.

NINGÚN, NINGUNO (-A, -OS, -AS)

(1) The negative pronoun *Ninguno (-a, -os, -as)* = "No one, none."

    E.g.: *Ninguna de ellas comprende eso.*

        None of them understands that.

(2) The adjective *Ningún, ninguna (-os, -as)* = "No, not any."

    E.g.: *Ninguna silla es cómoda.*

        No chair is comfortable.

NOTE:

Ninguno drops the final *-o (Ningún)* before a masculine singular noun.

E.g.: *Ningún libro se vende a más de quinientas pesetas.*

    No book sells for more than five hundred pesetas.

NO

(Adverb of negation) = "No, not."

(1) Used alone it means "No."

    E.g.: *¿Has terminado?* - *No.*

        "Have you finished?" "No."

(2) Used with a personal pronoun it means "Not."

E.g.: *No yo.*

　　　Not I.

　　　Ellos no.

　　　Not they.

(3) Used with a verb it means "Not" and always precedes the verb.

E.g.: *No comprendo.*

　　　I don't understand.

　　　¡No hables!

　　　Don't talk!

NO . . . NADA

(Negative construction) = "Nothing, not anything."

E.g.: *No hemos comprado nada.*

　　　We didn't buy anything.

NO . . . NADIE

(Negative construction) = "Nobody, not anybody."

E.g.: *No encontramos a nadie.*

　　　We didn't meet anybody.

NO . . . NI

(Negative construction) = "Neither . . . nor."

E.g.: *No tengo ni gato ni perro.*

　　　I have neither cat nor dog.

NO . . . NINGÚN, NINGUNO (-A)

(Negative construction) = "No, not a single one, not any."

E.g.: *No hay ninguna carta para Ud.*

　　　There is no letter for you.

¿NO ES VERDAD?

(Idiomatic expression) = "Isn't it true?" This expression (frequently abbreviated to *¿verdad?* or to *¿no?*) is the equivalent of the English expressions "Isn't it?, Don't you?, Aren't they?, Right?,' etc.

E.g.: *Aprendes el ruso, ¿no es verdad?*

　　　You're learning Russian, aren't you?

　　　Fuiste a México, ¿verdad?

　　　You went to Mexico, right?

　　　Llegaron ayer, ¿verdad?

　　　They arrived yesterday, didn't they?

　　　Puedes venir, ¿verdad?

　　　You can come, can't you?

NO HAY REMEDIO

(Verbal idiom) = "It can't be helped."

E.g.: *Tendremos que tomar otro vuelo. No hay remedio.*

　　　We'll have to take another flight. It can't be helped.

NO IMPORTA

Intransitive verb = "It doesn't matter."

E.g.: *No importa la hora, hay que terminar esto.*

　　　No matter the time (It doesn't matter what time it is), we must finish this.

NO LONGER
See *YA NO*

NO MÁS QUE

(Idiomatic construction) = "No more than, only."
E.g.: *Ella no trabaja más que cuatro días.*
      She only works four days.

NOBODY
See *NADIE*

NOR . . . EITHER
See *NI . . . TAMPOCO*

NOT ANYMORE
See **NO LONGER**

NOT ANY + noun

= *No* + noun (Negative construction).
E.g.: *No tengo bicicleta.*
      I don't have any bicycle.

NOT EVEN
See *NI SIQUIERA*

NOT NOW

= *Ahora no* (Adverbial idiom).
E.g.: *Ahora no puedo salir.*
      I cannot leave now.

NOT YET
See *TODAVÍA NO*

NOTHING
See *NADA*

NOUN

A noun *(un sustantivo)* is a word which names a person, thing, idea, or place. All nouns are either masculine or feminine.
E.g.: *El monumento.*   *La familia.*
      The monument.   The family.
A noun is either proper *(un nombre propio)* or common *(un nombre común)*. A proper noun is the name of a particular place, person, or thing and is capitalized.
E.g.: *Pedro.*   *Madrid.*   *La Alhambra.*
      Peter.   Madrid.   The Alhambra.
A common noun does not name a particular place, person, or thing and is not capitalized; but is generally preceded by a definite or indefinite article.
E.g.: *El coche.*   *La ventana.*   *Un hombre.*   *Una ciudad.*
      The car.   The window.   A man.   A city.
See **FEMININE NOUNS, identified by the ending**
See also **MASCULINE NOUNS, identified by the ending**

NOUN + *DE* + noun

This construction is the equivalent of the English use of nouns as adjectives.

E.g.: A grammar book = *Un libro de gramática.*
The airplane schedule = *El horario de los aviones.*
A mathematics teacher = *Un profesor de matemáticas.*

NOUNS, gender of

See **GENDER**

NOUNS, plural of

GENERAL RULES:

(1) Nouns ending in a vowel: Add *-s*:
E.g.: *El cuaderno → los cuadernos*
La muchacha → las muchachas

(2) Nouns ending in a consonant or y: Add *-es*:
E.g.: *La flor → las flores*
La pared → las paredes
El rey → los reyes

(3) Nouns ending in *-s* do not change in the plural unless the last syllable is accented *(-és, -ís)*.
E.g.: *El lunes → los lunes*
BUT: *Un francés → unos franceses*
El país → los países

(4) Nouns ending in *-z* change the *-z* to *-c* before adding *-es*.
E.g.: *La luz → las luces*
El lápiz → los lápices

(5) Nouns ending in *-n* or *-s* which have an accent mark on the last syllable drop the accent in the plural.
E.g.: *La lección → las lecciones*

EXCEPTION:

El país → los países

(6) If a noun of more than one syllable ends in *-n* and has no accent mark it takes an accent mark over the stressed vowel in the plural.
E.g.: *El joven → los jóvenes*

NOWHERE

(Adverb).

(a) If there is no movement: *En ninguna parte.*
E.g.: *No lo pude encontrar en ninguna parte.*
I could find him nowhere.

(b) If there is movement: *A ninguna parte.*
E.g.: *No vamos a ninguna parte.*
We are going nowhere.

NUESTRO (-A, -OS, -AS)

See **ADJECTIVES, POSSESSIVE**
See **PRONOUNS, POSSESSIVE**

NUMBERS, CARDINAL

(Los números cardinales).

Cero, uno (una, un), dos, tres, cuatro, cinco, seis, siete, ocho, nueve, diez, once, doce, trece, catorce, quince, diez y seis (or dieciséis), diez y siete (or diecisiete), diez y ocho (or dieciocho), diez y nueve (or diecinueve), veinte, veinte y uno (una, ún) (or veintiuno [una, ún]), veinte y dos (or veintidós), veinte y tres (or veintitrés), veinte y cuatro (or veinticuatro), veinte y cinco (or veinticinco), veinte y seis (or *veintiséis), veinte y siete* (or *veintisiete), veinte y ocho* (or *veintiocho), veinte y nueve* (or *veintinueve), treinta, treinta y uno (una, ún), treinta y dos, . . . cuarenta, cincuenta, sesenta, setenta, ochenta, noventa, ciento (cien), ciento uno (una, ún), ciento dos, . . . mil, dos mil, tres mil, cien mil, doscientos mil, cien mil, un millón (de), dos millones (de), cien millones (de).*

NOTE:

(1) When 16, 22, 23, and 26 are written as one word they have a written accent.

(2) *Uno* and the compounds of *ciento* are the only numbers which have a feminine form.

    E.g.: *Una corbata.*

         One necktie.

         Trescientas pesetas.

         Three hundred pesetas.

(3) *Uno* drops the final *-o* before a noun.

    E.g.: *Un caballero.*

         A gentleman.

    Ciento drops the final *-to* before a noun.

    E.g.: *Cien autobuses.*

         One hundred buses.

(4) The conjunction *y* is used only between 16 and 99.

    E.g.: *Veinte y cuatro.*

         Cincuenta y ocho.

         Noventa y nueve.

    BUT: *Ciento seis.*

         Ciento ochenta.

         Doscientos cuarenta y tres.

(5) Do NOT use *un* before *cien* and *mil.* If a noun follows *millón,* it must be preceded by *de.*

    E.g.: *Mil turistas.*

         A thousand tourists.

         Cuarenta millones de libras.

         Forty million pounds.

(6) Digits are separated by using periods (rather than commas as in English).

    E.g.: In Spanish: = In English:

         1.302.546   1,302,456

(7) Decimals are indicated by using a comma (rather than a period as in English).

    E.g.: In Spanish: = In English:

         $\pi = 3,141592 \ldots$ $\pi = 3.141592 \ldots$

NUMBERS, ORDINAL

(Los números ordinales). Ordinal numbers are adjectives.

Primero (-a, -os, -as), segundo (-a, -os, -as), tercero (-a, -os, -as), cuarto (-a, -os, -as), quinto (-a, -os, -as), sexto (-a, -os, -as), séptimo (-a, -os, -as), octavo (-a, -os, -as), noveno (-a, -os, -as), décimo (-a, -os, -as).

NOTES:

(1) Ordinal numbers beyond tenth are rarely used. Cardinal numbers are used instead.

    E.g.: *El quinto día de la semana.*

         The fifth day of the week.

    BUT: *La calle cuarenta y dos.*

         Forty-second street.

    And: *Carlos Primero.*

         Charles the First.

    BUT: *El papa Pío Doce.*

         Pope Pius the Twelfth.

(2) *Primero* and *tercero* drop the final -o in front of a masculine singular noun.

E.g.:　*El primer día.*

　　　The first day.

　　　El tercer hombre.

　　　The third man.

　　　La tercera puerta.

　　　The third door.

NUNCA

(Adverb) = "Never."

REMEMBER: If *Nunca* comes after the verb *no* or another negative word must be placed before the verb.

E.g.:　*Nunca he ido al Perú.*

　　　I have never gone to Peru.

　　　No he ido nunca al Perú.

　　　I have never gone to Peru.

O

O

(Conjunction) = "Or."

E.g.:　*Dos o tres personas.*

　　　Two or three persons.

NOTE:

O is replaced by *u* before words beginning with *o-* or *ho-*.

E.g.:　*Siete u ocho personas.*

　　　Seven or eight persons.

　　　Arañas u hormigas.

　　　Spiders or ants.

O'CLOCK

See TIME EXPRESSIONS

OBEDECER

(Transitive verb) = "To obey."

E.g.:　*Obedezco las leyes.*

　　　I obey the laws.

OCURRIR

(Intransitive verb) = "To happen, to occur."

E.g.:　*Ocurrió una cosa inolvidable.*

　　　Something unforgettable happened.

NOTE:

The reflexive *ocurrirse* is the passive construction = "To occur (to somebody), to have the idea."

E.g.:　*Se me ocurrió escribirles una carta.*

　　　It occurred to me to write them a letter.

　　　Se les ocurrió que no habían recibido noticias en dos meses.

　　　It occurred to them that they had not received news for two months.

OF COURSE

(Exclamation) = *¡Desde luego!* or *¡Naturalmente!*
E.g.: *¿Has comido? - ¡Desde luego!*
Have you eaten? - Of course!

OÍR

(Transitive verb) = "To hear."
PRES.: *oigo, oyes, oye, oímos, oís, oyen.*
IMPERF.: *o-ía, -ías, -ía, -íamos, -íais, -ían.*
PRETER.: *oí, oíste, oyó, oímos, oísteis, oyeron.*
FUT.: *oir-é, -ás, -á, -emos, -éis, -án.*
CONDIT.: *oir-ía, -ías, -ía, -íamos, -íais, -ían.*
SUBJ. PRES.: *oig-a, -as, -a, -amos, -áis, -an.*
SUBJ. IMPERF. 1: *oy-era, -eras, -era, -éramos, -erais, -eran.*
SUBJ. IMPERF. 2: *oy-ese, -eses, -es, -ésemos, -eseis, -esen.*
INFORMAL IMPERAT.: *oye (tú), no oigas (tú); oíd (vosotros), no oigáis (vosotros).*
FORMAL IMPERAT.: *oiga (Vd.); oigamos; oigan (Vds.).*
PRES PARTIC.: *oyendo.*
PAST PARTIC.: *oído.*
NOTES:
(1) This is a verb of perception. The English construction:
"To hear + (someone) + present participle" is rendered by:
(a) *Oír* + infinitive + personal *a* + person.
E.g.: *Oímos cantar a Felicia.*
We heard Felicia singing.
or (b) *Oír* + personal *a* + person + present participle.
E.g.: *Oímos a Felicia cantando en el pasillo.*
We heard Felicia singing in the hallway.
(2) If the infinitive has a direct object the word order is:
Oír + personal *a* + person + infinitive + object of the infinitive.
E.g.: *Oímos a Felicia cantar la canción.*
We heard Felicia singing the song.

OÍR DECIR QUE

(Verbal idiom). = "To hear that + clause."
E.g.: *He oído decir que es buena obra.*
I have heard that it is a good play.

OÍR HABLAR DE

(Verbal idiom) = "To hear (tell) of."
E.g.: *He oído hablar de ella.*
I have heard of her.

OÍR vs. ESCUCHAR

(1) *Oír* (Transitive verb) = "To hear."
E.g.: *Oigo un ruido.*
I hear a noise.
(2) *Escuchar* (Transitive verb) = "To listen to."
E.g.: *Escucho la radio.*
I listen to the radio.
See **ESCUCHAR**

¡OJALÁ (QUE) . . . !

(Idiomatic construction + subjunctive) = "Would that . . . ! I wish that . . . !" The *que* may be omitted. This (meaning literally: "May Allah grant (that) . . .") expresses:
(a) a wish that something may happen in the future.
    E.g.: *¡Ojalá que no llueva mañana!*
        I hope that it will not rain tomorrow!
(b) a wish concerning a situation which is contrary to fact.
    E.g.: *¡Ojalá que fueran libres!*
        I wish they were free.
NOTE:
In this case the verb is in the imperfect subjunctive.
(c) a wish concerning a situation that was contrary to fact in the past.
    E.g.: *¡Ojalá que tú hubieras ganado!*
        I wish you had won!
NOTE:
In this case the verb is in the pluperfect subjunctive.

OLER

(Transitive and intransitive verb) = "To smell."
PRES.: *huelo, hueles, huele, olemos, oléis, huelen.*
IMPERF.: *ol-ía, -ías, -ía, -íamos, -íais, -ían.*
PRETER.: *ol-í, -iste, -ió, -imos, -isteis, -ieron.*
FUT.: *oler-é, -ás, -á, -emos, -éis, -án.*
CONDIT.: *oler-ía, -ías, -ía, -íamos, -íais, -ían.*
SUBJ. PRES.: *huela, huelas, huela, olamos, oláis, huelan.*
SUBJ. IMPERF. 1: *oli-era, -eras, -era, -éramos, -erais, -eran.*
SUBJ. IMPERF. 2: *oli-ese, -eses, -ese, -ésemos, -eseis, -esen.*
INFORMAL IMPERAT.: *huele (tú), no huelas (tú); oled (vosotros), no oláis (vosotros).*
FORMAL IMPERAT.: *huela (Vd.); olamos; huelan (Vds.).*
PRES. PARTIC.: *oliendo.*
PAST PARTIC.: *olido.*
NOTE:
The preposition *a* is used with this verb: *Oler a* = "To smell of, to smell like."
E.g.: *Huele a rosas.*
    It smells of roses.

OLVIDAR. vs. OLVIDARSE

(1) *Olvidar* (Transitive verb) = "To forget."
    E.g.: *Olvidé mi cartera en casa.*
        I forgot my wallet at home.
(2) *Olvidarse* (Reflexive verb) = "To forget."
NOTE:
The person is the indirect object, while the item forgotten is the subject.
E.g.: *Se me olvidó el cuaderno.*
    I forgot my notebook.

    Se me olvidó traer mi cuaderno.
    I forgot to bring my notebook.

OMISSION OF SUBJECT PRONOUN

The subject pronoun is frequently omitted in Spanish. It is used only:
(1) to indicate stress:
    E.g.: *Tú estás cansado pero yo no.*
        You are tired but I am not.

(2) to avoid ambiguity:

    E.g.: *Está aquí.*

        He is here, she is here, you (formal, singular) are here.

    BUT: *Él está aquí.*

        He is here.

        Ella está aquí.

        She is here.

        Ud. está aquí.

        You are here.

(3) for contrast:

    E.g.: *Tú no fumas pero ella fuma mucho.*

        You don't smoke but she smokes a lot.

OMISSION OF THE DEFINITE ARTICLE

See **ARTICLES, DEFINITE**

ONE ANOTHER

See **EACH OTHER**

ONLY

(a) *No más que* (Idiomatic construction).

    E.g.: *No tengo más que una bicicleta.*

        I have only a bicycle.

(b) *Solamente* (Adverb).

    E.g.: *Tengo solamente una bicicleta.*

        I have only one bicycle.

ORDER OF OBJECT PRONOUNS

See **PRONOUN PAIRS**

ORDINAL NUMBERS

See **NUMBERS, ORDINAL**

ORTHOGRAPHIC CHANGES

See **ABSOLUTE SUPERLATIVES**

See also **ADJECTIVES**

See also **NOUNS**

See also **VERBS, SPELLING-CHANGE**

OTRA VEZ

(Adverbial idiom) = "Again, once again."

E.g.: *Hazlo otra vez.*

    Do it (once) again.

OUGHT TO

See *DEBER*

OUTSIDE, OUTDOORS

(1) (Adverbial construction) = *Fuera* or *al aire libre.*

    E.g.: *Los niños juegan al aire libre.*

        The children are playing outdoors.

        Dejamos el coche fuera.

        We left the car outside.

(2) Preposition = *Fuera de.*
    E.g.: *Esperan fuera de la oficina del director.*
         They are waiting outside the director's office.

OVER meaning "TURN THE PAGE"

= *Al otro lado* (Adverbial idiom).

P

PAGAR

(Transitive verb) = "To pay."
PRES.: *pag-o, -as, -a, -amos, -áis, -an.*
IMPERF.: *pag-aba, -abas, -aba, -ábamos, -abais, -aban.*
PRETER.: *pagué, pag-aste, -ó, -amos, -asteis, -aron.*
FUT.: *pagar-é, -ás, -á, -emos, -éis, -án.*
CONDIT.: *pagar-ía, -ías, -ía, -íamos, -íais, -ían.*
SUBJ. PRES.: *pagu-e, -es, -e, -emos, -éis, -en.*
SUBJ. IMPERF. 1: *pag-ara, -aras, -ara, -áramos, -arais, -aran.*
SUBJ. IMPERF. 2: *pag-ase, -ases, -ase, -ásemos, -aseis, -asen.*
INFORMAL IMPERAT.: *paga (tú), no pagues (tú); pagad (vosotros), no paguéis (vosotros).*
FORMAL IMPERAT.: *pague (Vd.); paguemos; paguen (Vds.).*
PRES. PARTIC.: *pagando*
PAST PARTIC.: *pagado.*

PARA

See **PARA vs. POR**

PARA vs. POR

Both *para* and *por* are prepositions, but their usages are quite different.
(1) **Para** is used:
    (a) To indicate purpose:
        E.g.: *Trabajo para ganar dinero.*
            I work (in order) to earn money.
    (b) To indicate destination:
        E.g.: *Salgo para África.*
            I am leaving for Africa.
    (c) To indicate use:
        E.g.: *Es una máquina para limpiar las alfombras.*
            It is a machine for cleaning carpets.
    (d) To indicate a point in time:
        E.g.: *El ataque ha sido fijado para el 25 de abril.*
            The attack has been set for April 25.
    (e) To indicate a deadline:
        E.g.: *Hay que rellenar estos formularios para el 15 de abril.*
            These forms must be filled out by April 15.
    (f) With an implied term of a comparison:
        E.g.: *Para niño toca bien el violín.*
            For a child, he plays the violin well.

(2) **Por** is used:

(a) To indicate cause or reason. It is the equivalent of:

"on account of, because of":

E.g.: *Me quedé en casa por el mal tiempo.*

I stayed home because of (on account of) the bad weather.

"in behalf of, for the sake of":

E.g.: *Lo hicieron por ti.*

They did it for your sake (in your behalf).

"in exchange for":

E.g.: *Vendí mi coche por mil dólares.*

I sold my car (in exchange) for a thousand dollars.

(b) To indicate the moment in time or the duration of time during which an action lasts.

E.g.: *Estudiamos por cinco horas ayer.*

We studied for five hours yesterday.

(c) To express "along, around, in, through (a place)."

E.g.: *Viajamos por Europa.*

We traveled around Europe.

Hay muchas moscas por aquí.

There are a lot of flies around here.

El ladrón entró por la ventana.

The thief entered through the window.

(d) To indicate the agent by whom or by which the action of a verb in the passive voice is performed. It also indicates the means by which something is done.

E.g.: *Este libro fue escrito por García Márquez.*

This book was written by García Márquez.

Ella me llamó por teléfono.

She called me on the telephone.

(e) To indicate the purpose of an action, after the verbs *enviar, ir, mandar, preguntar, venir.*

E.g.: *Enviamos por un médico.*

We sent for a doctor.

El director manda por sus ingenieros.

The director asks for his engineers.

María preguntó por ti.

Mary asked for (about) you.

La policía vino por él.

The police came for him.

Fuimos por un coche de segunda mano pero no encontramos ninguno.

We went (to look) for a secondhand car but didn't find any.

(f) In a number of idiomatic expressions. See below.

NOTE:

Remember that *buscar, esperar* and *pedir* do not take *por* or *para.* The word "for" is included in these verbs, which are transitive.

E.g.: *Busco mi cartera.*

I am looking for my wallet.

Los esperamos.

We are waiting for them.

Pido un café con leche.

I ask for coffee with milk.

PARA QUE

(Conjunctional construction) + subjunctive = "So that, in order that."

E.g.: *Trabaja mucho para que su padre esté contento de él.*

He works hard so that his father might be pleased with him.

PARECER vs. *PARECER QUE* vs. *PARECERSE A*

(1) *Parecer* (Intransitive verb) = "To appear, to seem."
  E.g.: *Margarita parece cansada.*
    Margaret seems tired.

NOTES:

(a) *Parecer* can also take the idiomatic construction like that used with *gustar* to indicate a person's opinion about something.
  E.g.: *Me parece buena la película.*
    = The film seems good to me.
      I like the film.

See **GUSTAR**

(b) The idiom *¿Qué te parece?* = "What do you think? What is your opinion?"

(2) *Parecer que* (Intransitive verb) + personal pronoun = "It seems (to . . .) that."
  E.g.: *Me parece que cuesta demasiado.*
    It seems to me that it costs too much.

(3) *Parecerse a* (Reflexive verb) = "To resemble, to look like."
  E.g.: *Te pareces a tu hermana.*
    You look like your sister.

    Ellas se parecen mucho.
    They resemble each other very much.

PARTICIPLE, PAST

The past participle *(el participio de pasado)* is an adjective form of the verb which conveys a sense of finished action. When used as a simple adjective, it agrees, like any adjective, with the noun it qualifies.

E.g.: *La obra presentada anoche.*
    The play presented last night.

    Los soldados matados en la guerra.
    The soldiers killed in the war.

See **PAST PARTICIPLES, AGREEMENT OF**

FORMATION:

(a) First conjugation verbs: Stem + *-ado*.
  E.g.: *Cantar → cantado.*

(b) Second and third conjugation verbs: Stem + *-ido*.
  E.g.: *Entender → entendido.*
    Salir → salido.

EXCEPTIONS:

Abrir → abierto.	*Morir → muerto.*
Cubrir → cubierto.	*Poner → puesto.*
Decir → dicho.	*Resolver → resuelto.*
Escribir → escrito.	*Romper → roto.*
Freír → frito.	*Ver → visto.*
Hacer → hecho.	*Volver → vuelto.*

USAGE:

The past participle is used to form all compound tenses of all verbs: present perfect, pluperfect, future perfect, past conditional, past preterite, past subjunctive, pluperfect subjunctive, and also the passive voice.

E.g.: *Yo he llegado.*
    Tú habías comido.
    Ella habrá vivido.
    Nosotros habríamos escrito.
    Vosotros hubierais bebido.
    Ellos hubiesen muerto.

See **PASSIVE VOICE**

PARTICIPLE, PRESENT (GERUND)

The present participle *(el participio de presente)*, or gerund *(el gerundio)*, is an adjective form of the verb which conveys a sense of ongoing action. It corresponds to the English verb ending: "-ing."

FORMATION:

(a) First conjugation verbs: Stem + *-ando.*

E.g.: *Escuch-ar* → *escuch-ando.*

(b) Second and third conjugation verbs: Stem + *-iendo.*

E.g.: *Comprend-er* → *comprend-iendo.*

Sal-ir → *sal-iendo.*

The present participle always ends in *-o.*

EXCEPTIONS:

Caer → *cayendo.*	*Oír* → *oyendo.*
Creer → *creyendo.*	*Pedir* → *pidiendo.*
Decir → *diciendo.*	*Poder* → *pudiendo.*
Dormir → *durmiendo.*	*Sentir* → *sintiendo.*
Ir → *yendo.*	*Traer* → *trayendo.*
Leer → *leyendo.*	*Venir* → *viniendo.*
Morir → *muriendo.*	

USAGE:

The present participle is used:

(1) with *estar*, to form the progressive form of verb tenses.

E.g.: *Están leyendo.*

They are reading.

Estábamos corriendo.

We were running.

(2) as a verb form.

E.g.: *Estaban en la cama mirando la televisión.*

They were in bed watching television.

(3) to express the English construction "By + present participle" ("By + -ing").

E.g.: *Trabajando seis días a la semana, ganaba mucho dinero.*

By working six days a week he earned a lot of money.

(4) after *Seguir* and *continuar*, to mean "To continue + -ing."

E.g.: *Siguieron cantando toda la noche.*

They continued to sing all night.

POSITION OF OBJECT PRONOUNS WITH THE PRESENT PARTICIPLE:

Object pronouns are placed after the present participle and connected to it, with a written accent to indicate the retention of stress in its normal position.

E.g.: *Yo estaba escuchándola.*

I was listening to her.

NOTE:

In the progressive tenses, the object pronouns may also be placed before *estar.*

E.g.: *Yo la estaba escuchando.*

I was listening to her.

PARTIR vs. *DEJAR* vs. *SALIR*

(1) *Partir* =

(a) "To start, to set out."

E.g.: *Partiremos a las ocho.*

We shall set out at eight o'clock.

(b) "To split, to divide."

E.g.: *Partió las nueces con un martillo.*

He split the nuts with a hammer.

(2) *Dejar* =
    (a) "To leave (out), to abandon."
        E.g.: *Dejaron sus maletas en el hotel.*
            They left their suitcases in the hotel.
    (b) "To let, to allow."
        E.g.: *No me dejan salir.*
            They don't let me go out.
(3) *Salir* = "To leave, to go out."
    E.g.: *Salió a las dos.*
        He left at two o'clock.

PARTS OF THE BODY, articles with

The definite articles are used rather than the possessive adjectives when:
(a) referring to parts of the body (or clothing) whose possessor is clear.
    E.g.: *Carmen se cortó el dedo.*
        Carmen cut her finger.

        Me pongo el sombrero.
        I put my hat on.
(b) talking about a person's physical appearance.
    E.g.: *Ella tiene los ojos verdes.*
        She has green eyes.

PASAR

(1) *Pasar* (Transitive verb) =
    (a) "To pass."
        E.g.: *¡Páseme el pan, por favor!*
            Pass me the bread, please!
    (b) "To spend (time)."
        E.g.: *Pasé el verano en Puerto Rico.*
            I spent the summer in Puerto Rico.
(2) *Pasar* (Intransitive verb) = "To pass, to go past."
    E.g.: *Pasaron por la calle principal.*
        They passed by the main street.
NOTE:
¡Pase Vd.! = "Please come in!"

PASSIVE VOICE

The passive voice *(la voz pasiva)* expresses an action performed upon the subject or one in which the subject is the result of the action.
E.g.: *La casa fue construida por mi abuelo.*
    The house was built by my grandfather.
NOTE:
Any active "transitive verb + direct object" construction can be turned into a passive construction, with the direct object becoming the subject and the subject, preceded by the preposition *por*, becoming the "agent" (or "doer") of the action.
E.g.: *Escribo el libro.* → *El libra es escrito por mí.*
    I write the book. → The book is written by me.
CONSTRUCTION:
The passive voice is constructed by using the verb *ser* + the past participle of the verb. *Ser* is conjugated in whatever tense is required.
E.g.: *El ladrón es detenido (ha sido detenido, será detenido,* etc.) *por la policía.*
    The thief is (has been, will be, etc.) arrested by the police.

NOTES:
(1) The past participle of a verb in the passive voice serves as an adjective and agrees in number and gender with the subject.
  E.g.: *Los ladrones fueron detenidos.*
    The thieves were arrested.
(2) The passive voice is not used very much in Spanish. If the agent is not mentioned (or implied), avoid using the passive voice by using the construction with the reflexive particle *se.* In this case, the subject usually follows the verb.
  E.g.: *Se terminó el edificio en tres meses.*
    The building was finished in three months.

PAST PARTICIPLE

See **PARTICIPLE, PAST**

PAST PARTICIPLES, AGREEMENT OF

(1) A past participle is invariable when used with the verb *haber* in all compound tenses.
  E.g.: *Los postres que han preparado.*
    The desserts they have prepared.
(2) A past participle agrees with the subject when used with the verb *ser* in the passive voice.
  E.g.: *Los soldados fueron heridos.*
    The soldiers were injured.
(3) A past participle agrees with the subject when used as an adjective with the verb *estar.*
  E.g.: *Las muchachas están cansadas.*
    The girls are tired.

PAST PRETERITE TENSE

The past preterite *(el pretérito perfecto)* is used only in the literary style, after *apenas* (hardly), *así que* (as soon as), *cuando* (when), *después de que* (after), *en cuanto* (as soon as), *luego que* (as soon as), and *tan pronto como* (as soon as). In the informal (or conversational) style the pluperfect is used rather than the preterite perfect.
E.g.: *En cuanto hubieron salido, sonó el teléfono.*
    As soon as they had left, the telephone rang.
The informal equivalent is:
En cuanto habían salido, sonó el teléfono.
FORMATION:
Preterite tense of *haber* + past participle.
E.g.: *Hube comido.*
    I had eaten.

    Hubieron entrado.
    They had entered.

PAST TENSES

There are 11 past tenses in Spanish:
The IMPERFECT
The PRETERITE
The PRESENT PERFECT
The PLUPERFECT
The PAST CONDITIONAL
The FUTURE PERFECT
The PAST PRETERITE
The IMPERFECT SUBJUNCTIVE (two forms)
The PAST SUBJUNCTIVE
The PLUPERFECT SUBJUNCTIVE
See the entry for each of these tenses: **IMPERFECT TENSE, PRETERITE TENSE, PRESENT PERFECT TENSE, PLUPERFECT TENSE, FUTURE PERFECT TENSE, PAST PRETERITE TENSE, CONDITIONAL TENSES, SUBJUNCTIVE MOOD**

PEDIR

(Transitive verb) = "To ask for."
PRES.: *pido, pides, pide, pedimos, pedís, piden.*
IMPERF.: *ped-ía, -ías, -ía, -íamos, -ías, -ían.*
PRETER.: *pedí, pediste, pidió, pedimos, pedisteis, pidieron.*
FUT.: *pedir-é, -ás, -á, -emos, -éis, -án.*
CONDIT.: *pedir-ía, -ías, -ía, -íamos, -íais, -ían.*
SUBJ. PRES.: *pid-a, -as, -a, -amos, -áis, -an.*
SUBJ. IMPERF. 1: *pidi-era, -eras, -era, -éramos, -erais, -eran.*
SUBJ. IMPERF. 2: *pidi-ese, -eses, -ese, -ésemos, -eseis, -esen.*
INFORMAL IMPERAT.: *pide (tú), no pidas (tú); pedid (vosotros), no pidáis (vosotros).*
FORMAL IMPERAT.: *pida (Vd.); pidamos; pidan (Vds.).*
PRES. PARTIC.: *pidiendo.*
PAST PARTIC.: *pedido.*
NOTES:
(1) The person is the indirect object and the thing asked for is the direct object.
    E.g.: *Le pido dinero a mi padre.*
        I ask my father for some money.
REMEMBER that the personal indirect object pronoun must be used in addition to the indirect object noun.
(2) *Pedir que* + subjunctive.
    E.g.: *Le pido a mi padre que me deje salir hasta las doce.*
        I ask my father to let me go out until midnight.
Do not confuse *pedir* with *preguntar*. See below.

PEDIR PRESTADO

(Verbal Idiom) = "To borrow."
E.g.: *Le pedí prestado el coche a Miguel.*
     I borrowed Michael's car.

PEDIR vs. PREGUNTAR

(1) *Pedir* (Transitive verb) = "To request, to demand, to ask for."
    E.g.: *Manuel me pidió un lápiz.*
        Manuel asked me for a pencil.
NOTE:
The person is an indirect object and the thing asked for is a direct object.
(2) *Preguntar* (Transitive verb) = "To inquire, to inquire of, to ask (for information)."
    E.g.: *Mi madre me preguntó tu nombre.*
        My mother asked me your name.
NOTES:
(1) *Preguntar por* = "To ask for, to inquire for."
    E.g.: *José preguntó por tí.*
        Joseph asked for you.
(2) *Hacer una pregunta* = "To ask a question."
    E.g.: *Este profesor hace muchas preguntas.*
        This teacher asks many questions.
See **HACER UNA PREGUNTA**

PENSAR + infinitive

(Idiomatic construction) = "To intend, to plan."
E.g.: *Pienso ir al Uruguay.*
     I intend to go to Uruguay.

PENSAR DE vs. *PENSAR EN*

(Idiomatic constructions).
(1) *Pensar de* = "To think of, to have an opinion about."
   E.g.: *¿Qué piensas de este libro?*
       What do you think of this book?
(2) *Pensar en* = "To think about."
   E.g.: *Pienso en my novia.*
       I am thinking about my fiancée.

PEOPLE

(1) "People (in general)" = (an indefinite number) = *La gente* (singular).
   E.g.: *Esta gente es muy pobre.*
       These people are very poor.
(2) "People" (a definite number) = *Personas.*
   E.g.: *Hay veinte personas.*
       There are twenty people.
(3) "The people (of a nation)" = (collective noun) = *El pueblo.*
   E.g.: *El pueblo de España tiene una historia muy larga.*
       The people of Spain have a long history.
(4) "The people (as a social class)" = (collective noun) = *El pueblo.*
   E.g.: *El pueblo se rebeló contra el rey.*
       The people revolted against the king.

PEOR

(1) (Comparative form of the adjective *malo*) = "Worse."
   E.g.: *Mi catarro está peor que el tuyo.*
       My cold is worse than yours.
(2) (Comparative form of the adverb *mal*) = "Worse."
   E.g.: *Carlota canta peor que Carmen.*
       Charlotte sings worse than Carmen.

PER

(Preposition) = *Por.*
E.g.: *Ganan mil pesetas por hora.*
       They earn one thousand pesetas per hour.

       Cincuenta kilómetros por hora.
       Fifty kilometres per hour.
BUT: *Un dólar la docena.*
       One dollar per dozen.

PERCEPTION, VERBS OF

Verbs of perception *(escuchar, oír, mirar, sentir, ver)*, when followed by a verb, take the infinitive or the gerund. The equivalent construction in English is a present participle.
E.g.: *Vimos entrar a María.*
       We saw Mary entering.
NOTE:
The word order is "Verb of perception + infinitive + noun or pronoun." If the direct object is a personal pronoun, it comes before the verb of perception.
E.g.: *La escuchamos tocar el violín.*
       We listen to her play the violin.

       Los sentimos acercarse.
       We felt them approach.

PERDER

(Transitive verb) = "To lose."
PRES.: *pierd-o, -es, -e, perdemos, perdéis, pierden.*
IMPERF.: *perd-ía, -ías, -ía, -íamos, -íais, -ían.*
PRETER.: *perd-í, -iste, -ió, -imos, -isteis, -ieron.*
FUT.: *perder-é, -ás, -á, -emos, -éis, -án.*
CONDIT.: *perder-ía, -ías, -ía, -íamos, -íais, -ían.*
SUBJ. PRES.: *pierd-a, -as, -a, perdamos, perdáis, pierdan.*
SUBJ. IMPERF. 1: *perdi-era, -eras, -era, -éramos, -erais, -eran.*
SUBJ. IMPERF. 2: *perdi-ese, -eses, -ese, -ésemos, -eseis, -esen.*
INFORMAL IMPERAT.: *pierde (tú), no pierdas (tú); perded (vosotros), no perdáis (vosotros).*
FORMAL IMPERAT.: *pierda (Vd.); perdamos; pierdan (Vds.).*
PRES. PARTIC.: *perdiendo.*
PAST PARTIC.: *perdido.*

PERDER DE VISTA

(Idiomatic expression) = "To lose sight of."
E.g.: *Perdimos de vista a nuestros compañeros.*
 We lost sight of our companions.

PERMITIR + verb

(Idiomatic construction) = "To let, to allow, to permit."
(1) This verb is an exception to the rule which requires a clause when there is a change of subject. The infinitive may be used after *permitir.*
 E.g.: *Mi padre no me permite manejar su coche.*
 My father doesn't let me drive his car.
(2) The regular construction *Permitir que* + subjunctive may also be used.
 E.g.: *Mi padre permite que yo maneje su coche.*
 My father allows me to drive his car.
See **SUBJUNCTIVE vs. INFINITIVE**

PERO vs. SINO

(Conjunctions). Both words mean "but," but their usage is quite different.
(1) *Pero* corresponds to the English "but" in most of its senses.
 E.g.: *Tengo este libro, pero no lo he leído.*
 I have this book but I haven't read it.
(2) *Sino* means "but on the contrary, but rather." It is used in an affirmative statement which contrasts with a preceding negative statement. A verb following *sino* is generally in the infinitive.
 E.g.: *No es japonés, sino chino.*
 He is not Japanese, but Chinese.
 No voy a dormir, sino a trabajar.
 I am not going to sleep, but to work.
NOTES:
(1) If a clause follows *sino* use *sino que.*
 E.g.: *Elena no leía, sino que miraba la televisión.*
 Helen was not reading, but watching television.

(2) The comparison must always be between two equivalent parts of speech, e.g., two adjectives, two nouns, two infinitives.

E.g.: *No es gorda sino delgada.*
She is not fat, but slim.

No es profesor sino médico.
He is not a teacher, but a doctor.

No vamos a dormir sino a trabajar.
We are not going to sleep, but to work.

No corren rápidamente sino lentamente.
They do not run fast, but slowly.

PERSON (Grammatical)

The "person" *(la persona)* is the form of the conjugation which indicates the person(s) who is (are) speaking, to whom one is speaking, or about whom one is speaking.

E.g.: *Yo trabajo.*   I work.
Tú trabajas.   You work.
Él, ella trabaja.   He, she works.
Nosotros (-as) trabajamos.   We work.
Vosotros (-as) trabajáis.   You work.
Ellos (-as) trabajan.   They work.

PERSONAL "A"

See **A (personal)**

PERSONAL PRONOUNS

See **PRONOUNS, PERSONAL**

PLACER

(Transitive verb) = "To please."
E.g.: *Nos place oír música moderna.*
We like to hear modern music.
NOTE:
The person is an indirect object.

to PLAY

(1) To play (a game) = *Jugar (a).*
E.g.: *Juegan al tenis.*
They play tennis.

Juego al ajedrez.
I play chess.

(2) To play (an instrument) = *Tocar.*
E.g.: *Tocas el piano.*
You play the piano.

(3) To play (a theater role) = *Hacer el papel (de).*
E.g.: *Hice el papel de Hamlet.*
I played the part of Hamlet.

PLEASE

(1) Accompanying a polite request = *¡Por favor!*
E.g.: *¡Escríbame pronto, por favor!*
Write me soon, please.

(2) Meaning "To give pleasure to" = *Dar gusto a* + indirect object.
E.g.: *Lo hicieron para darles gusto a sus hijos.*
They did it to please their children.

PLUPERFECT TENSE

The pluperfect *(el pluscuamperfecto)* expresses an action which was completed in the past before another action in the past.
FORMATION:
The imperfect tense of *haber* + past participle of the verb.
E.g.: *Había comido.*   I had eaten.
      Habías bebido.   You had drunk.
      Había entrado.   She had entered.
      Habíamos visto.   We had seen.
      Habíais escrito.   You had written.
      Habían viajado.   They had traveled.

NOTE:
Direct object pronouns come immediately before the auxiliary verb *haber.*
E.g.: *Yo no les había encontrado.*
      I had not met them.

NOTE:
In English, the use of the pluperfect is often overlooked.
E.g.: He said he saw him = He said he had seen him.
      He claimed he didn't do it = He claimed he had not done it.
In Spanish, the pluperfect is generally used in these cases.
E.g.: *Ella dijo que le había visto a Margarita.*
      She said that she had seen Margaret.

      Negaron que habían robado la joya.
      They denied that they had stolen the jewel.

See **SUBJUNCTIVE MOOD for the Pluperfect Subjunctive**

PLURAL OF ADJECTIVES
See **ADJECTIVES**

PLURAL OF NOUNS
See **NOUNS, plural of**

PLUSCUAMPERFECTO
See **PLUPERFECT TENSE**

POCO (-A, -OS, -AS)
(1) Adjective:
    (a) in the singular = "Little, small."
        E.g.: *Tenemos poco tiempo.*
              We have little time.
    (b) in the plural = "Few."
        E.g.: *El libro tiene pocas páginas.*
              The book has few pages.
(2) Adverb = "Little, not much."
    E.g.: *Ernesto estudia poco.*
          Ernest studies little.

PODER

(Transitive verb) = "To be able."
PRES.: *pued-o, -es, -e, podemos, podéis, pueden.*
IMPERF.: *pod-ía, -ías, -ía, -íamos, -íais, -ían.*
PRETER.: *pude, pudiste, pudo, pudimos, pudisteis, pudieron.*
FUT.: *podr-é, -ás, -á, -emos, -éis, -án.*
CONDIT.: *podr-ía, -ías, -ía, -íamos, -íais, -ían.*
SUBJ. PRES.: *pueda, puedas, pueda, podamos, podáis, puedan.*
SUBJ. IMPERF. 1: *pudi-era, -eras, -era, -éramos, -erais, -eran.*
SUBJ. IMPERF. 2: *pudi-ese, -eses, -ese, -ésemos, -eseis, -esen.*
INFORMAL IMPERAT.: -
FORMAL IMPERAT.: -
PRES. PARTIC.: *pudiendo.*
PAST PARTIC.: *podido.*

PONER

(Transitive verb) = "To put, to place."
PRES.: *pongo, pon-es, -e, -emos, -éis, -en.*
IMPERF.: *pon-ía, -ías, -ía, -íamos, -íais, -ían.*
PRETER.: *puse, pusiste, puso, pusimos, pusisteis, pusieron.*
FUT.: *pondr-é, -ás, -á, -emos, -éis, -án.*
CONDIT.: *pondr-ía, -ías, -ía, -íamos, -íais, -ían.*
SUBJ. PRES.: *pong-a, -as, -a, -amos, -áis, -an.*
SUBJ. IMPERF. 1: *pusi-era, -eras, -era, -éramos, -erais, -eran.*
SUBJ. IMPERF. 2: *pusi-ese, -eses, -ese, -ésemos, -eseis, -esen.*
INFORMAL IMPERAT.: *pon (tú), no pongas (tú); poned (vosotros), no pongáis (vosotros).*
FORMAL IMPERAT.: *ponga (Vd.); pongamos; pongan (Vds.).*
PRES. PARTIC.: *poniendo.*
PAST PARTIC.: *puesto.*

PONERSE + adjective

(Reflexive verb) = "To turn, to become (involuntarily)"
E.g.: *Al ver a su amigo, María se puso muy roja.*
When she saw her friend, Mary become very red.
See **BECOME**

PONERSE + noun

(Reflexive verb) = "To put on (clothing)."
E.g.: *Me pongo una camisa limpia.*
I'm putting on a clean shirt.

PONERSE A + infinitive

(Reflexive verb) = "To begin to, to start to."
E.g.: *Me puse a trabajar a las siete.*
I started to work at seven o'clock.

PONERSE DE ACUERDO

(Verbal idiom) = "To agree."
E.g.: *Los dos partidos se pusieron de acuerdo para terminar la discusión.*
The two parties agreed to end the discussion.

POR

See **PARA vs. POR**

POR AHORA

(Adverbial idiom) = "For now, for the moment, at the moment."
E.g.: *Por ahora no podemos decir nada.*
   For the moment we cannot say anything.

POR CASUALIDAD

(Adverbial idiom) = "By chance."
E.g.: *Se encontraron por casualidad en la calle.*
   They met by chance in the street.

POR CIERTO

(Adverbial idiom) = "Certainly, surely, for sure, for certain."
E.g.: *Por cierto han llegado a su destinación.*
   They have certainly arrived at their destination.

POR CONSIGUIENTE

(Adverbial idiom) = "Consequently, therefore."
E.g.: *No salí de casa, por consiguiente no vi el desfile.*
   I did not leave the house, therefore I did not see the parade.

POR DESGRACIA

(Adverbial idiom) = "Unfortunately."
E.g.: *Por desgracia, perdieron su llave.*
   Unfortunately, they lost their key.
Synonym: *Desgraciadamente.*

POR EJEMPLO

(Adverbial idiom) = "For example."
E.g.: *Hay que hacer algo, por ejemplo escribir una carta.*
   You have to do something; for example, write a letter.

POR ESCRITO

(Adverbial idiom) = "In writing."
E.g.: *¿Tenemos que hacerlo por escrito?*
   Do we have to do it in writing?

POR ESO

- (Adverbial idiom) = "Therefore, that's why, because of that."
E.g.: *Estaba enfermo. Por eso no pudo venir a la fiesta.*
   He was ill. That's why he couldn't come to the party.

POR FAVOR

(Adverbial idiom) = "Please."
E.g.: *Por favor, dame un beso.*
   Please give me a kiss.

POR FIN

(Adverbial idiom) = "Finally."
E.g.: *Por fin hemos terminado los cursos.*
   We have finally finished classes.
See **AL FIN**

POR LO GENERAL

(Adverbial idiom) = "Generally."
E.g.: *Por lo general me levanto a las siete.*
    I generally get up at seven.

POR LO TANTO

(Adverbial idiom) = "Consequently."
E.g.: *No comprendí, por lo tanto no pude contestar.*
    I did not understand, consequently I could not answer.

POR LO VISTO

(Adverbial idiom) = "Apparently."
E.g.: *Por lo visto habrán salido.*
    Apparently they must have gone out.

POR POCO

(Adverbial idiom) = "Almost + verb."
E.g.: *Por poco salí mal en el examen.*
    I almost failed the examination.
NOTE:
It is often followed by the present tense to mean the past.
E.g.: *Por poco choco con el camión.*
    I almost crashed into the truck.

¿POR QUÉ vs. PARA QUÉ?

Both expressions mean "Why?," but their meanings are quite different.
(a) *¿Por qué?* = "Why (for what reason)?"
    E.g.: *¿Por qué no vienes conmigo?*
        Why don't you come with me?
(b) *¿Para qué?* = "Why (for what purpose)?"
    E.g.: *¿Para qué quieres comprar este libro?*
        Why do you want to buy this book?

POR QUÉ vs. PORQUE vs. PORQUÉ

(1) *¿Por qué?* = (interrogative expression) = "Why" (for what reason, because of what)?"
    E.g.: *¿Por qué no hiciste el trabajo?*
        Why didn't you do the work?
(2) *Porque* (conjunction) = "Because." It is followed by the indicative.
    E.g.: *No hice el trabajo porque estaba cansado.*
        I didn't do the work because I was tired.
(3) *El porqué* (masculine noun) = "The cause, the reason, the whys and wherefores."
    E.g.: *Estudiamos el porqué de la guerra.*
        We studied the cause of the war.

POR SUPUESTO

(Idiomatic adverbial exclamation) = "Of course, naturally!"
E.g.: *¿Quieres ir al cine? - ¡Por supuesto!*
    "Do you want to go to the movies?" "Of course!"

POR vs. PARA

See **PARA vs. POR**

PORQUE vs. *A CAUSA DE*
See ***A CAUSA DE* vs. *PORQUE***

POSITION OF OBJECT PRONOUNS
See **PRONOUNS, OBJECT OF VERB**
See also **PRONOUN PAIRS**

POSSESSION

Possession is expressed by the preposition *de*. This construction corresponds to the English " 's" or " 's.' "

E.g.: *El libro de Pedro.*
Peter's book.

La casa de los Delgado.
The Delgados' house.
See **ADJECTIVES, POSSESSIVE**
See also **PRONOUNS, POSSESSIVE**

POTENCIAL (EL TIEMPO)
See **CONDITIONAL TENSES**

PREGUNTAR

(Transitive verb) = "To ask (a question)."
NOTE:
The person of whom the question is asked is the indirect object.
E.g.: *Le preguntaré a Pedro dónde vive.*
I shall ask Peter where he lives.

PREGUNTAR POR

(Intransitive verb) = "To inquire."
E.g.: *Mi hermana preguntó por ti ayer.*
My sister inquired about you yesterday.

PREGUNTAR vs. *PEDIR*
See ***PEDIR* vs. *PREGUNTAR***

PREOCUPAR vs. *PREOCUPARSE (DE* or *POR)*

(1) *Preocupar* (Transitive verb) = "To worry, to bother."
    E.g.: *Tu salud me preocupa muchísimo.*
        Your health worries me a lot.
(2) *Preocuparse* (Reflexive verb) = "To worry, to concern oneself."
    E.g.: *¡No te preocupes!*
        Don't worry!
See **to WORRY**

PREPOSITION

A preposition *(una preposición)* is an invariable word which serves to establish a link with another word (called the object of the preposition). Examples of prepositions: *a, con, de, debajo de, delante de, para, por, sin, sobre,* etc.

E.g.: *Ella va a Madrid.*
> She goes to Madrid.

Ellos trabajan con mi padre.
> They work with my father.

Hablo de su hermana.
> I am talking about his sister.

El libro está sobre la mesa.
> The book is on the table.

When the object of a preposition is a verb, it is always in the infinitive.

E.g.: *Trabajo para ganar mi vida.*
> I work (in order) to earn a living.

PREPOSITION + infinitive

When a verb introduces an infinitive, it does so in one of five ways: (a) without any preposition, (b) with the preposition *a*, (c) with the preposition *con*, (d) with the preposition *de*, or (e) with the preposition *en*.

There are no clear-cut rules for the choice of preposition. This must be learned through practice.

See **VERBS + (A, CON, DE, EN, or no preposition) + infinitive**

See also **DE or A (with verbs)**

PRESENT PARTICIPLE

See **PARTICIPLE, PRESENT**

PRESENT PERFECT TENSE

The present perfect tense *(el presente perfecto)* describes an action that took place in the recent past.

FORMATION:

The auxiliary verb *haber* + past participle.

E.g.: *Hemos escrito la carta.*
> We have written the letter.

PRESENT TENSE

The present tense *(el presente)* describes an action taking place at the present moment.

E.g.: *Ella habla ahora.*
> She speaks now.

As in English, it is also used:

(1) To describe an action that will take place in the near future:

E.g.: *Voy a Madrid mañana.*
> I am going to Madrid tomorrow.

(2) To describe a future action after a conditional *si.*

E.g.: *Si vas a España, iré contigo.*
> If you go to Spain, I shall go with you.

NOTE:

While in English there are three forms of the present, there are only two in Spanish. There is no emphatic form.

	In English:	*In Spanish:*
Simple Present:	I work.	*Trabajo.*
Progressive Present:	I am working.	*Estoy trabajando.*
Emphatic Present:	I do work.	*Trabajo.*

PRETERITE TENSE

The preterite *(el pretérito)* is a tense which expresses a completed action in the past.
FORMATION:
(a) *-ar* verbs: Stem + *é, aste, ó, amos, asteis, aron.*
(b) *-er* and *-ir* verbs: Stem + *í, iste, ió, imos, isteis, ieron.*
    E.g.: *Hablé, cantaste, llegó, estudiamos, bailasteis, marcharon.*
          Comí, bebiste, perdió, entendimos, descendisteis, perdieron.
          Viví, escribiste, salió, fingimos, huisteis, sufrieron.

IRREGULAR PRETERITES:
ANDAR: *anduve, anduviste, anduvo, anduvimos, anduvisteis, anduvieron.*
CABER: *cupe, cupiste, cupo, cupimos, cupisteis, cupieron.*
CONDUCIR: *conduje, condujiste, condujo, condujimos, condujisteis, condujeron.*
DAR: *di, diste, dio, dimos, disteis, dieron.*
DECIR: *dije, dijiste, dijo, dijimos, dijisteis, dijeron.*
ESTAR: *estuve, estuviste, estuvo, estuvimos, estuvisteis, estuvieron.*
HABER: *hube, hubiste, hubo, hubimos, hubisteis, hubieron.*
HACER: *hice, hiciste, hizo, hicimos, hicisteis, hicieron* (and all the compounds of *hacer*; e.g.: DESHACER, SATISFACER).
IR: *fui, fuiste, fue, fuimos, fuisteis, fueron.*
PODER: *pude, pudiste, pudo, pudimos, pudisteis, pudieron.*
PONER: *puse, pusiste, puso, pusimos, pusisteis, pusieron* (and all the compounds of *poner*; e.g.: COMPONER, DISPONER, PROPONER).
PRODUCIR: *produje, produjiste, produjo, produjimos, produjisteis, produjeron.*
QUERER: *quise, quisiste, quiso, quisimos, quisisteis, quisieron.*
SABER: *supe, supiste, supo, supimos, supisteis, supieron.*
SER: *fui, fuiste, fue, fuimos, fuisteis, fueron.*
TENER: *tuve, tuviste, tuvo, tuvimos, tuvisteis, tuvieron* (and all the compounds of *tener*; e.g.: CONTENER, DETENER, MANTENER.)
TRAER: *traje, trajiste, trajo, trajimos, trajisteis, trajeron.*
TRADUCIR: *traduje, tradujiste, tradujo, tradujimos, tradujisteis, tradujeron.*
VENIR: *vine, viniste, vino, vinimos, vinisteis, vinieron.*
Also:
Verbs whose stem ends in *-e,* in the third persons singular and plural; the endings *-ió* and *-ieron* change to *-yó* and *-yeron.*
E.g.: *Creyó. Leyeron.*

USAGE:
The preterite is used:
(1) to express past actions which lasted a specific amount of time.
    E.g.: *Vivieron cuatro años en Chile.*
        They lived four years in Chile.
(2) to express actions whose (a) beginning, (b) end, or (c) duration is known.
    E.g.: (a) *Empezó a llover a las dos.*
          It began to rain at two o'clock.
       (b) *Estudié hasta las once.*
          I studied until eleven o'clock.
       (c) *Pasé una hora en la biblioteca.*
          I spent one hour in the library.
(3) to express a series of actions in the past.
    E.g.: *Entré en el restaurante, llamé al camarero y pedí una paella.*
        I went into the restaurant, I called the waiter, and I ordered a paella.
(4) to express a past action which was repeated a specific number of times.
    E.g.: *Visitaron las Canarias cuatro veces.*
        They visited the Canary Islands four times.
See **IMPERFECT vs. PRETERITE**

PRETERITE vs. IMPERFECT
See **IMPERFECT vs. PRETERITE**

PROBABILITY
The concept of probability can be rendered by:
(1) The adverb *Quizá(s)* or *tal vez.*
   E.g.: *Quizá han llegado.*
      They have probably arrived.
(2) The future tense.
   E.g.: *¿A qué hora llegarán?*
      At what time will they (probably) arrive?
(3) *Deber de* + infinitive.
   E.g.: *Deben de haber llegado.*
      They must have arrived.
(4) The impersonal construction *Es posible* (or *probable*) *que* + subjunctive.
   E.g.: *Es posible que hayan llegado.*
      It's possible that they have arrived.

PROGRESSIVE TENSES
The progressive tenses *(los tiempos progresivos)* express an action continuing at the time in question. They consist of the verb *estar* + present participle of the verb. The most commonly used progressive tenses are:
(a) The present progressive.
   E.g.: *Estoy leyendo.*
      I am reading.
(b) The imperfect progressive.
   E.g.: *Estabas leyendo.*
      You were reading.
(c) The future progressive
   E.g.: *Estará leyendo.*
      He will be reading.
(d) The present subjunctive progressive.
   E.g.: *Es preciso que estemos trabajando cuando él llegue.*
      It is important that we be working when he arrives.

PROHIBIR
(Transitive verb) = "To prohibit, to forbid."
PRES.: prohib-o, -es, -e, -imos, -ís, -en.
IMPERF.: prohib-ía, -ías, -ía, -íamos, -íais, -ían.
PRETER.: prohib-í, -iste, -ió, -imos, -isteis, -ieron.
FUT.: prohibir-é, -ás, -á, -emos, -éis, -án.
CONDIT.: prohibir-ía, -ías, -ía, -íamos, -íais, -ían.
SUBJ. PRES.: prohib-a, -as, -a, -amos, -áis, -an.
SUBJ. IMPERF. 1: prohibi-era, -eras, -era, -éramos, -erais, -eran.
SUBJ. IMPERF. 2: prohibi-ese, -eses, -ese, -ésemos, -eseis, -esen.
INFORMAL IMPERAT.: prohibe (tú), no prohibas (tú); prohibid (vosotros), no prohibáis (vosotros).
FORMAL IMPERAT.: prohiba (Vd.); prohibamos; prohiban (Vds.).
PRES. PARTIC.: prohibiendo.
PAST PARTIC.: prohibido.

NOTE:

This is a verb of influence which can be followed by the infinitive even if there is a change of subject between the main clause and the subordinate clause.

E.g.: *Su madre le prohibe a María que salga con él.*

Her mother forbids Mary to go out with him.

Su madre le prohibe a María salir con él.

Her mother forbids Mary to go out with him.

See **SUBJUNCTIVE vs. INFINITIVE**

PRONOUN

A pronoun *(un pronombre)* is a word which is used as a substitute for a noun (or sometimes an idea or a clause) which is expressed elsewhere in the context.

E.g.: *Hay un coche en la calle. Lo veo desde aquí.*

There is a car in the street. I see it from here.

PRONOUN PAIRS

When there are two object pronouns, the indirect object pronoun (which is usually a person) precedes the direct object pronoun (which is usually a thing.)

E.g.: *Pedro me los da.*

Peter gives them to me.

María te lo lee.

Mary reads it to you.

Juan se la envía.

John sends it to him (her, you, them).

Arturo nos la canta.

Arthur sings it to us.

Carmen os los dice.

Carmen tells them to you.

This rule applies also when the pronouns come after the verb.

E.g.: *¡Escríbamela!*

Write it to me!

Quieren llevárnoslo.

They want to bring it to us.

Estaban describiéndomela.

They were describing it to me.

NOTE:

Le and *les* change to *se* when they come before *lo, la, los* or *las.* This is done to avoid the repetition of the "*l*" sound.

E.g.: *Pedro se la dió.*

Peter gave it to him (her, you, them).

If the meaning of *se* is not clear, it can be explained by adding *a él, a ella, a ellos, a ellas, a Vd.,* or *a Vds.*

REMEMBER, however, that the *se* must still be expressed even though its meaning needs to be clarified.

E.g.: *El profesor se la contestó a ellos.*

The teacher answered it to them.

See **PRONOUNS, OBJECT OF VERB**

PRONOUNS, DEMONSTRATIVE

Demonstrative pronouns *(los pronombres demostrativos)* replace the noun while pointing to it and distinguishing it from others. They agree in number and gender with the noun they replace.

E.g.: *Esta mesa y aquélla.*

This table and that one.

There are three forms in Spanish, corresponding to:
(a) what is near the speaker, (b) what is near the listener, and (c) what is far from both speaker and listener.

PRONOUNS, DEMONSTRATIVE

		Masculine	Feminine	Neuter
(a)	This (one)	*éste*	*ésta*	*esto*
	These (ones)	*éstos*	*éstas*	
(b)	That (one)	*ése*	*ésa*	*eso*
	Those (ones)	*ésos*	*ésas*	
(c)	That (one)	*aquél*	*aquélla*	*aquello*
	Those (ones)	*aquéllos*	*aquéllas*	

The neuter forms *esto, eso* and *aquello* refer to ideas, concepts, statements, etc., and are invariable.
E.g.: *Pedro habla siempre en clase, y eso la molesta a la profesora.*
   Peter always talks in class, and that bothers the teacher.
NOTE:
The forms of the demonstrative pronouns differ from the demonstrative adjectives only in that they have a written accent (except the neuter forms).

PRONOUNS, DOUBLE OBJECT
See **PRONOUN PAIRS**

PRONOUNS, INDEFINITE
Indefinite pronouns *(los pronombres indefinidos)* replace indefinite or unspecified persons or things which may or may not be otherwise mentioned in the sentence.
FORMS:
(1) *Algo* = "Something."
   E.g.: *Quiero comer algo.*
      I want to eat something.
(2) *Alguien* = "Somebody, someone."
   E.g.: *Alguien está en el cuarto.*
      Somebody is in the room.
NOTE:
The personal *a* is used before *alguien* when it is a direct object.
E.g.: *He visto a alguien en el cuarto.*
   I saw somebody in the room.
(3) *Alguno (-a, -os, -as)* = "Somebody, someone, anybody, anyone."
   E.g.: *Hay alguna de las muchachas aquí.*
      There is (some)one of the girls here.
(4) *Nada* = "Nothing, not . . . anything."
   E.g.: *Nada me interesa.*
      Nothing interests me.
NOTE:
If *nada* comes after the verb, a negative word must precede the verb.
E.g.: *No veo nada.*
   I don't see anything.
(5) *Nadie* = "Nobody, no one, not anybody, not anyone."
   E.g.: *Nadie comprende esto.*
      Nobody understands this.

NOTE:

If *nadie* comes after the verb, a negative word must precede the verb. Also, remember that the personal *a* is used when *nadie* is a direct object.

E.g.: *No encontré a nadie en la calle.*

 I didn't meet anyone in the street.

(6) *Ninguno* = "None, not any, no one, not one."

E.g.: *De los libros no he leído ninguno.*

 Of the books, I haven't read any.

(7) *Todo el mundo* = "Everybody."

E.g.: *Todo el mundo quiere cantar.*

 Everybody wants to sing.

(8) *Todo* = "Everything."

E.g.: *Todo cuesta mucho aquí.*

 Everything costs a lot here.

(9) *Todos (-as)* = "All (of them)."

E.g.: *Todos han salido temprano.*

 They have all left early.

(10) *Unos (-as)* = "A few, some, any."

E.g.: *De estas novelas he leído unas.*

 Of those novels, I have read a few.

PRONOUNS, INTERROGATIVE

The interrogative pronouns *(los pronombres interrogativos)* are used to ask a question concerning a person or a thing.

(1) *¿Qué?* = "What?"

It can be (a) subject, (b) direct object, or (c) object of a preposition.

E.g.: (a) *¿Qué hace ese ruido?*

  What makes that noise?

 (b) *¿Qué dices?*

  What do you say?

 (c) *¿Con qué escribes?*

  With what do you write?

(2) *¿Quién?* = Who(m)?"

It can be (a) subject, (b) direct object, or (c) object of a preposition.

E.g.: (a) *¿Quién? llama?*

  Who is calling?

 (b) *¿A quién miras?*

  Whom are you looking at?

 (c) *¿Para quién es el regalo?*

  For whom is the present?

(3) *¿Cuál(es)?* = "Which one(s)?"

It can be (a) subject, (b) direct object or, (c) object of a preposition.

E.g.: (a) *¿Cuál es el mejor?*

  Which one is the best?

 (b) *¿A cuáles miras?*

  Which ones are you looking at?

 (c) *¿En cuál vives?*

  In which one do you live?

(4) *¿Cuántos (-as)?* = "How many?"

It can be (a) subject, (b) direct object, or (c) object of a preposition.

E.g.: (a) *¿Cuántos han llegado?*

  How many have arrived?

 (b) *¿A cuántas has visto?*

  How many did you see?

 (c) *¿Con cuántos has venido?*

  With how many did you come?

PRONOUNS, MULTIPLE
See **PRONOUN PAIRS**

PRONOUNS, OBJECT OF PREPOSITION
Pronouns which are introduced by a preposition always come immediately after that preposition.
FORMS:
mí, ti, sí, él, ella, Vd., nosotros (-as), vosotros (-as), ellos (-as), Vds.
E.g.: *Trabajo con él.*
    I work with him.

    Compro un libro para vosotros.
    I buy a book for you.
NOTE:
The preposition *con* combines with *mí, ti* and *sí* to form:
Conmigo = with me.
Contigo = with you.
Consigo = with himself (herself, oneself, themselves).
E.g.: *Han llevado los libros consigo.*
    They have taken the books with them(selves).

PRONOUNS, OBJECT OF VERB
Object pronouns are placed before the verb of which they are the object EXCEPT:
(a) with affirmative commands, when they are placed after the verb and connected to it.
    E.g.: *¡Dámelas!*
        Give them to me!
(b) with an infinitive, when they may be placed:
    - after the infinitive (and connected to it):
    E.g.: *Quiero leerlos.*
        I want to read them.
    - before the verb which introduces the infinitive:
    E.g.: *Los quiero leer.*
        I want to read them.
(c) with a present participle, when they can be placed:
    - after the present participle (and connected to it):
    E.g.: *Estamos preparándolas.*
        We are preparing them.
    - before the verb which introduces the present participle:
    E.g.: *Las estamos preparando.*
        We are preparing them.
NOTE:
When there are two object pronouns, the indirect object pronoun always precedes the direct object pronoun.
E.g.: *Me lo ha dicho.*
    He told it to me.
REMEMBER that the indirect object pronouns *le* and *les* change to *se* in front of *lo, la, los*, and *las*.
See **PRONOUN PAIRS**

PRONOUNS, ORDER OF
See **PRONOUNS, OBJECT OF VERB**

PRONOUNS, PERSONAL
(Los pronombres personales).
NOTE:
The term ''personal pronouns'' is a misnomer because they are used not only for persons but also for things and, in some cases, for adjectives and ideas.

FORMS:

PRONOUNS, PERSONAL

	Singular			Plural		
Person:	1st	2nd	3rd	1st	2nd	3rd
SUBJECT:	yo	tú	él, ella, Vd.	nosotros (-as)	vosotros (-as)	ellos(-as), Vds.
DIRECT OBJECT:	me	te	lo, la	nos	os	los, las
INDIRECT OBJECT:	me	te	le	nos	os	les
OBJ. OF PREPOSITIONS:	mí	ti	él, ella, Vd.	nosotros (-as)	vosotros (-as)	ellos (-as), Vds.
REFLEXIVE:	me	te	se	nos	os	se

PRONOUNS, POSSESSIVE

(Los pronombres posesivos). These pronouns replace the noun while indicating its possessor. FORMS:

If the noun belongs to ONE OWNER:

Masc. Sing. Nouns:	el mío	el tuyo	el suyo
Fem. Sing. Noun:	la mía	la tuya	la suya
Masc. Plur. Noun:	los míos	los tuyos	los suyos
Fem. Plur. Noun:	las mías	las tuyas	las suyas

If the noun belongs to SEVERAL OWNERS:

Masc. Sing. Noun:	el nuestro	el vuestro	el suyo
Fem. Sing. Noun:	la nuestra	la vuestra	la suya
Masc. Plur. Noun:	los nuestros	los vuestros	los suyos
Fem. Plur. Noun:	las nuestras	las vuestras	las suyas

NOTES:

(1) Like all pronouns, possessive pronouns agree in number and gender with the noun they replace, not with the possessor.
   E.g.: *Mi casa es más pequeña que la suya.*
      My house is smaller than his (hers, yours, theirs).

(2) The corresponding English construction makes the gender of the owner clear. This is not the case in Spanish. In order to be more specific, replace or supplement *el suyo, la suya,* etc. with *el (la) de él (ella, ellos, ellas, Vd., Vds.).*
   E.g.: *Mi casa es más pequeña que la de ella.*
      My house is smaller than hers.

(3) With the verb *ser,* the possessive article is not used before possessive pronouns.
   E.g.: *Esta camisa es mía.*
      This shirt is mine.

PRONOUNS, RECIPROCAL
   See **VERBS, REFLEXIVE**

PRONOUNS, REFLEXIVE

Reflexive pronouns *(los pronombres reflexivos)* reflect the action of the verb back onto the subject. They are used with (and are part of) reflexive verbs.
See **VERBS, REFLEXIVE**

PRONOUNS, RELATIVE

Relative pronouns *(los pronombres relativos)* connect a relative clause to the noun or pronoun which they stand for.

E.g.: *El libro que compré.*

The book (which) I bought.

(*que* stands for the book; *compré* relates to it)

The noun or pronoun which the relative pronoun stands for is called "the antecedent."

NOTE:

Although relative pronouns are frequently omitted in English, they must always be expressed in Spanish.

E.g.: The book I bought.

= The book which I bought.

= *El libro que compré.*

FORMS:

(1) *Que* = "Who, whom, which, that."

It is the most frequently used relative pronoun. It is used for:

(a) persons, as subject or direct object.

E.g.: *La mujer que habla.*

The woman who speaks.

El hombre que encontré.

The man (whom) I met.

(b) things, as subject, direct object, or object of prepositions.

E.g.: *El libro que está sobre la mesa.*

The book which is on the table.

El libro que compré.

The book which I bought.

El libro en que leí esto.

The book in which I read this.

(2) *Quien(es)* = "Who, whom."

It is used for persons as object of prepositions.

E.g.: *El hombre a quien conocí.*

The man whom I met.

La mujer con quien trabajo.

The woman with whom I work.

NOTE:

The personal *a* is used when *quien* is direct object.

(3) *El cual, la cual, los cuales, las cuales* = "Who, whom, which."

These are used when the relative pronoun does not immediately follow its antecedent.

E.g.: *Hablo de la hija de la Sra. Márquez, la cual estudia en la universidad.*

I am talking about the daughter of Mrs. Marquez, who (i.e., the daughter) studies at the university.

(4) *El que, la que, los que, las que* = "He who, the one who, she who, they who, those who."

E.g.: *Los que dicen eso son tontos.*

Those who say that are fools.

NOTE:

The neuter forms: *lo que* and *lo cual* (= "Which") are used to refer to abstract ideas, concepts, or entire clauses.

E.g.: *Llegaron tarde, lo cual me molestó mucho.*

They arrived late, which bothered me very much.

(5) *Cuyo (-a, -os, -as)* = "Whose."
(Possessive relative pronoun). It refers both to persons and things. As all pronouns, it agrees with the noun it replaces, not with the gender of the possessor.
E.g.: *La muchacha cuyo hermano habla.*
　　　The girl whose brother speaks.

NOTE:

Every relative pronoun must have an antecedent. If there is no expressed antecedent, the neuter personal pronoun *lo* must be used.
E.g.: *No comprendo lo que dices.*
　　　I don't understand what (= that which) you are saying.

PROXIMATE FUTURE

This corresponds to the English construction "To be going to + verb." Similarly, in Spanish the construction is: *"Ir a + infinitive."*
E.g.: *Voy a estudiar.*
　　　I am going to study.

　　　¿Vais a salir?
　　　Are you going to go out?

PUNCTUATION

(La puntuación). Punctuation rules are slightly different in Spanish than in English.
GENERAL RULES:
(1) A comma is placed at the end of a restrictive relative clause.
E.g.: *El libro que compré, es muy caro.*
　　　The book (which) I bought is very expensive.
(2) In addition to the normal marks at the end of the sentence, an inverted question mark (¿) or an inverted exclamation mark (¡) is placed at the beginning of a question or an exclamation.
E.g.: *¿Qué dices?*
　　　What do you say?

　　　¡Es increíble!
　　　It's incredible!

NOTE:

The question or exclamation does not necessarily start at the beginning of the sentence.
E.g.: *Si hubieran venido, ¿nos habrían acompañado?*
　　　If they had come, would they have accompanied us?
(3) Parentheses suggest an unclear meaning and should be avoided. This can be done by phrasing the statement with more care.
E.g.: He said that he (John) did not know if he (James) would do it.
　　　Dijo que Juan no sabía si Jaime lo haría.
(4) Each statement in a dialogue is indicated by a new line beginning with a dash.
E.g.: *-¡Hola, María!*
　　　-Buenos días, Pedro.
　　　-¿Quieres beber algo?
　　　-Sí, con mucho gusto.
　　　"Hello, Mary."
　　　"Good morning, Peter."
　　　"Do you want to have a drink?"
　　　"Yes, gladly."

PUNCTUATION MARKS

Punctuation marks *(los signos de puntuación)* are in almost all cases identical to those used in English. There are, however, a few additional marks in Spanish:

The period	= *el punto*	.
The comma	= *la coma*	,
The semicolon	= *el punto y coma*	;
The colon	= *dos puntos*	:
The question mark at the beginning of the question:	= *el punto de interrogación*	? ¿
The exclamation point at the beginning of the sentence:	= *el punto de exclamación*	! ¡
The suspension points	= *los puntos de suspensión*	. . .
The parentheses	= *los paréntesis*	( )
The quotation marks	= *las comillas*	« »
The dash	= *la raya* or *el guión*	—
The asterisk	= *el asterisco*	*

QUE vs. QUÉ

(1) The relative pronoun *Que* = "who, whom, that, which." It is used as (a) subject, (b) direct object, (c) object of a preposition.

E.g.: (a) *El periódico que está sobre la mesa.*
The newspaper which is on the table.

(b) *El periódico que leo.*
The newspaper which I read.

(c) *El periódico en que he leído eso.*
The newspaper in which I read that.

See **PRONOUNS, RELATIVE**

(2) The conjunction *Que* = "that."

E.g.: *María dice que no vendrá.*
Mary says that she will not come.

(3) The interrogative pronoun *Qué* = "What . . . ?"

E.g.: *¿Qué es el flamenco?*
What is flamenco?

See **PRONOUNS, INTERROGATIVE**

(4) The interrogative adjective *Qué* = "What, which?"

E.g.: *¿Qué día vendrán?*
What day will they come?

See **ADJECTIVES, INTERROGATIVE**

NOTE:

The interrogative adjective is also used as an exclamative adjective.

E.g.: *¡Qué cosa increíble!*
What an incredible thing!

See **EXCLAMATIONS**

QUERER

(Transitive verb) = "To wish, to want, to like, to love."
PRES.: *quiero, quieres, quiere, queremos, queréis, quieren.*
IMPERF.: *quer-ía, -ías, -ía, -íamos, -íais, -ían.*
PRETER.: *quis-e, -iste, -iso, -imos, -isteis, -ieron.*
FUT.: *querr-é, -ás, -á, -emos, -éis, -án.*
CONDIT.: *querr-ía, -ías, -ía, -íamos, -íais, -ían.*
SUBJ. PRES.: *quier-a, -as, -a, queramos, queráis, quieran.*
SUBJ. IMPERF. 1: *quisi-era, -eras, -era, -éramos, -erais, -eran.*
SUBJ. IMPERF. 2: *quisi-ese, -eses, -ese, -ésemos, -eseis, -esen.*
INFORMAL IMPERAT.: *quiere (tú), no quieras (tú); quered (vosotros); no queráis (vosotros).*
FORMAL IMPERAT.: *quiera (Vd.); queramos; quieran (Vds.).*
PRES. PARTIC.: *queriendo.*
PAST PARTIC.: *querido.*
NOTES:
(1) This verb has several meanings:
    (a) "To want."
        E.g.: *Yo quiero ir con María.*
          I want to go with Mary.
    (b) "To love."
        E.g.: *Yo quiero a María.*
          I love Mary.
(2) In the imperfect subjunctive *querer* expresses a polite request.
    E.g.: *Quisiera ir con María.*
        I should like to go with Mary.

QUIEN(ES) vs. QUIÉN(ES)

(1) The relative pronoun *Quien(es)* = "Who, whom." It can be used as (a) direct object, (b) object of a preposition. While it can be used as subject, *que* is generally preferred in this case.
    E.g.: (a) *El hombre a quien veo.*
          The man whom I see.
      (b) *El hombre con quien hablo.*
          The man with whom I speak.
See **PRONOUNS, RELATIVE**
(2) The interrogative pronoun *Quién(es)* = "Who, whom?"
    It can be used as (a) subject, (b) direct object, (c) object of a preposition.
    E.g.: (a) *¿Quién habla?*
          Who speaks?
      (b) *¿A quién has visto?*
          Whom did you see?
      (c) *¿De quién hablas?*
          Of whom are you speaking?
See **PRONOUNS, INTERROGATIVE**

QUITAR

(Transitive verb) = "To remove."
NOTE:
The thing removed is the direct object. The person from whom it is removed is the indirect object.
E.g.: *No puedo quitar esta mancha en mi falda.*
    I can't remove this stain on my skirt.

QUIZÁ(S)

(Adverb) = "Perhaps, probably."

It is followed by:

(a) the indicative if certainty is implied:

    E.g.: *Quizá(s) vendrán pronto.*

        Perhaps (= probably) they will come soon.

(b) the subjunctive if uncertainty is implied.

    E.g.: *Quizá(s) lleguen mañana.*

        Perhaps they might come tomorrow.

See **PROBABILITY**

R

RECIPROCAL PRONOUNS

See **VERBS, RECIPROCAL**

RECIPROCAL VERBS

See **VERBS, RECIPROCAL**

REFLEXIVE PRONOUNS

See **PRONOUNS, REFLEXIVE**

REFLEXIVE VERBS

See **VERBS, REFLEXIVE**

REGAR

(Transitive verb) = "To water, to irrigate."

PRES.: *rieg-o, -as, -a, regamos, regáis, riegan.*

IMPERF.: *reg-aba, -abas, -aba, -ábamos, -abais, -aban.*

PRETER.: *regu-é, reg-aste, -ó, -amos, -asteis, -aron.*

FUT.: *regar-é, -ás, -á, -emos, -éis, -án.*

CONDIT.: *regar-ía, -ías, -ía, -íamos, -íais, -ían.*

SUBJ. PRES.: *riegu-e, -es, -e, -emos, -éis, -en.*

SUBJ. IMPERF. 1: *reg-ara, -aras, -ara, -áramos, -arais, -aran.*

SUBJ. IMPERF. 2: *reg-ase, -ases, -ase, -ásemos, -aseis, -asen.*

INFORMAL IMPERAT.: *riega (tú), no riegues (tú); regad (vosotros), no reguéis (vosotros).*

FORMAL IMPERAT.: *riegue (Vd.); reguemos; rieguen (Vds.).*

PRES. PARTIC.: *regando.*

PAST PARTIC.: *regado.*

REGULAR VERBS

Verbs are generally divided into three conjugations according to the ending of the infinitive: *-ar, -er,* and *-ir.*

FIRST CONJUGATION: -*ar*
E.g.: *Hablar* (To talk, to speak)
PRES.: habl-o, -as, -a, -amos, -áis, -an.
IMPERF.: habl-aba, -abas, -aba, -ábamos, -abais, -aban.
PRETER.: habl-é, -aste, -ó, -amos, -asteis, -aron.
FUT.: hablar-é, -ás, -á, -emos, -éis, -án.
CONDIT.: hablar-ía, -ías, -ía, -íamos, -íais, -ían.
SUBJ. PRES.: habl-e, -es, -e, -emos, -éis, -en.
SUBJ. IMPERF. 1: habl-ara, -aras, -ara, -áramos, -arais, -aran.
SUBJ. IMPERF. 2: habl-ase, -ases, -ase, -ásemos, -aseis, -asen.
IMPERAT.: habla (tú), no hables (tú); hablad (vosotros), no habléis (vosotros).
FORMAL IMPERAT.: hable (Vd.); hablemos; hablen (Vds.).
PRES. PARTIC.: hablando.
PAST PARTIC.: hablado.
SECOND CONJUGATION: -*er*
E.g.: *Comer* (To eat)
PRES.: com-o, -es, -e, -emos, -éis, -en.
IMPERF.: com-ía, -ías, -ía, -íamos, -íais, -ían.
PRETER.: com-í, -iste, -ió, -imos, -isteis, -ieron.
FUT.: comer-é, -ás, -á, -emos, -éis, -án.
CONDIT.: comer-ía, -ías, -ía, -íamos, -íais, -ían.
SUBJ. PRES.: com-a, -as, -a, -amos, -áis, -an.
SUBJ. IMPERF. 1: comi-era, -eras, -era, -éramos, -erais, -eran.
SUBJ. IMPERF. 2: comi-ese, -eses, -ese, -ésemos, -eseis, -esen.
IMPERAT.: come (tú), no comas (tú); comed (vosotros), no comáis (vosotros).
FORMAL IMPERAT.: coma (Vd.); comamos; coman (Vds.).
PRES. PARTIC.: comiendo.
PAST PARTIC.: comido.
THIRD CONJUGATION: -*ir*
E.g.: *Vivir* (To live)
PRES.: viv-o, -es, -e, -imos, -ís, -en.
IMPERF.: viv-ía, -ías, -ía, -íamos, -íais, -ían.
PRETER.: viv-í, -iste, -ió, -imos, -isteis, -ieron.
FUT.: vivir-é, -ás, -á, -emos, -éis, -án.
CONDIT.: vivir-ía, -ías, -ía, -íamos, -íais, -ían.
SUBJ. PRES.: viv-a, -as, -a, -amos, -áis, -an.
SUBJ. IMPERF. 1: vivi-era, -eras, -era, -éramos, -erais, -eran.
SUBJ. IMPERF. 2: vivi-ese, -eses, -ese, -ésemos, -eseis, -esen.
IMPERAT.: vive (tú), no vivas (tú); vivid (vosotros), no viváis (vosotros).
FORMAL IMPERAT.: viva (Vd.); vivamos; vivan (Vds.).
PRES. PARTIC.: viviendo.
PAST PARTIC.: vivido.

REÍR

(Intransitive verb) = "To laugh."
PRES.: río, ríes, ríe, reímos, reís, ríen.
IMPERF.: re-ía, -ías, -ía, -íamos, -íais, -ían.
PRETER.: reí, reíste, rió, reímos, reísteis, rieron.
FUT.: reir-é, -ás, -á, -emos, -éis, -án.
CONDIT.: reir-ía, -ías, -ía, -íamos, -íais, -ían.
SUBJ. PRES.: rí-a, -as, -a, riamos, riáis, rían.
SUBJ. IMPERF. 1: ri-era, -eras, -era, -éramos, -erais, -eran.
SUBJ. IMPERF. 2: ri-ese, -eses, -ese, -ésemos, -eseis, -esen.
INFORMAL IMPERAT.: ríe (tú), no rías (tú); reíd (vosotros), no riáis (vosotros).
FORMAL IMPERAT.: ría (Vd.); riamos; rían (Vds.).
PRES. PARTIC.: riendo.
PAST PARTIC.: reído.

REÑIR

(Transitive verb) = "To scold, to quarrel."
PRES.: *riño, riñes, riñe, reñimos, reñís, riñen.*
IMPERF.: *reñ-ía, -ías, -ía, -íamos, -íais, -ían.*
PRETER.: *reñí, reñiste, riñó, reñimos, reñisteis, riñeron.*
FUT.: *reñir-é, -ás, -á, -emos, -éis, -án.*
CONDIT.: *reñir-ía, -ías, -ía, -íamos, -íais, -ían.*
SUBJ. PRES.: *riñ-a, -as, -a, -amos, -áis, -an.*
SUBJ. IMPERF. 1: *riñ-era, -eras, -era, -éramos, -erais, -eran.*
SUBJ. IMPERF. 2: *riñ-ese, -eses, -ese, -ésemos, -eseis, -esen.*
INFORMAL IMPERAT.: *riñe (tú), no riñas (tú); reñid (vosotros), no riñáis (vosotros).*
FORMAL IMPERAT.: *riña (Vd.); riñamos; riñan (Vds.).*
PRES. PARTIC.: *riñendo.*
PAST PARTIC.: *reñido.*

REQUESTS

There are several ways of making requests:
(1) *Me quiere* (or *puede*) + infinitive.
    E.g.: *¿Me quiere traer aquella caja?*
        Would you bring me that box?

        ¿Me puede traer aquella caja?
        Could you bring me that box?
(2) For very polite requests use the imperfect subjunctive (first form, ending in *-ra*) of the verb
poder or *querer*.
    E.g.: *¿Pudiera acompañarme, por favor?*
        Could you please accompany me?

        Quisiera hacerle una pregunta.
        I should like to ask you a question.

REUNIR

(Transitive verb) = "To join, to assemble, to gather together."
PRES.: *reúno, reúnes, reúne, reunimos, reunís, reúnen.*
IMPERF.: *reun-ía, -ías, -ía, -íamos, -íais, -ían.*
PRETER.: *reun-í, -iste, -ió, -imos, -isteis, -ieron.*
FUT.: *reunir-é, -ás, -á, -emos, -éis, -án.*
CONDIT.: *reunir-ía, -ías, -ía, -íamos, -íais, -ían.*
SUBJ. PRES.: *reún-a, -as, -as, reunamos, reunáis, reúnan.*
SUBJ. IMPERF. 1: *reuni-era, -eras, -era, -éramos, -erais, -eran.*
SUBJ. IMPERF. 2: *reuni-ese, -eses, -ese, -ésemos, -eseis, -esen.*
INFORMAL IMPERAT.: *reúne (tú), no reúnas (tú); reunid (vosotros), no reunáis (vosotros).*
FORMAL IMPERAT.: *reúna (Vd.); reunamos; reúnan (Vds.).*
PRES. PARTIC.: *reuniendo.*
PAST PARTIC.: *reunido.*

REZAR

(Transitive verb) = "To pray."
PRES.: rez-o, -as, -a, -amos, -áis, -an.
IMPERF.: rez-aba, -abas, -aba, -ábamos, -abais, -aban.
PRETER.: recé, rezaste, rezó, rezamos, rezasteis, rezaron.
FUT.: rezar-é, -ás, -á, -emos, -éis, -án.
CONDIT.: rezar-ía, -ías, -ía, -íamos, -íais, -ían.
SUBJ. PRES.: rec-e, -es, -e, -emos, -éis, -en.
SUBJ. IMPERF. 1: rez-ara, -aras, -ara, -áramos, -arais, -aran.
SUBJ. IMPERF. 2: rez-ase, -ases, -ase, -ásemos, -aseis, -asen.
INFORMAL IMPERAT.: reza (tú), no reces (tú); rezad (vosotros), no recéis (vosotros).
FORMAL IMPERAT.: rece (Vd.); recemos; recen (Vds.).
PRES. PARTIC.: rezando.
PAST PARTIC.: rezado.

ROBAR

(Transitive verb) = "To steal."
NOTE:
The thing stolen is the direct object. The person from whom it is stolen is the indirect object.
E.g.: *El ladrón le robó el reloj a Juan.*
The thief stole the watch from John.

ROGAR

(Transitive verb) = "To ask, to beg, to pray."
PRES.: rueg-o, -as, -a, rogamos, rogáis, ruegan.
IMPERF.: rog-aba, -abas, -aba, -ábamos, -abais, -aban.
PRETER.: rogué, rog-aste, -ó, -amos, -asteis, -aron.
FUT.: rogar-é, -ás, -á, -emos, -éis, -án.
CONDIT.: rogar-ía, -ías, -ía, -íamos, -íais, -ían.
SUBJ. PRES.: ruegu-e, -es, -e, roguemos, roguéis, rueguen.
SUBJ. IMPERF. 1: rog-ara, -aras, -ara, -áramos, -arais, -aran.
SUBJ. IMPERF. 2: rog-ase, -ases, -ase, -ásemos, -aseis, -asen.
INFORMAL IMPERAT.: ruega (tú), no ruegues (tú); rogad (vosotros), no roguéis (vosotros).
FORMAL IMPERAT.: ruegue (Vd.); roguemos; rueguen (Vds.).
PRES. PARTIC.: rogando.
PAST PARTIC.: rogado.

ROMPER

(Transitive verb) = "To break."
PRES.: romp-o, -es, -e, -emos, -éis, -en.
IMPERF.: romp-ía, -ías, -ía, -íamos, -íais, -ían.
PRETER.: romp-í, -iste, -ió, -imos, -isteis, -ieron.
FUT.: romper-é, -ás, -á, -emos, -éis, -án.
CONDIT.: romper-ía, -ías, -ías, -íamos, -íais, -ían.
SUBJ. PRES.: romp-a, -as, -a, -amos, -áis, -an.
SUBJ. IMPERF. 1: rompi-era, -eras, -era, -éramos, -erais, -eran.
SUBJ. IMPERF. 2: rompi-ese, -eses, -ese, -ésemos, -eseis, -esen.
INFORMAL IMPERAT.: rompe (tú), no rompas (tú); romped (vosotros), no rompáis (vosotros).
FORMAL IMPERAT.: rompa (Vd.); rompamos; rompan (Vds.).
PRES. PARTIC.: rompiendo.
PAST PARTIC.: roto.

S

SABER

(Transitive verb) = "To know."
PRES.: *sé, sabes, sabe, sabemos, sabéis, saben.*
IMPERF: *sab-ía, -ías, -ía, -íamos, -íais, -ían.*
PRETER.: *supe, supiste, supo, supimos, supisteis, supieron.*
FUT.: *sabr-é, -ás, -á, -emos, -éis, -án.*
CONDIT.: *sabr-ía, -ías, -ía, -íamos, -íais, -ían.*
SUBJ. PRES.: *sep-a, -as, -a, -amos, -áis, -an.*
SUBJ. IMPERF. 1: *supi-era, -eras, -era, -éramos, -erais, -eran.*
SUBJ. IMPERF. 2: *supi-ese, -eses, -ese, -ésemos, -eseis, -esen.*
INFORMAL IMPERAT.: *sabe (tú), no sepas (tú); sabed (vosotros), no sepáis (vosotros).*
FORMAL IMPERAT.: *sepa (Vd.); sepamos; sepan (Vds.).*
PRES. PARTIC.: *sabiendo.*
PAST PARTIC.: *sabido*
NOTE:
Saber in the preterite means "To find out, to learn."
E.g.: *Supe la noticia anoche.*
    I learned the news last night.
See **SABER vs. CONOCER vs. PODER below.**

SABER vs. CONOCER vs. PODER

(1) *Saber* = "To know a fact, to know how."
    Eg.: *Yo sé la fecha del nacimiento del rey Fernando.*
        I know the date of birth of king Ferdinand.
        Ella no sabe conducir.
        He doesn't know how to drive.
(2) *Conocer* = "To be acquainted with." It always refers to a person or a place.
    Eg.: *No conozco a tu hermana.*
        I don't know your sister.
        ¿Conoces el museo del Prado?
        Do you know the Prado Museum?
(3) *Poder* = "To be able to."
    Eg.: *Pudimas selir por la ventana.*
        We were able to leave by the window.
See **CONOCER vs. SABER**

SACAR DE QUICIO

(Verbal idiom) = "To irritate, to get on someone's nerves."
E.g.: *Este trabajo me saca de quicio.*
    This work gets on my nerves.
See **FUERA DE SÍ**

SACAR UNA FOTO(GRAFÍA)

(Verbal idiom) = "To take a picture."
E.g.: *Cuando voy de vacaciones, siempre saco muchas fotografías.*
    When I go on vacation, I always take a lot of pictures.

SACAR UNA NOTA

(Verbal idiom) = "To get a grade (on a paper or assignment)."
E.g.: *Pedro sacó una buena nota en su examen de historia.*
   Peter received a good grade on his history exam.

SALIR

(Intransitive verb) = "To leave, to go out (of)."
PRES.: *salgo, sal-es, -e, -imos, -ís, salen.*
IMPERF.: *sal-ía, -ías, -ía, -íamos, -íais, -ían.*
PRETER.: *sal-í, -iste, -ió, -imos, -isteis, -ieron.*
FUT.: *saldr-é, -ás, -á, -emos, -éis, -án.*
CONDIT.: *saldr-ía, -ías, -ía, -íamos, -íais, -ían.*
SUBJ. PRES.: *salg-a, -as, -a, -amos, -áis, -an.*
SUBJ. IMPERF. 1: *sali-era, -eras, -era, -éramos, -erais, -eran.*
SUBJ. IMPERF. 2: *sali-ese, -eses, -ese, -ésemos, -eseis, -esen.*
INFORMAL IMPERAT.: *sal (tú), no salgas (tú); salid (vosotros), no salgáis (vosotros).*
FORMAL IMPERAT.: *Salga (Vd.); salgamos; salgan (Vds.).*
PRES. PARTIC.: *saliendo.*
PAST PARTIC.: *salido.*
NOTE:
Salir requires the preposition *de* before an object (as opposed to the English verb "to leave,"
which is transitive).
E.g.: *Salimos de la escuela.*
   We leave the school.

SALIR vs. IRSE vs. MARCHARSE

All three verbs mean "To leave, to go," but there are slight differences in their meaning.
(1) *Salir (de)* = "To leave, to go out, to come out."
   Eg.: *Salimos de la escuela a las cuatro.*
      We leave school at four o'clock.
      Siempre salen los sábados.
      They always go out on Saturdays.
(2) *Irse* = "To go away, to leave, to depart."
   Eg.: *Nos vamos a las cuatro.*
      We leave at four o'clock.
(3) *Marcharse* = "To go away, to leave."
   E.g.: *Nos marchamos a las cuatro.*
      We leave at four o'clock.

SANO Y SALVO

(Adjectival idiom) = "Safe and sound."
E.g.: *Salió de la ruinas sano y salvo.*
   He came out of the ruins safe and sound.

SAN(TO)

(Noun) = "Saint."
NOTE:
The ending *-to* is dropped before masculine names which do not begin with *Do-* or *To-*.
E.g.: *San José.*
   Saint Joseph.
BUT: *Santo Tomás.*
   Saint Thomas.
   Santo Domingo.
   Saint Dominic.

SATISFACER

(Transitive verb) = "To satisfy."
PRES.: *satisfago, satisfac-es, -e, -emos, -éis, -en.*
IMPERF.: *satisfac-ía, -ías, -ía, -íais, -ían.*
PRETER.: *satisfic-e, -iste, satisfizo, satisfic-imos, -isteis, -ieron.*
FUT.: *satisfar-é, -ás, -á, -emos, -éis, -án.*
CONDIT.: *satisfar-ía, -ías, -ía, -íamos, -ías, -ían.*
SUBJ. PRES.: *satisfag-a, -as, -a, -amos, -áis, -an.*
SUBJ. IMPERF. 1: *satisfici-era, -eras, -éramos, -erais, -eran.*
SUBJ. IMPERF. 2: *satisfici-ese, -eses, -ese, -ésemos, -eseis, -esen.*
INFORMAL IMPERAT.: *satisfaz (tú) or satisface (tú), no satisfagas (tú); satisfaced (vosotros), no satisfagáis (vosotros).*
FORMAL IMPERAT.: *satisfaga (Vd.); satisfagamos; satisfagan (Vds.).*
PRES. PARTIC.: *satisfaciendo.*
PAST PARTIC.: *satisfecho.*

SE

(1) *Se* (Reflexive pronoun, third person singular and plural)
See **PRONOUNS, REFLEXIVE**
(2) *Se* can also be used as a substitute for the passive voice, if the subject of the verb in the passive voice is a thing and the agent is not expressed. This construction usually precedes the subject.
E.g.: *Se habla portugués en Brasil.*
Portuguese is spoken in Brazil.

Se cierran las tiendas a las seis.
The stores close at six.
See **PASSIVE VOICE**
(3) *Se* replaces the indirect object pronouns *le* and *les* when they precede the direct object pronoun *lo, la, los,* or *las.*
Eg.: *Se lo dije.*
= I told him (or her) it.
I told it to him or to her.
See **PRONOUN PAIRS**
See also **PRONOUNS, OBJECT OF VERB**
(4) *Se* is used with many verbs to express the concept of "becoming."
E.g.: *Se calman.*
They are calming down (becoming calm).

Enfadarse.
To become angry.

SEASONS

The definite article is used with the names of seasons:
E.g. *La primavera.* Spring.
El verano. Summer.
El otoño. Fall.
El invierno. Winter.
EXCEPTIONS:
(a) after the verbs *pasar* and *ser*:
E.g.: *Era verano cuando se casaron.*
It was summer when they got married.

Pasamos un verano magnífico en Suiza.
We spent a wonderful summer in Switzerland.
(b) in a phrase with the preposition *de*:
E.g.: *Es un día de invierno.*
It is a winter day.

(c) It is frequently omitted after *en*:
    E.g.: *En verano hace mucho calor.*
        It is very hot in summer.

SEGUIR

(Transitive verb) = "To follow."
PRES.: *sigo, sigues, sigue, seguimos, seguís, siguen.*
IMPERF.: *segu-ía, -ías, -ía, -íamos, -íais, -ían.*
PRETER.: *seguí, seguiste, siguió, seguimos, seguisteis, siguieron.*
FUT.: *seguir-é, -ás, -á, -emos, -éis, án.*
CONDIT.: *seguir-ía, -ías, -ía, -íamos, -íais, -ían.*
SUBJ. PRES.: *sig-a, -as, -a, -amos, -áis, -an.*
SUBJ. IMPERF. 1: *sigui-era, -eras, -era, -éramos, erais, eran.*
SUBJ. IMPERF. 2: *sigui-ese, -eses, -ese, -ésemos, -eseis, -esen.*
INFORMAL IMPERAT.: *sigue (tú), no sigas (tú); seguid (vosotros), no sigáis (vosotros).*
FORMAL IMPERAT.: *siga (Vd.); sigamos; sigan (Vds.).*
PRES. PARTIC.: *siguiendo.*
PAST PARTIC.: *seguido.*
NOTE:
The construction *Seguir* + present principle = "To continue + present participle (or infinitive)."
E.g.: *Siguieron hablando.*
    They continued talking (They continued to talk).

SEGÚN

(Preposition) = "According to, in accordance with."
E.g.: *Según el presidente no habrá guerra.*
    According to the president, there will be no war.

SELF

(Reflexive pronoun) = "Myself, yourself, etc."
FORMS:

Yo mismo (-a)	I myself
Tú mismo (-a)	You yourself
Él (ella) mismo (-a)	He himself, she herself
Sí mismo (-a)	Oneself
Nosotros (-as) mismos (-as)	We ourselves
Vosotros (-as) mismos (-as)	You yourselves
Ellos (-as) mismos (-as)	They themselves

USAGE:
These forms are used for emphasis only. They are not needed in the normal construction of reflexive verbs.
E.g.: *Me corté el pelo.*
    I cut my hair.
BUT: for emphasis:
    Me corté el pelo yo mismo.
    I cut my hair myself.

SENTIR

(Intransitive verb) = "To feel, to be or feel sorry."
PRES.: *sient-o, -es, -e, sentimos, sentís, sienten.*
IMPERF.: *sent-ía, -ías, -ía, -íamos, -íais, -ían.*
PRETER.: *sentí, sentiste, sintió, sentimos, sentisteis, sintieron.*
FUT.: *sentir-é, -ás, -á, -emos, -éis, -án.*
CONDIT.: *sentir-ía, -ías, -ía, -íamos, -ías, -ían.*
SUBJ. PRES.: *sient-a, -as, -a, sintamos, sintáis, sientan.*
SUBJ. IMPERF. 1: *sinti-era, -eras, -era, -éramos, -erais, -eran.*
SUBJ. IMPERF. 2: *sinti-ese, -eses, -ese, -ésemos, -eseis, -esen.*
INFORMAL IMPERAT.: *siente (tú), no sientas (tú); sentid (vosotros), no sintáis (vosotros).*
FORMAL IMPERAT.: *sienta (Vd.); sintamos; sientan (Vds.).*
PRES. PARTIC.: *sintiendo.*
PAST PARTIC.: *sentido.*

SENTIR vs. SENTIRSE

(1) *Sentir* (Transitive verb) =
   (a) "To feel:"
      E.g.: *Siento un dolor en la pierna.*
          I feel a pain in my leg.
   (b) "To sense:"
      E.g.: *Siento que va a llover esta tarde.*
          I feel (sense) that it's going to rain this afternoon.
   (c) "To regret:"
      E.g.: *Siento que estés enfermo.*
          I regret that you are ill.
NOTE:
The subjunctive is required in this case since *sentir* expresses an emotion.
(2) *Sentirse* (Reflexive verb) = "To feel (an emotion, a state of health)."
     E.g.: *Me siento un poco enfermo.*
        I feel a little ill.

SEQUENCE OF TENSES

See **SUBJUNCTIVE MOOD**
See also **"SI" CLAUSES**

SER

(Intransitive verb) = "To be."
PRES.: *soy, eres, es, somos, sois, son.*
IMPERF.: *era, eras, era, éramos, erais, eran.*
PRETER.: *fui, fuiste, fue, fuimos, fuisteis, fueron.*
FUT.: *ser-é, -ás, -á, -emos, -éis, -án.*
CONDIT: *ser-ía, -ías, -ía, -íamos, -íais, -ían.*
SUBJ. PRES.: *se-a, -as, -a, -amos, -áis, -an.*
SUBJ. IMPERF. 1: *fu-era, -eras, -era, -éramos, -erais, -eran.*
SUBJ. IMPERF. 2: *fu-ese, -eses, -ese, -ésemos, -eseis, -esen.*
INFORMAL IMPERAT.: *sé (tú), no seas (tú); sed (vosotros), no seáis (vosotros).*
FORMAL IMPERAT.: *sea (Vd.); seamos; sean (Vds.).*
PRES. PARTIC.: *siendo.*
PAST PARTIC.: *sido.*

USAGE:
Ser is used.
(1) with a predicate adjective, noun, or pronoun to indicate that the subject and the predicate refer to the same thing.
    E.g.: *María es profesora.*
        Mary is a teacher.
        Fidel es alto.
        Fidel is tall.
(2) with the preposition *de* to indicate:
    (a) ownership;
        E.g.: *El coche es de Martín.*
            The car is Martin's.
    (b) origin:
        E.g.: *Mi abuelo es de Granada.*
            My grandfather is from Granada.
    (c) material.
        E.g.: *La mesa es de madera.*
            The table is (made) of wood.
(3) with the preposition *para* to indicate for what or whom something is intended.
    E.g.: *Este regalo es para mi madre.*
        This present is for my mother.
(4) in impersonal expressions (= "It + verb + adjective or noun").
    E.g.: *Es imposible comprender eso.*
        It is impossible to understand that.
(5) with an adjective to indicate an essential or inherent quality, a characteristic which is relatively permanent (e.g.: color, size, shape, nationality, etc.).
    E.g.: *México es una federación.*
        Mexico is a federation.
        El gato es negro.
        The cat is black.
        Esta novela es aburrida.
        This novel is boring.
(6) to express dates or the time of day.
    E.g.: *Es el cuatro de enero.*
        It is January fourth.
        Son las tres.
        It is three o'clock.
(7) to form the passive voice: *Ser* + past participle.
    E.g.: *Los aztecas fueron conquistados por Cortés.*
        The Aztecs were conquered by Cortés.
See **SER vs. ESTAR**

SER AFICIONADO A

(Verbal idiom) = "To be fond of."
E.g.: *Magdalena es aficionada a las novelas policíacas.*
    Madeline is fond of detective novels.

SER vs. ESTAR

Both verbs mean "To be," but their usage is quite different:
(1) *Estar* is used:
    (a) to express the location, situation, or position of the subject.
        E.g.: *Mi padre está en Toledo.*
            My father is in Toledo.
            Los coches están delante de la casa.
            The cars are in front of the house.

(b) to express the condition or state of the subject.

E.g.: *Estoy contento.*

I am glad.

El autobús estaba lleno.

The bus was full.

Las ventanas están abiertas.

The windows are open.

María está sentada.

Mary is seated.

(c) to form the progressive tenses (with the present participle).

E.g.: *Estamos trabajando.*

We are working.

Estaban leyendo.

They were reading.

2) *Ser* is used:

(a) with adjectives to express an inherent characteristic or quality of the subject.

E.g.: *Mi sobrino es profesor.*

My nephew is a teacher.

Mi casa es de ladrillo.

My house is (made) of brick.

La bailarina es esbelta.

The ballerina is svelte.

(b) to describe the subject.

E.g.: *Pedro es alto.*

Peter is tall.

Mi abuelo es viejo.

My grandfather is old.

¿Quién es?

Who is it?

(c) to express the time, the date, or where an event takes place.

E.g.: *Son las cuatro.*

It is four o'clock.

Es el diez de octubre.

It is the tenth of October.

La exposición es en el Prado.

The exhibit is in the Prado.

(d) with impersonal expressions.

E.g.: *Es posible que venga.*

It is possible that he may come.

Es difícil comprender eso.

It is difficult to understand that.

(e) to construct the passive voice (with the past participle).

E.g.: *El soldado fue matado.*

The soldier was killed.

Sus poemas fueron publicados el año pasado.

His poems were published last year.

SERVIR DE

(Verbal idiom) = "To serve as."

E.g.: *La mesa sirve de cama.*

The table serves as a bed.

SERVIR PARA

(verbal idiom) = "To serve for, to be good for, to be useful for."
E.g.: *Esta máquina sirve para firmar los cheques.*
　　 This machine is (serves) for signing checks.

SEVERAL

(1) *Varios (-as)* or *algunos (-as)* (Adjective).
　　E.g.: *Encontramos a varias personas en la discoteca.*
　　　　 We met several people at the disco.
(2) *Algunos (-as)* (Pronoun).
　　E.g.: *Algunos de ellos hablan alemán.*
　　　　 Several of them speak German.

SHALL and WILL

"Shall" and "will" are used to form the future tense in English. The corresponding construction in Spanish is the future tense.
E.g.: *Iré a la universidad.*
　　 I shall go to the university.
　　 Ellos llegarán.
　　 They will arrive.
NOTE:
If "shall" and "will" are used to express determination or will, use *Querer* + infinitive.
E.g.: *El chico no quiere obedecer.*
　　 The child will not obey.
The future may also be used in this case.
E.g.: *Iré a la fiesta, digan lo que digan.*
　　 I will go the party no matter what they say.

SHOULD

See **DEBER**

"SI" CLAUSES

A clause introduced by *si* expresses a supposition. The subordinate *si* clause describes the condition, while the main clause describes the result clause of this condition. There are three kinds of *Si* clauses:

(1) THE SUPPOSITION IS POSSIBLE:

Conditional Clause	Result Clause
Si + present indic.	(a) present indic.
	(b) future
	(c) imperative

E.g.: (a) *Si hace frío, me quedo en casa.*
　　　　 If it's cold, I stay home.
　　 (b) *Si hace frío, me quedaré en casa.*
　　　　 If it's cold, I shall stay home.
　　 (c) *Si hace frío, ¡quédate en casa!*
　　　　 If it's cold, stay home!

(2) THE SUPPOSITION IS CONTRARY TO FACT IN THE PRESENT:

Conditional Clause	Result Clause
Si + imperfect subjunctive (*-ra* or *-se* form)	present conditional or imperfect subjunctive (*-ra* form only)

E.g.: *Si hiciera (or hiciese) frío, me quedaría (or me quedara) en casa.*
   If it were cold, I would stay home.

(3) THE SUPPOSITION IS CONTRARY TO FACT IN THE PAST:

Conditional Clause	Result Clause
Si + pluperfect subjunctive (*-ra* or *-se* form)	conditional perfect or pluperfect subjunctive (*-ra* form only)

E.g.: *Si hubiera (or hubiese) hecho frío, me habría (or hubiera) quedado en casa.*
   If it had been cold, I would have stayed home.

NOTE:
The present subjunctive is never used in "*Si*" clauses.

SÍ vs. *SI*

(1) *Sí* (Third person reflexive pronoun used after prepositions) = "Himself, herself, itself, yourself, oneself, themselves, yourselves."
   E.g.: *Pedro trabaja para sí mismo.*
      Peter works for himself.

   María canta para sí.
      Mary sings for herself.

   El problema se solucionará de sí mismo.
      The problem will resolve itself.

   Siempre hablan de sí mismos.
      They are always talking about themselves.

(2) *Sí* (Adverb) = "Yes, certainly, indeed."
   E.g.: *¿Hablas español? - Sí, lo hablo.*
      "Do you speak Spanish?" "Yes, I speak it."

   Yo no como carne pero ella sí.
      I don't eat meat, but she does.

(3) *Si* (Conjunction) =
   (a) "If."
      E.g.: *Si llueve, me quedo en casa.*
         If it rains, I stay home.

See *"SI"* **CLAUSES**
   (b) "Whether."
      E.g.: *Te pregunto si comprendes.*
         I am asking you if you understand.

SIEMPRE

(Adverb) = "Always."
E.g.: *Siempre come mucho.*
   He always eats a lot.

SIN

(Preposition) = "Without."
(1) As with all prepositions, a verb following *Sin* must be in the infinitive.
   E.g.: *Se marcharon sin decir adiós.*
      They left without saying goodbye.
(2) A noun taken in the general sense takes no article following *Sin.*
   E.g.: *Salió sin abrigo.*
      He went out without a coat.
NOTES:
(1) Do not confuse with the conjunctional construction *Sin que.*
See **SIN QUE**
(2) Remember that a double negative is allowed in Spanish, and *Sin* may be followed by a negative word.
   E.g.: *Salió sin decir nada.*
      He left without saying anything.

SIN DUDA

(Adverbial idiom) = "Undoubtedly, without a doubt."
E.g.: *Regresarán mañana sin duda.*
   They will undoubtedly return tomorrow.

SIN EMBARGO

(Adverbial idiom) = "However, nevertheless."
E.g.: *Tenía dolor de cabeza; sin embargo fue a la escuela.*
   He had a headache; nevertheless, he went to school.

SIN QUE

(Conjunctional construction) + subjunctive = "Without."
E.g.: *Roban el equipaje de los viajeros sin que ellos se den cuenta.*
   They steal the travelers' luggage without their realizing it.
See **SIN**

SINCE + time expression

= *Desde* + time expression.
   E.g.: *Vivo en Valladolid desde 1985.*
      = I live in Valladolid since 1985.
         I have been living in Valladolid since 1985.
NOTE:
The present tense is used in Spanish (as opposed to the progressive present perfect in English).

SINGULAR

"Singular" *(el singular)* means that there is only one. For example, "book" *(libro)* is singular and "books" *(libros)* is plural.

SINO vs. PERO

See **PERO vs. SINO**

SINO vs. SINO QUE

(1) *Sino* (Conjunction) = "But (rather), but (instead)." It is used:

    (a) to contrast a negative clause with an affirmative clause when the verbs in both clauses are in the infinitive.

        E.g.: *No quieren beber sino comer.*

            They don't want to drink, but to eat.

    (b) to express contrast between two nouns, adjectives, or adverbs.

        E.g.: *No es un león sino un tigre.*

            It's not a lion but a tiger.

            El paquete no es ligero sino pesado.

            The package is not light but (rather) heavy.

            No trabajan alegremente sino tristemente.

            They are not working happily but (rather) sadly.

(2) *Sino que* (Conjunctional construction) must be used when contrasting two clauses which have two different conjugated verbs.

        E.g.: *No se quedó en Madrid sino que salió para Córdoba.*

            He didn't stay in Madrid but left for Cordoba.

See **PERO vs. SINO**

to SIT

(1) To express the action "to sit" = *Sentarse.*

    E.g.: *Entraron y se sentaron en las butacas.*

        They entered and sat down in the armchairs.

(2) To express the state "to be sitting" = *Estar sentado (-a, -os, -as).*

    Eg.: *Estaban sentados cuando entré.*

        They were sitting when I came in.

SIZES and MEASUREMENTS

(1) Vocabulary:

La longitud	= the length
La anchura	= the width
La altura	= the height
La profundidad	= the depth

    E.g.: *¿Cuál es la altura de los Pirineos?*

        What is the height of the Pyrenees?

        ¿Cuál es la longitud del itinerario?

        How long is the itinerary?

(2) Measurements (of clothing, etc.) = *El número.*

    E.g.: *¿Cuál es su número de zapatos?*

        What is your shoe size?

(3) Height (of people) = *La talla.*

    E.g.: *Un hombre de talla mediana.*

        A man of medium height.

(4) "To be . . . tall" = *Medir*

    E.g.: *Mido 1 metro 75 centímetros.*

        I am 1 meter 75 centimeters tall.

(5) Weight: "To weigh . . ." = *Pesar.*

    E.g.: *Peso 75 kilos.*

        I weigh 75 kilos.

CLOTHING SIZES (with approximate British and American equivalents):

Men's suits:

U.S.:	36	38	40	42	44	46
G.B.:	36	38	40	42	44	46
Spain:	46	48	50	52	54	56

Women's dresses:

U.S.:	8	10	12	14	16	18
G.B.:	10	12	14	16	18	20
Spain:	38	40	42	44	46	48

Shirts:

U.S.:	14	14½	15	15½	16	16½	17
G.B.:	14	14½	15	15½	16	16½	17
Spain:	36	37	38	39	41	42	43

Socks:

U.S.:	9½	10	10½	11	11½
G.B.:	9½	10	10½	11	11½
Spain:	38	39	40	41	42

Men's shoes:

U.S.:	8	8½	9½	10½	11½	12
G.B.:	7	7.5	8.5	9.5	10.5	11
Spain:	41	42	43	44	45	46

Women's shoes:

U.S.:	6	6½	7	7½	8	8½
G.B.:	4.5	5	5.5	6	6.5	7
Spain:	38	38	39	39	40	41

NOTE:

The definite article is used before units of weights and measures, as opposed to the English construction which requires the indefinite article.

E.g.: *Dos mil pesos el kilo.*

Two thousand pesos a kilo.

SO + adjective or adverb

= *Tan* + adjective or adverb.

E.g.: *¡Ella es tan inteligente!*

She is so intelligent!

¡Corren tan rápidamente!

They run so fast!

SO MANY, SO MUCH + noun

= *Tanto (-a, -os, -as)* (Adjective).

E.g.: *¡Tienes tantas amigas!*

You have so many girlfriends!

¡Hay tanto trabajo!

There is so much work!

SOBRAR

(1) *Sobrar* (Transitive verb) = "To exceed, to surpass."

E.g.: *El total sobra dos millones.*

The total exceeds two million.

(2) *Sobrar* (Intransitive verb) = "To remain, to be left over."

E.g.: *Nos sobran doscientas pesetas.*

= There remain two hundred pesetas to us.

We have two hundred pesetas left over.

NOTE:

The person is the indirect object.

SOBRE

(Preposition) = "About, on, over, on the subject of, upon."
E.g.: *El libro está sobre la mesa.*
The book is on the table.

Escribió un artículo sobre su viaje.
He wrote an article about his trip.

SOME

(Plural indefinite article) = *Unos (-as).*
E.g.: *Tengo unos libros sobre la historia de España.*
I have some books on Spanish history.
NOTE:
When "some" is not emphasized it can simply be omitted (as it is in English).
E.g.: *Tengo libros en mi cuarto.*
I have (some) books in my room.

SOMETIMES

= *Algunas veces* or *A veces* (Adverbs).
E.g.: *Vamos al teatro algunas veces (or a veces).*
Sometimes we go to the theater.

SOMEWHERE

(a) If there is no movement = *En alguna parte* (Prepositional adverbial idiom).
E.g.: *Estoy seguro de que lo encontrarás en alguna parte.*
I'm sure you will find him somewhere.
(b) If there is movement = *A alguna parte* (Prepositional adverbial idiom).
E.g.: *Iremos a alguna parte del país que no conocemos.*
We shall go somewhere in the country which we do not know.

SOMEWHERE ELSE

(a) If there is no movement = *En otra parte* (Prepositional adverbial idiom).
E.g.: *Viven en otra parte.*
They live somewhere else.
(b) If there is movement = *A otra parte* (Prepositional adverbial idiom).
E.g.: *Vamos a ir a otra parte.*
We are going to go somewhere else.

SOÑAR (CON)

(Transitive and intransitive verb) = "To dream of, about."
E.g.: *Alberto sueña con su novia cada noche.*
Albert dreams of his fiancé every night.

SPELLING-CHANGE VERBS
See VERBS, SPELLING-CHANGE

to SPEND

(Transitive verb)
(1) "To spend (money)" = *Gastar.*
E.g.: *Ellos gastan mucho dinero.*
They spend a lot of money.
(2) "To spend (time)" = *Pasar.*
E.g.: *Pasamos dos meses en las islas Canarias.*
We spent two months in the Canary Islands

STEM

The "stem" *(el tema)* of a word is that part which expresses its core of meaning. To the stem are added the endings and inflections.

E.g.: *Habl-ar*   *Com-er*   *Viv-ir*
      (Stem) (ending)   (Stem) (ending)   (Stem) (ending)

      Conduc-tor   *Prodigios-amente*   *Talent-osa*
      (Stem) (ending)   (Stem) (ending)   (Stem) (ending)

STEM-CHANGING VERBS
See **VERBS, STEM-CHANGING**

STRESS

Spanish words are stressed according to the following rules:
(a) words which end in a vowel, *-n*, or *-s* are stressed on the next-to-last syllable:
   E.g.: *imposible; agradable; americano; hablaron; cuadernos*
(b) words which end in a consonant other than *-n* or *-s* are stressed on the last syllable:
   E.g.: *ciudad; encontrar; español; papel; reloj; feliz.*
(c) words which do not follow the above two rules carry a written accent where the stress falls:
   E.g.: *adiós; débil; lección; rápidamente.*
See **ACCENTS**

SUBJECT

The subject *(el sujeto)* is the word or group of words about which the verb expresses an action or state.

E.g.: *Los libros están sobre la mesa.*
      The books are on the table.

SUBJECT PRONOUNS
See **PRONOUNS, PERSONAL**

SUBJUNCTIVE MOOD

The subjunctive mood *(el subjuntivo)* presents the action of the verb as contingent, or dependent, upon some emotion, desire, wish, will power, doubt, etc. It occurs only in subordinate clauses.

E.g.: *Quiero que ella trabaje.*
      I want her to work.

      Es preciso que ella trabaje.
      It is necessary that she work.

      Dudo que ella trabaje.
      I doubt that she works.

TENSES:

There are four tenses in the subjunctive mood:

PRESENT:

FORMATION:

(a) *-ar* verbs:
   Stem of the first person singular of the present indicative + *e, es, e, emos, éis, en.*
(b) *-er* and *-ir* verbs:
   Stem of the first person singular of the present indicative + *a, as, a, amos, áis, an.*
   E.g.: *Es importante que hables español.*
        It is important that you speak Spanish.

NOTES:
(1) If the first person singular of the indicative present is irregular, the same irregularity carries over to the subjunctive.

E.g.: *Tener: tengo → tenga, tengas . . .*
(2) Verbs ending in *-car*, *-gar*, and *-zar*: *-c* changes to *-qu*, *-g* to *-gu*, and *-z* to *-c*, respectively. These are the same changes that occur in the preterite.

E.g.: *Buscar → busque.*

Navegar → navegue.

Lanzar → lance.
(3) Verbs ending in *-ar* and *-er* with stem changes in the present indicative also have these changes in the subjunctive.

E.g.: *Cerrar → cierre.*

Dormir → duerma.

Pedir → pida.
(4) Verbs ending in *-iar* and *-uar* take a written accent over the *i* or the *u* to maintain the correct stress.

E.g.: *Enviar: envíe, envíes, envíe, enviemos, enviéis, envíen.*

Actuar, actúes, actúe, actuemos, actúeis, actúen.

IRREGULAR FORMS:

DAR: *dé, des, dé, demos, déis, den.*

ESTAR: *esté, estés, esté, estemos, estéis, estén.*

HABER: *haya, hayas, haya, hayamos, hayáis, hayan.*

IR: *vaya, vayas, vaya, vayamos, vayáis, vayan.*

SABER: *sepa, sepas, sepa, sepamos, sepáis, sepan.*

SER: *sea, seas, sea, seamos, seáis, sean.*

IMPERFECT:

FORMATION:
(a) **-ar** verbs: Drop the *-ron* ending of the third person plural of the preterite and add the endings:
 - for the IMPERFECT 1: *-ra, -ras, -ra, -ramos, -ráis, -ran.*

E.g.: *No creían que nosotros habláramos inglés.*

They didn't think that we spoke English.

 - for the IMPERFECT 2: *-se, -ses, -se, -semos, -séis, -sen.*

E.g.: *No creían que nosotros hablásemos inglés.*

They didn't think that we spoke English.
(b) **-er** verbs: Drop the *-ron* ending of the third person plural of the preterite and add the endings:
 - for the IMPERFECT 1: *-ra, -ras, -ra, -ramos, -rais, -ran.*

E.g.: *No pensaba que vinieran conmigo.*

I didn't think they would come with me.

 - for the IMPERFECT 2: *-se, -ses, -se, -semos, -seis, -sen.*

E.g.: *No pensaba que viniesen conmigo.*

I didn't think they would come with me.

PERFECT (or PAST):

FORMATION:

The present subjunctive of *haber* + past participle of the verb.

E.g.: *Temo que hayan hecho muchos errores.*

I fear that they have made many errors.

PLUPERFECT:

FORMATION:

The imperfect subjunctive of *haber* + past participle of the verb.

E.g.: *Estaban tristes que te hubieras herido.*

They were sad that you had hurt yourself.

Estaban tristes que te hubieses herido.

They were sad that you had hurt yourself.

NOTES:

(1) Since there is no longer any future tense in the subjunctive, the present subjunctive is used instead.

E.g.: *Es posible que ella venga mañana.*

It is possible that she will come tomorrow.

(2) The subjunctive mood is frequently found in a subordinate clause introduced by *que*, but BEWARE: This does not mean that *que* is always followed by the subjunctive. It is incorrect to think: "There is a subjunctive because there is a *que*"! The reason for the presence of a subjunctive will always be that the clause is contingent upon a concept of emotion, desire, wish, will power, doubt, etc., or a construction which requires the subjunctive.

USAGE:

The subjunctive mood is used in subordinate clauses when:

(1) The main verb expresses:

(a) an emotion (sorrow, joy, fear, surprise, anger, etc).

Some common expressions of emotion which require the subjunctive in the noun clause that follows:

Alegrarse de, sentir, sorprenderse de, temer, tener miedo de.

E.g.: *Me alegro que estés aquí.*

I am glad that you are here.

Temo que hagan errores.

I fear that they (might) make mistakes.

Ella se sorprende que sepas eso.

She is surprised that you (should) know that.

(b) a desire, demand, will or wish, preference, prohibition.

Some common expressions of desire, demand, will, wish, preference, or prohibition which require the subjunctive:

Aconsejar, decir, dejar, desear, esperar, exigir, hacer, insistir en, mandar, ¡ojalá que!, pedir, permitir, preferir, prohibir, querer, rogar, suplicar.

E.g.: *Quiero que escribas la carta.*

I want you to write a letter.

Prohiben que fumemos.

They forbid us to smoke.

(c) an expression of necessity, uncertainty, or possibility.

Some common expressions of necessity, uncertainty, or possibility which require the subjunctive:

Es dudoso, es importante, es imposible, es lástima, es mejor, es menester, es necesario, es preciso, es posible, es preferible, es probable, importa, más vale.

E.g.: *Es dudoso que escriban.*

It is doubtful that they will write.

Es posible que nos llamen.

It is possible that they (might) call us.

Es menester que estudies.

It is necessary that you (should) study.

(2) The subordinate clause is introduced by certain conjunctions, namely:

(a) *A fin de que* = in order that, so that

(b) *A menos que* = unless

(c) *Antes de que* = before

(d) *Con tal que* = provided that

(e) *En caso de que* = in case

(f) *Para que* = so that, in order that

(g) *Sin que* = without

E.g.: (a) *Estudio a fin de que pueda obtener un empleo.*

I study so that I might be able to obtain a job.

(b) *Te acompañaré a menos que no tenga dinero.*

I shall accompany you unless I don't have any money.

(c) *Iremos a la tienda antes de que vuelvan mis padres.*
We shall go to the store before my parents return.

(d) *Lo compraremos con tal que no cueste demasiado.*
We shall buy it provided that it does not cost too much.

(e) *No salgo en caso de que me llame María.*
I'm not going out in case Mary should call me.

(f) *Te escribo para que sepas la noticia.*
I am writing so that you might know the news.

(g) *Se levantarán sin que tú te des cuenta de lo que hacen.*
They will get up without your realizing what they are doing.

NOTE:

The following conjunctions are followed by the subjunctive in the adverbial clause that follows only if anticipation, doubt, indefiniteness, or uncertainty is implied. Otherwise, they take the indicative:

(h) *Así que* = as soon as
(i) *Aunque* = although, even though
(j) *Cuando* = when
(k) *De manera que* = so that, in such a way that
(l) *De modo que* = so that, in such a way that
(m) *Después (de) que* = after
(n) *En cuanto* = as soon as
(o) *Hasta que* = until
(p) *Luego que* = as soon as
(q) *Mientras* = while
(r) *Tan pronto como* = as soon as

E.g.: (h) *Te llamaré así que vuelva.*
I shall call you as soon as I return.

BUT: *Yo te llamé así que volví.*
I called you as soon as I returned.

(i) *Saldremos aunque haga frío.*
We shall go out even if it is cold.

BUT: *Salimos aunque hacía frío.*
We went out although it was cold.

(j) *Me levantaré cuando me sienta mejor.*
I shall get up when I feel better.

BUT: *Me levanté cuando me sentía mejor.*
I got up when I felt better.

(k) *Lo explica claramente de manera que todos lo entiendan.*
He explains it well so that everyone might understand.

BUT: *Lo explica muy mal de manera que nadie lo comprende.*
He explains it very badly, so (that) nobody understands.

(l) *Se preparó mucho de modo que pueda obtener buenos resultados.*
He prepared himself a lot so that he might obtain good results.

BUT: *Se preparó muy poco de modo que no obtuvo buenos resultados.*
He prepared himself very little, so he did not get good results.

(m) *Ella irá al centro después de que lleguen sus amigas.*
She will go downtown after her friends arrive.

BUT: *Ella fue al centro después de que llegaron sus amigas.*
She went downtown after her friends arrived.

(n) *Nos levantaremos en cuanto suene el despertador.*
We shall get up as soon as the alarm rings.

BUT: *Nos levantamos en cuanto sonó el despertador.*
We got up as soon as the alarm rang.

(o) *¡Espere hasta que vuelva yo!*
Wait until I return!

BUT: *Esperé hasta que volviste.*
I waited until you returned.

(p) *Luego que me lo pidas te lo daré.*
As soon as you ask for it, I shall give it to you

BUT: *Luego que me lo pediste te lo di.*
As soon as you asked for it, I gave it to you.

(q) *Prepararé la comida mientras tú pongas la mesa.*
I shall prepare the meal while you set the table.

BUT: *Preparé la comida mientras tú pusiste la mesa.*
I prepared the meal while you set the table.

(r) *Saldrán tan pronto como termine el* BUT: *Salieron tan pronto como terminó el*
     espectáculo.   *espectáculo.*
     They will go out as soon as the show   They went out as soon as the show
     ends.   ended.

(3) The main clause contains a superlative, or an expression having superlative value, to indicate
    that the statement is only an opinion.
    E.g.: *Es la mejor película que jamás hayamos visto.*
          It is the best movie we have ever seen.

          No hay nadie que pueda ayudarme.
          There is nobody who can help me.

(4) The main clause contains a relative pronoun whose antecedent is indefinite or uncertain.
    E.g.: *¿Hay alguien aquí que hable chino?*
          Is there anybody here who speaks Chinese?

          Busco un libro que contenga poemas de amor.
          I am looking for a book which contains (might contain) love poems.

(5) The main clause contains certain indefinite relative pronouns, namely:
    (a) *cualquiera (cualesquiera)* = whatever, any
    (b) *cuandoquiera* = whenever
    (c) *dondequiera* = wherever
    (d) *por* + adjective or adverb + **que** = however, no matter how
    (e) *quienquiera* = whoever
    E.g.: (a) *Leerán cualquiera revista que encuentren.*
              They will read whatever magazine they find.
          (b) *Cuandoquiera que vengan me alegraré de verlos.*
              Whenever they come, I shall be glad to see them.
          (c) *Dondequiera que estén, tenemos que encontrarles.*
              Wherever they may be, we have to find them.
          (d) *Por peligroso que sea hay que hacerlo.*
              No matter how dangerous it is, it has to be done.
          (e) *Quienquiera que diga eso es estúpido.*
              Whoever says that is stupid.

(6) The *"Si"* clause of a conditional contrary-to-fact sentence. In this case, the imperfect or
    pluperfect subjunctive is used.
    E.g.: *Si pudiera, iría a Guatemala.*
          If I could, I would go to Guatemala.

NOTE:
When the main verb and the subordinate verb have the same subject, do not use the subjunctive.
Use the infinitive construction.
E.g.: *Quiero que vayas a casa.*
      I want you to go home.
BUT: *Quiero ir a casa.*
      I want to go home.

AGREEMENT OF TENSES IN THE SUBJUNCTIVE:
(1) If the main verb is in the present, future, or present perfect, or in the imperative mood, then
    the verb in the dependent clause will generally be in the present or present perfect subjunctive.
    E.g.: *Miguel quiere que vayamos a su casa.*
          Michael wants us to go to his house.

          Miguel querrá que vayamos con él.
          Michael will want us to go with him.

          Miguel ha pedido que estemos aquí a las cuatro.
          Michael has asked that we be here at four o'clock.

(2) If the main verb is in the preterite, imperfect, or pluperfect tense, or in the conditional mood, then the subjunctive verb must be in the imperfect or pluperfect subjunctive tense.

E.g.: *Se alegraron de que nosotros ganásemos* (or *ganáramos*) *el premio.*
They rejoiced that we won the prize.

Tendríamos miedo de que tú llegaras (or *llegases*) *tarde.*
We would be afraid that you would arrive late.

Ellos habían temido que nosotros llegáramos (or *llegásemos*) *tarde.*
They had been afraid that we might arrive late.

SUBJUNCTIVE vs. INDICATIVE

See **INDICATIVE vs. SUBJUNCTIVE**
See also **SUBJUNCTIVE MOOD**

SUBJUNCTIVE vs. INFINITIVE

(1) When the subject of the subordinate clause is different from the subject of the main clause, use the subjunctive in the subordinate clause.

E.g.: *No quiero que te marches.*
I do not want you to leave.

(2) When the subject of the subordinate clause is the same as the subject of the main clause, use the infinitive in the subordinate clause.

E.g.: *No quiero marcharme.*
I do not want to leave.

NOTE:
Before an infinitive, a preposition is used rather than a conjunction:

CONJUNCTION	PREPOSITION
+ subjunctive	+ infinitive
a fin de que	*a fin de*
antes de que	*antes de*
después de que	*después de*
hasta que	*hasta*
para que	*para*
sin que	*sin*

(3) Verbs of influence, such as *aconsejar, dejar, permitir, prohibir,* may be followed by an infinitive even if there is a change of subject.

E.g.: *Les aconsejé irse* or *Les aconsejé que se fueran.*
I advised them to leave.

Mis padres me prohiben fumar or *Mis padres prohiben que yo fume.*
My parents forbid me to smoke.

See the entries for ***ACONSEJAR, DEJAR, PERMITIR,*** and ***PROHIBIR***

to SUCCEED

(1) Meaning "To be successful" = *Tener éxito.*

E.g.: *Marta tiene mucho éxito en sus estudios.*
Martha succeeds very well in her studies.

(2) Meaning "To follow" = *Suceder.*

E.g.: *El hijo sucedió a su padre como presidente de la compañía.*
The son succeeded his father as president of the company.

SUCEDER

(Transitive and intransitive verb).

(1) "To happen"

E.g.: *¿Qué sucede en el Oriente Medio?*
What's happening in the Middle East?

(2) "To succeed, to follow"

E.g.: *El príncipe sucedió al trono.*

The prince succeeded to the throne.

SUCH

= *Tal(es)* (Adjective).

E.g.: *Nunca he visto tales montañas.*

I have never seen such mountains.

SUCH AS

= *Tal(es) como.*

E.g.: *Enseñan lenguas tales como el chino y el japonés.*

They teach such languages as Chinese and Japanese.

to SUIT (meaning "to fit")

(Idiomatic construction) = *Sentar* or *quedar* + indirect object.

E.g.: *Esta chaqueta te sienta (or queda) bien.*

This jacket suits you well.

SUPERLATIVE + "in the . . ."

The proposition *de,* not *en,* is used before the complement of the superlative expression.

E.g.: *La mejor estudiante de la escuela.*

The best student in the school.

SUPERLATIVE of ADJECTIVES

See **ADJECTIVES, SUPERLATIVE OF**

SUPERLATIVE of ADVERBS

See **ADVERBS, COMPARATIVE AND SUPERLATIVE**

SUPERLATIVE, ABSOLUTE

(Idiomatic construction). To express the absolute degree of an adjective, add the ending *-ísimo (-a, -os, -as).* It has the same meaning as *Muy* + adjective.

E.g.: *El español es facilísimo.*

Spanish is very easy.

NOTES:

(1) Adjectives ending in a vowel drop the final vowel before adding *-ísimo.*

E.g.: *Carolina es guapísima.*

Caroline is very pretty.

(2) Adjectives ending in *-co, -go,* and *-z* change to *-qu, -gu,* and *-c* before *-ísimo.*

E.g.: *Fresco → fresquísimo.*

Largo → larguísimo.

Feliz → felicísimo.

(3) The absolute superlative form of adverbs is formed by dropping the final vowel and adding *-ísimamente* to the feminine of the adjective.

E.g.: *Andaba lentísimamente.*

He was walking very slowly.

to be SUPPOSED TO (meaning "ought")

(Idiomatic construction) = *Deber* + infinitive.

E.g.: *Debemos estudiar este libro.*

We are supposed to study this book.

See *DEBER*

SUYO (-A, -OS, -AS)
See **ADJECTIVES, POSSESSIVE**
See **PRONOUNS, POSSESSIVE**

SYLLABICATION

A syllable *(una sílaba)* is a sound or group of sounds forming a unit of the spoken language. For example, the English word "figure" consists of two sounds or syllables:

fig - ure.

(Most dictionaries indicate the division of words into syllables.)

BEWARE: Rules for division into syllables *(el silabeo)* are not the same in Spanish as in English. The Spanish word *figura,* for example, consists of three syllables:

fi - gu - ra.

Spanish syllables tend to end on a vowel rather than a consonant as is often the case in English. Knowing how to divide words into syllables is important for the correct division of words at the end of a line and for the correct pronunciation of words.

BASIC RULES OF SYLLABICATION:

(1) Do not split one syllable words.

(2) Make the division between consonants, except if the second consonant is *l* or *r.*

E.g.: *ver-bo; es-tán; ven-der.*

BUT: *pue-blo; o-bra.*

(3) Remember that *ch, ll,* and *rr* are treated as single letters and sounds in Spanish and therefore cannot be split.

E.g.: *pe-cho; la-dri-llo; ca-ta-rro.*

(4) When there are three consonants, the last one goes with the following vowel, except if it is *l* or *r.*

E.g.: *trans-por-te.*

BUT: *cen-tral.*

(5) Adjacent vowels which do not form diphthongs or triphthongs form separate syllables.

E.g.: *re-al, i-de-a, to-a-lla.*

Here are a few examples of how words are split in Spanish:

A-é-re-o.

Con-ver-sa-ción.

Gua-te-ma-la.

Mo-men-to.

O-í-do.

Par-ti-cu-lar.

T

to TAKE

(1) Meaning "To carry (something or someone someplace)" = *Llevar.*

E.g.: *Los alumnos llevan sus libros a clase.*

The students take their books to class.

Juan llevó a Margarita al cine.

John took Margaret to the movies.

(2) Meaning "To take in one's hand, to take (a bus, etc.)" = *Tomar* or *Coger.*

E.g.: *El mono toma el plátano en la mano.*

The monkey picks up the banana in its hand.

Mi hermano toma el autobús.

My brother takes the bus.

Cogió a su hermanita por la mano.

She took her little sister by the hand.

TAL VEZ

(Adverbial idiom) = "Perhaps."
Followed by:
(a) the indicative if certainty is implied.
     E.g.: *Tal vez vendrán pronto.*
          Perhaps (= probably) they will come soon.
(b) the subjunctive if uncertainty is implied.
     E.g.: *Tal vez lleguen mañana.*
          Perhaps they might arrive tomorrow.

to TALK TO vs. to TALK ABOUT

(1) "To talk to" = *Hablar* + indirect object.
     E.g.: *Le hablamos a nuestra prima.*
          We talk to our cousin.

          Les hablamos.
          We talk to them.
(2) "To talk about" = *Hablar de* + object of preposition.
     E.g.: *Ella habla de Jaime.*
          She talks about James.

          Ella habla de él.
          She talks about him.

TAN + adjective or adverb + COMO

This is the comparative construction of equality = "As + adjective + as."
E.g.: *Guillermo es tan fuerte como Miguel.*
     William is as strong as Michael.

     Corre tan rápidamente como yo.
     He runs as fast as I.
See ADJECTIVES, COMPARISON OF
See also ADVERBS, COMPARATIVE AND SUPERLATIVE OF

TAN PRONTO COMO

(Conjunctional construction) = "As soon as."
Followed by:
(a) the indicative if it refers to a present or past action.
     E.g.: *Siempre empiezan tan pronto como llegan.*
          They always start as soon as they arrive.

          Empezaron tan pronto como llegaron.
          They began as soon as they arrived.
(b) The subjunctive if it refers to a future action.
     E.g.: *Empezarán tan pronto como lleguen.*
          They will begin as soon as they arrive.

TANTO vs. TANTO (-A, -OS, -AS)

(1) *Tanto* (Adverb) = "So much."
     E.g.: *¡Ellos trabajan tanto!*
          They work so much!
(2) *Tanto (-a, -os, -as)* (Adjective) = "As much, as many, so much, so many."
     E.g.: *¡Tienes tantas ideas!*
          You have so many ideas!
NOTE:
Tanto (-a, -os, -as) . . . como = "As many . . . as, as much . . . as."
E.g.: *Tenemos tantos libros como Uds.*
     We have as many books as you.

TARDAR EN + infinitive

(Intransitive verb) = "To be late in, to be slow in + present participle."

E.g.: *Los muchachos tardaron en volver a su residencia.*

The boys were late in returning to their dormitory.

TEMPERATURE

(1) Referring to the weather = *La temperatura.*

E.g.: *La temperatura mediana en el verano es de treinta grados.*

The average temperature in the summer is thirty degrees.

(2) Referring to a medical condition = *La fiebre.*

E.g.: *El niño tiene una fiebre elevada.*

The child has a high temperature.

NOTE:

In Hispanic countries, as in most parts of the world, the Celsius gradations are used. The conversion formulas are:

$$C = 5/9 \ (F - 32)$$
$$F = 9/5 \ (C + 32)$$

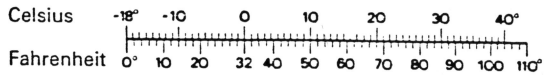

TENER

(Transitive verb) = "To have, to hold, to keep."

PRES.: *tengo, tienes, tiene, tenemos, tenéis, tienen.*

IMPERF.: *ten-ía, -ías, -ía, -íamos, -íais, -ían.*

PRETER.: *tuve, tuviste, tuvo, tuvimos, tuvisteis, tuvieron.*

FUT.: *tendr-é, -ás, -á, -emos, -éis, -án.*

CONDIT.: *tendr-ía, -ías, -ía, -íamos, -íais, -ían.*

SUBJ. PRES.: *teng-a, -as, -a, -amos, -áis, -an.*

SUBJ. IMPERF. 1: *tuvi-era, -eras, -era, -éramos, -erais, -eran.*

SUBJ. IMPERF. 2: *tuvi-ese, -eses, -ese, -ésemos, -eseis, -esen.*

INFORMAL IMPERAT.: *ten (tú), no tengas (tú); tened (vosotros), no tengáis (vosotros).*

FORMAL IMPERAT.: *tenga (Vd.); tengamos; tengan (Vds.).*

PRES. PARTIC.: *teniendo.*

PAST PARTIC.: *tenido.*

TENER CALOR/FRÍO

(Verbal idiom) = "To be hot, cold [talking about a person]."

E.g.: *Tengo calor porque llevo un abrigo.*

I am hot because I'm wearing an overcoat.

Mi abuela siempre tiene frío.

My grandmother is always cold.

TENER CELOS (DE)

(Transitive verb) = "To be jealous (of)."

E.g.: *Tengo celos de Marta.*

I'm jealous of Martha.

TENER CUIDADO

(Verbal idiom) = "To be careful."

E.g.: *¡Ten cuidado cuando manejas!*

Be careful when you drive!

TENER DOLOR (DE CABEZA, DE DIENTES, etc.)

(Verbal idiom) = "To have an . . . ache."
E.g.: *Tengo dolor de cabeza.*
    I have a headache.
    Ella tiene dolor de estómago.
    She has a stomach ache.

TENER ÉXITO

(Verbal idiom) = "To be successful."
E.g.: *Julio Iglesias tuvo mucho éxito en la Argentina.*
    Julio Iglesias was very successful in Argentina.

TENER GANAS DE + infinitive

(Verbal idiom) = "To feel like, to have an urge to + infinitive."
E.g.: *Tengo ganas de ir al cine.*
    I feel like going to the movies.

TENER HAMBRE

(Verbal idiom) = "To be hungry."
E.g.: *Los niños tienen hambre después de jugar.*
    The children are hungry after playing.

TENER LA CULPA DE

(Verbal idiom) = "To be to blame for."
E.g.: *Pedro tiene la culpa de lo que ha pasado.*
    Peter is to blame for what happened.

TENER LUGAR

(Verbal idiom) = "To take place."
E.g.: *El partido de béisbol tendrá lugar la semana próxima.*
    The baseball game will take place next week.

TENER MIEDO (DE)

(Verbal idiom) = "To be afraid of, to."
E.g.: *Mi hermana tiene miedo de las arañas.*
    My sister is afraid of spiders.
    El niño tiene miedo de salir durante la noche.
    The child is afraid to go out at night.

TENER POR

(Verbal idiom) = "To consider."
E.g.: *Lo tenemos por cierto que vendrán.*
    We consider it certain that they will come.

TENER PRISA

(Verbal idiom) = "To be in a hurry."
E.g.: *Teníamos prisa porque el tren iba a salir en dos minutos.*
    We were in a hurry because the train was going to leave in two minutes.

TENER QUE + infinitive

(Verbal idiom) = "To have to, must + infinitive."
E.g.: *Tengo que ir al dentista.*
    I have to go to the dentist.

TENER QUE VER CON

(Verbal idiom) = "To have to do with."
E.g.: *Eso no tiene nada que ver con el problema.*
That has nothing to do with the problem.

TENER RAZÓN

(Verbal idiom) = "To be right [talking about a person]."
E.g.: *Este profesor cree que siempre tiene razón.*
This teacher thinks he is always right.
NOTE:
No tener razón = "To be wrong."

TENER SED

(Verbal idiom) = "To be thirsty."
E.g.: *Tenía mucha sed después de correr.*
I was very thirsty after running.

TENER SUEÑO

(Verbal idiom) = "To be sleepy."
E.g.: *Me acosté a las ocho porque tenía mucho sueño.*
I went to bed at eight o'clock because I was very sleepy.

TENER SUERTE

(Verbal idiom) = "To be lucky."
E.g.: *Tengo suerte. Gané cien mil pesetas en la lotería.*
I am lucky. I won 100,000 pesetas in the lottery.

TENER VERGÜENZA (DE)

(Idiomatic expression) = "To be ashamed (of)."
E.g.: *¿No tienes vergüenza de mentir así?*
Aren't you ashamed of lying like that?

TENSE

The tense *(el tiempo)* of a verb indicates at what moment the action takes place relative to the moment of speech. This can be not only the present, the past, or the future but also the future in a past context, the past in a past context, etc.
See the heading for each tense.

TENSES, COMPOUND

The compound tenses are:
(1) the present perfect (indicative and subjunctive).
(2) the pluperfect (indicative and subjunctive).
(3) the future perfect.
(4) the preterite perfect.
(5) the conditional perfect.
See the appropriate listing for each tense.

THAN

"Than" introduces the second term of a comparison:
(a) *Que* (Conjunction) before a noun or pronoun.
    E.g.: *Guillermo es más inteligente que Arturo.*
        William is more intelligent than Arthur.

(b) *De* (Preposition) before a numeral.

      E.g.: *Carmen tiene más de siete sobrinos.*

          Carmen has more than seven nieces and nephews.

THANKS TO

    = *Gracias a* (Prepositional idiom).

    E.g.: *Pude hacerlo gracias a tí.*

          I was able to do it thanks to you.

THAT

    (1) Demonstrative adjective = *Este (-a, -os, -as).*

See **ADJECTIVES, DEMONSTRATIVE**

    (2) Demonstrative pronoun = *Eso.*

See **PRONOUNS, DEMONSTRATIVE**

    (3) "That one" = *Éste (-a).*

See **PRONOUNS, DEMONSTRATIVE**

    (4) Before a relative pronoun = *Él, la, los, las.*

See **PRONOUNS, DEMONSTRATIVE**

    (5) Relative pronoun = *Que* or *quien(es).*

See **PRONOUNS, RELATIVE**

    (6) Conjunction = *Que.*

See **CONJUNCTIONS**

THE LESS . . . THE LESS

    = *Cuanto menos . . . tanto menos* (Correlative pronouns).

    E.g.: *Cuanto menos estudias, tanto menos comprenderás.*

          The less you study the less you will understand.

THE MORE . . . THE MORE

    = *Cuanto más . . . más* (Correlative pronouns).

    E.g.: *Cuanto más trabajo, más gano.*

          The more I work the more I earn.

THE ONE(S)

The corresponding Spanish construction is: Personal pronoun + relative pronoun.

    E.g.: *El que me gusta cuesta quinientos pesos.*

          The one I like costs five hundred pesos.

REMEMBER to make the personal pronoun ("the one[s]") agree in number and gender with the noun it replaces.

    E.g.: *Los de que hablo cuestan mucho.*

          Those (= the ones) of which I am speaking cost a lot.

THERE IS/ARE

    = *Hay* (Impersonal verb).

    E.g.: *Hay un perro.*

          There is a dog.

          Hay muchos automóviles.

          There are many cars.

See **HAY**

NOTE:
Hay is a variant of the present tense of the verb *Haber*. It is conjugated in all tenses:
IMPERF.: *había* (= there was, there were).
PRETER.: *hubo* (= there was, there were).
FUT.: *habrá* (= there will be).
CONDIT.: *habría* (= there would be).
SUBJ. PRES.: *haya* (= [that] there be).
PRES. PERF.: *ha habido* (= there has been, there have been).
PLUPERF.: *había habido* (= there had been).
See **HABER**

to THINK ABOUT vs. to THINK OF
See **PENSAR DE vs. PENSAR EN**

THIRSTY
= *Tener sed* (Idiomatic construction).
E.g.: *Cuando tengo sed, tomo un refresco.*
    When I am thirsty I have a drink.

TIEMPO vs. *HORA* vs. *VEZ (VECES)*
See **HORA vs. TIEMPO vs. VEZ (VECES)**

TILDE
The tilde *(la eñe)* [˜] is the diacritical mark over the letter *n* indicating that it is to be pronounced *ni* rather than *n*.
E.g.: *El cañón. La mañana.*

TIME EXPRESSIONS
(1) O'clock:
    (a) "What time is it?"   = *"¿Qué hora es?"*
    (b) "It is one o'clock"   = *"Es la una."*
        "It is two o'clock, three o'clock, four o'clock, etc."
                            = *"Son las dos, las tres, las cuatro, etc."*
    (c) "Quarter past . . ."   = *". . . y cuarto."*
        E.g.: *Son las tres y cuarto.*
            It is a quarter past three.
    (d) "A quarter of (or to.) . . "   = *". . . menos cuarto."*
        E.g.: *Son las cinco menos cuarto.*
            It is a quarter of (or to) five.
    (e) "Half past . . ."   = *". . . y media."*
        E.g.: *Son las nueve y media.*
            It is half past nine.
    (f) "Noon"   = *"Mediodía."*
    (g) "Midnight"   = *"Medianoche."*
    (h) a.m.   = *"de la mañana."*
        E.g.: *Son las seis de la mañana.*
            It is six a.m.
NOTE:
When no specific time is stated: *"por la mañana"* or *"por la tarde."*
E.g.: *Estudio por la mañana.*
      I study during the a.m.

E.g.: *Doy un paseo por la tarde.*
I take a walk in the p.m.
  (i) p.m.   = *"de la tarde."*
    E.g.: *Juego al fútbol a las dos de la tarde.*
      I play soccer at two p.m.
  (ii) early a.m.   = *"de la madrugada."*
    E.g.: *A las tres de la madrugada.*
      At three a.m.
  (iii) after sundown, p.m. = *"de la noche."*
    E.g.: *Me acuesto a las diez de la noche.*
      I go to bed at ten p.m.
  (iv) The definite article is used before the hour but not before minutes past or before the hour.
    E.g.: *Las cuatro y veinte.*
      Four twenty.

      Las seis menos diez.
      Ten of (or to) six.
  (v) The 24 hour clock is used for all official schedules and timetables.
    E.g.: *El tren sale a las 19h.43.*
      The train leaves at 7:43 p.m.
  (vi) The abbreviation for *hora* is *h.*
(2) Calendar expressions:
  (a) Today   = *Hoy.*
  (b) Tomorrow   = *Mañana.*
  (c) Day after tomorrow   = *Pasado mañana.*
  (d) Yesterday   = *Ayer.*
  (e) Day before yesterday   = *Anteayer.*
  (f) The following (or next) day = *El día siguiente.*
  (g) The day before   = *El día antes.*
  (h) A week (a month, 3 years) ago = *Hace una semana (un mes, 3 años).*
  (i) A week from today   = *En una semana.*
  (j) A year from now   = *En un año.*

TIME vs. HOUR vs. TIMES

(1) (a) "Time" meaning "o'clock" = *Hora.*
      E.g.: *¿Qué hora es?*
        What time is it?

NOTE:
The word *hora* is omitted in stating the time:
E.g.: *Son las cuatro.*
  It is four o'clock.
See **TIME EXPRESSIONS**
  (b) "Time" meaning "duration, period, length of time" = *Tiempo.*
    E.g.: *Pasaron mucho tiempo en México.*
      They spent much time in Mexico.

      No tenemos tiempo para leer.
      We don't have time to read.
  (c) "Time" meaning "point of time" = *Momento.*
    E.g.: *En este momento no puedo venir.*
      I cannot come at this time.
(2) "Hour" = *Hora.*
  E.g.: *Trabajé por seis horas.*
    I worked for six hours.

(3) "Time(s)" = *Vez, veces.*
    E.g.: *Visitamos el museo tres veces.*
          We visited the museum three times.

NOTE:
In arithmetic expressions, use *por.*
E.g.: *Dos por cinco son diez.*
     Two times five are ten.

TITLES, articles with

(1) When talking about someone, the definite article is used before a title (EXCEPT before *Don, Doña, Santo, San, Santa*).
    E.g.: *El doctor Calderón.*
         Doctor Calderón.
    BUT: *Doña Lucía.*
         Lucy.
         San Juan.
         Saint John.
(2) When addressing the person the article is not used.
    E.g.: *Buenas tardes, doctor Calderón.*
         Good afternoon, doctor Calderón.

TO (meaning "as far as, all the way to")

(Preposition) = *Hasta.*
E.g.: *Ella sabe contar hasta mil.*
     She can count up to one thousand.
     Viajamos hasta la frontera.
     We traveled as far as the border.

TO (meaning "in order to")

(Preposition) = *Para* + infinitive.
E.g.: *Vamos a clase para aprender el español.*
     We go to class (in order) to learn Spanish.

TOCAR

(Transitive verb) = "To touch, to feel, to play (music)."
PRES.: *toc-o, -as, -a, -amos, -áis, -an.*
IMPERF.: *toc-aba, -abas, -aba, -ábamos, -abais, -aban.*
PRETER.: *toqué, toc-aste, -ó, -amos, -asteis, -aron.*
FUT.: *tocar-é, -ás, -á, -emos, -éis, -án.*
CONDIT.: *tocar-ía, -ías, -ía, -íamos, -íais, -ían.*
SUBJ. PRES.: *toqu-e, -es, -e, -emos, -éis, -en.*
SUBJ. IMPERF. 1: *toc-ara, -aras, -ara, -áramos, -arais, -aran.*
SUBJ. IMPERF. 2: *toc-ase, -ases, -ase, -ásemos, -aseis, -asen.*
INFORMAL IMPERAT.: *toca (tú), no toques (tú); tocad (vosotros), no toquéis (vosotros).*
FORMAL IMPERAT.: *toque (Vd.); toquemos; toquen (Vds.).*
PRES. PARTIC.: *tocando.*
PAST PARTIC.: *tocado.*
NOTE:
The idiomatic construction *Tocarle a uno* = "To be one's turn, to concern one."
E.g.: *A tí te toca contestar.*
     It's your turn to answer.
     Eso no me toca a mí.
     That doesn't concern me.

TOCAR vs. *JUGAR*

Both verbs mean "To play", but note the difference in usage:
(1) *Tocar* = "To play (an instrument)."
    E.g.: *Benito toca el piano.*
        Benito plays the piano.
(2) *Jugar (a)* = "To play (a sport, a game)."
    E.g.: *Juego al básquetbol.*
        I play basketball.

TODAVÍA

(Adverb) = "Still."
E.g.: *María duerme todavía.*
    Mary is still sleeping.

TODAVÍA NO

(Adverbial idiom) = "Not yet."
E.g.: *Todavía no he visto la película.*
    I haven't seen the film yet.

TODO EL MUNDO

(Nominal idiom) = "Everybody."
E.g.: *Todo el mundo tiene que trabajar.*
    Everybody has to work.

TODO (-A, -OS, -AS)

(1) *Todo (-a, -os, -as)* (Adjective) = "All, whole, entire."
    E.g.: *Todas las muchachas.*
        All the girls.
        Toda la clase.
        The whole class.
(2) *Todo (-a, -os, -a)* (Pronoun) = "All, everything, everybody."
    E.g.: *Todos han llegado.*
        All have arrived.
        Todos dicen eso.
        Everybody says that.
        Todo cuesta mucho aquí.
        Everything costs a lot here.
(3) *Todo* (Adverb) = "All, completely, entirely."
    E.g.: *Estoy todo cansado.*
        I am all tired out.

TOO + adjective + verb

= *Demasiado* + adjective + *para* + infinitive.
E.g.: *Estoy demasiado enfermo para levantarme.*
    I am too ill to get up.

TOO MANY/MUCH + noun

= *Demasiados, (-a, -os, -as)* (Adjective of quantity) + noun.
E.g.: *Hay demasiados automóviles.*
    There are too many automobiles.
    El profesor nos da demasiado trabajo.
    The teacher gives us too much work.

TOWARD(S)

= *Hacia* (Preposition)

E.g.: *Anduvieron hacia la salida.*

They walked towards the exit.

TRADUCIR

(Transitive verb) = "To translate."

PRES.: *traduzco, traduc-es, -e, -imos, -ís, -en.*

IMPERF.: *traduc-ía, -ías, -ía, -íamos, -íais, -ían.*

PRETER.: *traduj-e, -iste, -o, -imos, -isteis, -eron.*

FUT.: *traducir-é, -ás, -á, -emos, -éis, -án.*

CONDIT.: *traducir-ía, -ías, -ía, -íamos, -íais, -ían.*

SUBJ. PRES.: *traduzc-a, -as, -a, -amos, -áis, -an.*

SUBJ. IMPERF. 1: *traduj-era, -eras, -era, -éramos, -erais, -eran.*

SUBJ. IMPERF. 2: *traduj-ese, -eses, -ese, -ésemos, -eseis, -esen.*

INFORMAL IMPERAT.: *traduce (tú), no traduzcas (tú); traducid (vosotros), no traduzcáis (vosotros).*

FORMAL IMPERAT.: *traduzca (Vd.); traduzcamos; traduzcan (Vds.).*

PRES PARTIC.: *traduciendo.*

PAST PARTIC.: *traducido.*

TRAER

(Transitive verb) = "To bring."

PRES.: *traigo, tra-es, -e, -emos, -éis, -en.*

IMPERF.: *tra-ía, -ías, -ía, -íamos, -íais, -ían.*

PRETER.: *traj-e, -iste, -o, -imos, -isteis, -eron.*

FUT.: *traer-é, -ás, -á, -emos, -éis, -án.*

CONDIT.: *traer-ía, -ías, -ía, -íamos, -íais, -ían.*

SUBJ. PRES.: *traig-a, -as, -a, -amos, -áis, -an.*

SUBJ. IMPERF. 1: *traj-era, -eras, -era, -éramos, -erais, -eran.*

SUBJ. IMPERF. 2: *traj-ese, -eses, -ese, -ésemos, -eseis, -esen.*

INFORMAL IMPERAT.: *trae (tú), no traigas (tú); traed (vosotros), no traigáis (vosotros).*

FORMAL IMPERAT.: *traiga (Vd.); traigamos; traigan (Vds.).*

PRES. PARTIC.: *trayendo.*

PAST PARTIC.: *traído.*

TRANSITIVE VERBS

See **VERBS, TRANSITIVE**

TRANSPORTATION, means of

Generally the preposition *en* precedes means of transportation.

E.g.: *Viajamos en avión, en coche, en barco, en tren, en bicicleta, en motocicleta.*

We travel by airplane, by car, by ship, by train, by bicycle, by motorcycle.

BUT: *A pie.*

On foot.

A caballo.

On horseback.

TRAS

(Preposition) = "After, behind [in stating order of succession]."

E.g.: *El huevo vino tras la gallina.*

The egg came after the chicken.

TRATAR DE + infinitive

(Verbal idiom) = "To try + infinitive."

E.g.: *Traté de resolver el problema de matemáticas.*
    I tried to solve the mathematics problem.

TRATARSE DE

(Reflexive verb) = "To be a matter of, to be a question of, to have to do with."

E.g.: *¿De qué se trata?*
    What is it about? What's up?

    Se trata de un crimen horrible.
    It is a matter of a horrible crime.

    Se trataba de un acuerdo político.
    It had to do with a political agreement.

TROPEZAR CON

(Intransitive verb) = "To stumble upon, to meet by chance."

E.g.: *Tropezamos con Margarita ayer.*
    We met Margaret (by chance) yesterday.

See **ENCONTRAR** and **DAR CON**

TÚ vs. *TU*

(1) *Tú* = subject pronoun, second person singular.
    E.g.: *Tú tienes un coche muy elegante.*
        You have a very elegant car.
(2) *Tu* = possessive adjective, second person singular.
    E.g.: *Tu coche es muy elegante.*
        Your car is very elegant.

TÚ vs. *USTED*

See **USTED(ES) vs. TÚ/VOSOTROS(-AS)**

TUYO (-A, -OS, -AS)

See **ADJECTIVES, POSSESSIVE**
See also **PRONOUNS, POSSESSIVE**

U

U

(Conjunction) = "Or." *U* is used instead of *o* before words beginning with *o-* or *ho-*.

E.g.: *Siete u ocho.*
    Seven or eight.

    Mujeres u hombres.
    Men or women.

UN POCO (DE)

(1) *Un poco* (Adverbial idiom) = "A little bit, slightly."
    E.g.: *Ella estudia un poco cada día.*
        She studies a little every day.
(2) *Un poco de* + noun (Adverbial expression of quantity) = "A little, a bit of."
    E.g.: *¡Dame un poco de vino, por favor!*
        Give me a little wine, please!

UN (-O, -A, -OS, -AS)

(Indefinite article)
(1) *Un* (Masculine singular) = "A, an."
   E.g.: *Tengo un amigo.*
      I have a friend.
(2) *Una* (Feminine singular) = "A, an."
   E.g.: *Tengo una amiga.*
      I have a (girl) friend.
(3) *Unos (-as)* (Masculine and feminine plural) = "Some, a few."
   E.g.: *Tengo unos amigos en Toledo.*
      I have some friends in Toledo.
(2) *Uno* (Indefinite pronoun) = "One, someone."
   E.g.: *Uno no puede pasar por aquí.*
      One may not go through here.
See **ARTICLE, INDEFINITE**
See **PRONOUN, INDEFINITE**

UNCERTAINTY

The concept of uncertainty is conveyed by:
(a) *Dudar que* + subjunctive.
   E.g.: *Dudamos que ellos vengan.*
      We doubt that they will come.
(b) *No estar seguro de que* + subjunctive.
   E.g.: *No estoy seguro de que él comprenda.*
      I am not sure that he understands.

UNLESS

= *A menos que* (conjunction) + subjunctive.
E.g.: *Daremos un paseo a menos que llueva.*
   We shall go for a walk unless it should rain.

UNO

(Indefinite subject pronoun). *Uno* can be used, particularly with reflexive verbs, when there is no specified subject.
E.g.: *Uno se levanta muy temprano en el ejército.*
   One gets up very early in the army.

UNTIL

(1) "Until" (Preposition) = *Hasta.*
   E.g.: *Nos quedaremos aquí hasta el lunes.*
      We shall stay here until Monday.
(2) "Until" (Conjunction) =
   (a) *Hasta que* + indicative.
      E.g.: *Estudié hasta que volviste.*
         I studied until you returned.
   (b) *Hasta que* + subjunctive (when referring to a future action).
      E.g.: *Estudiaré hasta que vuelvas.*
         I shall study until you return.

UPON + verb (-ing)

= *Al* + infinitive (Prepositional construction).
E.g.: *Al entrar, vi a mi hermana.*
   Upon entering I saw my sister.
See **GERUND**

UPSIDE DOWN

= *Al revés* (Adverbial idiom).

E.g.: *Tienes tu libro al revés.*
> You are holding your book upside down.

USED TO (meaning "accustomed to")

(a) "To be used to" = *Estar acostumbrado a* + infinitive or noun.

E.g.: *Estamos acostumbrados a trabajar por la noche.*
> We are used to working during the night.

Estoy acostumbrado al frío:
> I am used to the cold.

(b) "To become used to" = *Acostumbrarse a* + infinitive or noun.

E.g.: *Me acostumbro a hablar español.*
> I'm getting used to speaking Spanish.

Se acostrumbraron al clima.
> They became used to the climate.

USED TO (meaning habitual action)

Habitual or repeated actions in the past are conveyed by the imperfect tense.

E.g.: *Ellos vivían en el Paraguay.*
> They used to live in Paraguay.

Mi familia y yo íbamos a la playa cada verano.
> My family and I used to go to the beach every year.

See **IMPERFECT TENSE**

USEFUL CLASSROOM EXPRESSIONS
see **CLASSROOM EXPRESSIONS**

USTED(ES) vs. *TÚ/VOSOTROS (-AS)*

(a) *Usted* (abbreviated *Ud.* or *Vd.*; plural *ustedes,* abbreviated *Uds.* or *Vds.*) is the formal subject and prepositional object pronoun. In Latin America, however, *Vds.* is both formal and informal. It always takes the third person of the verb.

E.g.: *¿Cómo está Vd.?*
> How are you?

Vds. han ganado el premio.
> You (plur.) have won the prize.

The origin of this expression is *Vuestra Merced* ("Your honor.")

(b) *Tú* is the informal subject pronoun, second person singular (plural: *vosotros (-as)*). It is used with friends, people of the same age as the speaker, and members of the family.

E.g.: *¿Cómo estás (tú), mamá?*
> How are you, Mom?

Vosotros seréis bienvenidos a mi casa, amigos.
> You will be welcome in my house, friends.

V

VALER

(Transitive and intransitive verb) = "To be worth, to be valid."
PRES.: *valgo, val-es, -e, -emos, -éis, -en.*
IMPERF.: *val-ía, -ías, -ía, -íamos, -íais, -ían.*
PRETER.: *val-í, -iste, -ió, -imos, -isteis, -ieron.*
FUT.: *valdr-é, -ás, -á, -emos, -éis, -án.*
CONDIT.: *valdr-ía, -ías, -ía, -íamos, -íais, -ían.*
SUBJ. PRES.: *valg-a, -as, -a, -amos, -áis, -an.*
SUBJ. IMPERF. 1: *vali-era, -eras, -era, -éramos, -erais, -eran.*
SUBJ. IMPERF. 2: *vali-ese, -eses, -ese, -ésemos, -eseis, -esen.*
INFORMAL IMPERAT.: *val (tú), no valgas (tú); valed (vosotros), no valgáis (vosotros).*
FORMAL IMPERAT.: *valga (Vd.); valgamos; valgan (Vds.).*
PRES. PARTIC.: *valiendo.*
PAST PARTIC.: *valido.*
USAGE:
(a) = "To be worth."
    E.g.: *¿Cuánto vale este coche?*
        How much is this car worth?
(b) = "To be useful, to be valid."
    E.g.: *Estas ideas no valen.*
        These ideas are no good.

VALER LA PENA

(Verbal idiom) = "To be worthwhile, to be worth the trouble."
(1) *Valer la pena* + infinitive.
    E.g.: *No vale la pena visitar ese museo.*
        It is not worthwhile to visit that museum.
(2) *Valer la pena que* + subjunctive.
    E.g.: *Vale la pena que ellos aprendan la lengua.*
        It is worthwhile for them to learn the language.

¡VAMOS!

(First person plural imperative of *ir*) = "Let's go."
Use the subjunctive for the negative form.
E.g.: *¡No vayamos!*
    Let's not go!
NOTES:
(1) For stronger emphasis use the imperative of the reflexive verb *irse*:
    E.g.: *¡Vámonos!*
        Let's go, let's get going!
(2) *¡Vamos!* also has the idiomatic meaning: "Come on, now!"
    E.g.: *¡Vamos!, no es tan peligroso!*
        Come now, it's not that dangerous!

VARIOS (-AS)

(Adjective) = "Several, some, a number of."
E.g.: *Vimos varias obras de teatro en Buenos Aires.*
    We saw several plays in Buenos Aires.

VENCER

(Transitive verb) = "To overcome."
PRES.: *venzo, venc-es, -e, -emos, -éis, -en.*
IMPERF.: *vencía, -ías, -ía, -íamos, -íais, -ían.*
PRETER.: *venc-í, -iste, -ió, -imos, -isteis, -ieron.*
FUT.: *vencer-é, -ás, -á, -emos, -éis, -án.*
CONDIT.: *vencer-ía, -ías, -ía, -íamos, -íais, -ían.*
SUBJ. PRES.: *venz-a, -as, -a, -amos, -áis, -an.*
SUBJ. IMPERF. 1: *venci-era, -eras, -era, -éramos, -erais, -eran.*
SUBJ. IMPERF. 2: *venci-ese, -eses, -ese, -ésemos, -eseis, -esen.*
INFORMAL IMPERAT.: *vence (tú), no venzas (tú); venced (vosotros), no venzáis (vosotros).*
FORMAL IMPERAT.: *venza (Vd.); venzamos; venzan (Vds.).*
PRES. PARTIC.: *venciendo.*
PAST PARTIC.: *vencido.*

VENIR

(Intransitive verb) = "To come."
PRES.: *vengo, vienes, viene, venimos, venís, vienen.*
IMPERF.: *ven-ía, -ías, -ía, -íamos, -íais, -ían.*
PRETER.: *vine, viniste, vino, vinimos, vinisteis, vinieron.*
FUT.: *vendr-é, -ás, -á, -emos, -éis, -án.*
CONDIT.: *vendr-ía, -ías, -ía, -íamos, -íais, -ían.*
SUBJ. PRES.: *veng-a, -as, -a, -amos, -áis, -an.*
SUBJ. IMPERF. 1: *vini-era, -eras, -era, -éramos, -erais, -eran.*
SUBJ. IMPERF. 2: *vini-ese, -eses, -ese, -ésemos, -eseis, -esen.*
INFORMAL IMPERAT.: *ven (tú), no vengas (tú); venid (vosotros), no vengáis (vosotros).*
FORMAL IMPERAT.: *venga (Vd.); vengamos; vengan (Vds.).*
PRES PARTIC.: *viniendo.*
PAST PARTIC.: *venido.*

VER

(Transitive verb) = "To see."
PRES.: *veo, ves, ve, vemos, veis, ven.*
IMPERF.: *ve-ía, -ías, -ía, -íamos, -íais, -ían.*
PRETER.: *vi, viste, vio, vimos, visteis, vieron.*
FUT.: *ver-é, -ás, -á, -emos, -éis, -án.*
CONDIT.: *ver-ía, -ías, -ía, -íamos, -íais, -ían.*
SUBJ. PRES.: *ve-a, -as, -a, -amos, -áis, -an.*
SUBJ. IMPERF. 1: *vi-era, -eras, -era, -éramos, -erais, -eran.*
SUBJ. IMPERF. 2: *vi-ese, -eses, -ese, -ésemos, -eseis, -esen.*
INFORMAL IMPERAT.: *ve (tú), no veas (tú); ved (vosotros), no veáis (vosotros).*
FORMAL IMPERAT.: *vea (Vd.); veamos; vean (Vds.).*
PRES. PARTIC.: *viendo.*
PAST PARTIC.: *visto.*
NOTE:
This is a verb of perception. The English construction "To see + present participle" is rendered by *Ver* + infinitive or gerund.
E.g.: *Vimos a Margarita entrar (or entrando) en el almacén.*
   We saw Margaret entering the department store.
See **VERBS OF PERCEPTION**

VER vs. MIRAR

See **MIRAR vs. VER**

VERBS + (*A, CON, DE, EN,* or no preposition) + infinitive

acabar de = to have just
acercarse a = to approach
acertar a = to manage
acordarse de = to remember
acostumbrarse a = to become accustomed
alegrarse de = to rejoice
amenazar con = to threaten
aprender a = to learn
apresurarse a = to hasten
aspirar a = to aspire
atreverse a = to dare
ayudar a = to help
cesar de = to stop
comenzar a = to begin
consentir en = to agree
consistir en = to consist of
contar con = to count on
convenir en = to agree
convidar a = to invite
correr a = to run
deber (de) = must, to have to
decidirse a = to decide
dedicarse a = to dedicate oneself
dejar = to let, to allow
dejar de = to stop
desear = to desire
disponerse a = to prepare
empeñarse en = to be determined
empezar a = to begin
encargarse de = to attend to
enseñar a = to teach

esperar = to hope, to expect
hacer = to make, to do
insistir en = to insist
invitar a = to invite
ir a = to be going to
llegar a = to succeed
lograr = to manage, to succeed
necesitar = to need
negarse a = to refuse
obligar a = to force
oír = to hear
olvidar de = to forget
pensar = to think
poder = to be able
ponerse a = to begin
preferir = to prefer
pretender = to try
principiar a = to begin
prometer = to promise
querer = to want
regresar a = to return
resignarse a = to resign oneself
saber = to know
salir a = to go out
soler = to be in the habit
soñar con = to dream
tardar en = to be slow
tratar de = to try
venir a = to come
ver = to see
volver a = to . . . again

See **PREPOSITIONS + infinitive**
See also **DE or A (with verbs)**

VERBS ENDING IN: -*CAR*

These verbs change the *c* to *qu* before the letter *e*; i.e., in the first person singular of the preterite, in all the persons of the subjunctive present, and in the formal imperative.
E.g.: *Buscar* = "To look for, to seek."
PRETER.: *busqué, (buscaste, buscó, buscamos, buscasteis, buscaron).*
SUBJ. PRES.: *busque, busques, busque, busquemos, busquéis, busquen.*
FORMAL IMPERAT.: *busque (Vd.), busquen (Vds.).*
Verbs of this type:

acercarse = to approach
comunicar = to communicate
dedicar = to dedicate
desembocar = to empty
destacarse = to stand out
indicar = to indicate
intensificar = to intensify

mascar = to chew
pescar = to fish
platicar = to chat
practicar = to practice
sacar = to take out
significar = to mean
simplificar = to simplify
tocar = to touch, to play (music)

VERBS ENDING IN: *-CER*

If the *-cer* is preceded by a consonant, these verbs change the *c* to *z* before *a* and *o*, i.e., in the first person singular of the present indicative, in all persons of the present subjunctive, and in the formal imperative.
E.g.: *Vencer* = "To overcome, to vanquish."
PRES.: *venzo, (vences, vence, vencemos, vencéis, vencen).*
SUBJ. PRES.: *venza, venzas, venza, venzamos, venzáis, venzan.*
FORMAL IMPERAT.: *venza (Vd.), venzan (Vds.).*
Verbs of this type:
convencer = to convince
ejercer = to exert

VERBS ENDING IN: *-CIR*

When the *-cir* is preceded by a consonant, these verbs change the *c* to *z* before the letters *o* and *a*: i.e., in the first person singular of the present indicative, in all persons of the present subjunctive, and in the formal imperative.
E.g.: *Esparcir* = "To spread, to scatter."
PRES.: *esparzo, (esparces, esparce, esparcimos, esparcís, esparcen).*
SUBJ. PRES.: *esparza, esparzas, esparza, esparzamos, esparzáis, esparzan*
FORMAL IMPERAT.: *esparza (Vd.), esparzan (Vds.).*

VERBS ENDING IN: *-DUCIR*

These verbs insert a *z* before the *c* in the first person singular of the present indicative and in all persons of the subjunctive present. They also have additional changes in the preterite and in the imperfect subjunctive. Note also the stem change in the present, and both forms of the imperfect subjunctive.
E.g.: *Traducir* = "To translate."
PRES.: *traduzco, (traduces, traduce, traducimos, traducís, traducen).*
SUBJ. PRES.: *traduzca, traduzcas, traduzca, traduzcamos, traduzcáis, traduzcan.*
PRETERITE: *traduje, tradujiste, tradujo, tradujimos, tradujisteis, tradujeron.*
SUBJ. IMPERF. 1: *tradujera, tradujeras, tradujera, tradujéramos, tradujerais, tradujeran.*
SUBJ. IMPERF. 2: *tradujese, tradujeses, tradujese, tradujésemos, tradujeseis, tradujesen.*
Verbs of this type:
conducir = to drive, to lead
inducir = to induce
introducir = to introduce
producir = to produce

VERBS ENDING IN: *-GAR*

These verbs change the *g* to *gu* before *e*, i.e., in the first person singular of the preterite, in all persons of the present subjunctive, and in the formal imperative.
E.g.: *Llegar* = "To arrive."
PRETER.: *llegué, (llegaste, llegó, llegamos, llegasteis, llegaron).*
SUBJ. PRES.: *llegue, llegues, llegue, lleguemos, lleguéis, lleguen.*
FORMAL IMPERAT.: *llegue (Vd.), lleguen (Vds.).*
Verbs of this type:
cargar = to load
entregar = to hand (over)
jugar = to play [NOTE: this verb also has a *ue* change.]
navegar = to sail, to navigate
pagar = to pay
rogar = to pray, to beg, to ask [NOTE: this verb also has a *ue* change.]

VERBS ENDING IN: *-GER*

These verbs change the *g* to *j* before *a* and *o*, i.e., in the first person singular of the present indicative, in all persons of the preterite, and in the formal imperative.
E.g.: *Escoger* = "To choose."
PRES.: *escojo, (escoges, escoge, escogemos, escogéis, escogen).*
SUBJ. PRES.: *escoja, escojas, escoja, escojamos, escojáis, escojan.*
FORMAL IMPERAT.: *escoja (Vd.), escojan (Vds.).*
Verbs of this type:
proteger = to protect
recoger = to pick up

VERBS ENDING IN: *-GIR*

These verbs change the *g* to *j* before *a* and *o*, i.e., in the first person singular of the present indicative, in all persons of the present subjunctive, and in the formal imperative.
E.g.: *Dirigir* = "To direct."
PRES.: *dirijo, (diriges, dirige, dirigimos, dirigís, dirigen).*
SUBJ. PRES.: *dirija, dirijas, dirija, dirijamos, dirijáis, dirijan.*
FORMAL IMPERAT.: *dirija (Vd.), dirijan (Vds.).*
Verbs of this type:
elegir = to elect
exigir = to urge, to demand

VERBS ENDING IN: *-GUAR*

These verbs change the *gu* to *gü* before *e*, i.e., in the first person singular of the preterite, in all persons of the present subjunctive, and in the formal imperative.
E.g.: *Averiguar* = "To find out, to inquire."
PRETER: *averigüé, (averiguaste, averiguó, averiguamos, averiguasteis, averiguaron).*
SUBJ. PRES.: *averigüe, averigües, averigüe, averigüemos, averigüéis, averigüen.*
FORMAL IMPERAT.: *averigüe (Vd.), averigüen (Vds.).*

VERBS ENDING IN: *-GUIR*

These verbs change the *gu* to *g* before *a* and *o*, i.e., in the first person singular of the present indicative, in all persons of the present subjunctive, and in the formal imperative.
E.g.: *Distinguir* = "To distinguish."
PRES.: *distingo, (distingues, distingue, distinguimos, distinguís, distinguen).*
SUBJ. PRES.: *distinga, distingas, distinga, distingamos, distingáis, distingan.*
FORMAL IMPERAT.: *distinga (Vd.), distingan (Vds.).*
Verbs of this type:
conseguir = to get, to obtain (NOTE: this verb also has an *i* change)
seguir = to follow (NOTE: this verb also has an *i* change)

VERBS ENDING IN: *-IAR*

Some verbs of this type require a written accent over the *i* in the first, second, and third persons singular and in the third person plural of the present indicative; in the subjunctive present; and in the formal imperative.
E.g.: *Enviar* = "To send."
PRES.: *envío, envías, envía, (enviamos, enviais), envían.*
SUBJ. PRES.: *envíe, envíes, envíe, (enviemos, envieis), envíen.*
FORMAL IMPERAT.: *envíe (Vd.), envíen (Vds.).*
Verbs of this type:
criar = to grow, to rear, to raise

VERBS ENDING IN: *-QUIR*

These verbs change the *qu* to *c* before *a* and *o*, i.e., in the first person singular of the present indicative, in all persons of the present subjunctive, and in the formal imperative.
E.g.: *Delinquir* = "To be guilty."
PRES.: *delinco, (delinques, delinque, delinquimos, delinquís, delinquen).*
SUBJ. PRES.: *delinca, delincas, delinca, delincamos, delincáis, delincan.*
FORMAL IMPERAT.: *delinca (Vd.), delincan (Vds.)*

VERBS ENDING IN: *-UAR*

These verbs have a written accent on the *u* in the first, second, and third persons singular and the third person plural of the present indicative and present subjunctive, and in the formal imperative.
E.g.: *Continuar* = "To continue."
PRES.: *continúo, continúas, continúa, (continuamos, continuáis), continúan.*
SUBJ. PRES.: *continúe, continúes, continúe, (continuemos, continuéis), continúen.*
FORMAL IMPERAT.: *continúe (Vd.), continúen (Vds.).*

VERBS ENDING IN: *-UIR* (except *-GUIR*)

These verbs insert *y* (except before *i*) and change unaccented *i* between vowels to *y* in the first person singular of the present indicative, in the third persons singular and plural of the preterite, in all persons of the present and imperfect subjunctives, in the formal imperative, and in the present participle.
E.g.: *Construir* = "To build."
PRES.: *construyo, construyes, construye, (construimos, construís), construyen.*
PRETERITE: *(construí, construiste), construyó, (construimos, construisteis), construyeron.*
SUBJ. PRES.: *construya, construyas, construya, construyamos, construyáis, construyan.*
SUBJ. IMPERF. 1: *construyera, construyeras, construyera, construyéramos, construyerais, construyeran.*
SUBJ. IMPERF. 2: *construyese, construyeses, construyese, construyésemos, construyeseis, construyesen.*
FORMAL IMPERAT.: *construya (Vd.), construyan (Vds.).*
PRES. PARTIC.: *construyendo.*
Verbs of this type:
constituir = to constitute
destruir = to destroy

VERBS ENDING IN: VOWEL + *CER*

These verbs insert a *z* before the *c* in the first person plural of the present indicative and in all persons of the present subjunctive.
E.g.: *Conocer* = "To know."
PRES.: *conozco, (conoces, conoce, conocemos, conocéis, conocen).*
SUBJ. PRES.: *conozca, conozcas, conozca, conozcamos, conozcáis, conozcan.*
Verbs of this type:

aparecer = to appear	*parecer* = to seem
establecer = to establish	*pertenecer* = to belong
merecer = to merit	*prevalecer* = to prevail
nacer = to be born	

VERBS ENDING IN: VOWEL + *ER*

Some verbs of this type change the unaccented *i* to *y* in the third person singular and third person plural of the preterite, in all persons of the imperfect subjunctive, and in the present participle.

E.g.: *Creer* = "To believe, to think."
PRETER.: *(creí, creíste), creyó, (creímos, creísteis, creyeron).*
SUBJ. IMPERF. 1: *creyera, creyeras, creyera, creyéramos, creyerais, creyeran.*
SUBJ. IMPERF. 2: *creyese, creyeses, creyese, creyésemos, creyeseis, creyesen.*
PRES. PART.: *creyendo.*
Verbs of this type:
leer = to read
poseer = to possess

VERBS ENDING IN: -*ZAR*

These verbs change the *z* to *c* before *e* in the first person singular of the preterite, in all persons of the present subjunctive, and in the formal imperative.
E.g.: *Cruzar* = "To cross."
PRETER.: *cruce, (cruzaste, cruzó, cruzamos, cruzasteis, cruzaron).*
SUBJ. PRES.: *cruce, cruces, cruce, crucemos, crucéis, crucen.*
FORMAL IMPERAT.: *cruce (Vd.), crucen (Vds.).*
Verbs of this type:
alcanzar = to reach
almorzar = to eat lunch
caracterizar = to characterize
comenzar = to begin (NOTE: this verb also has an *ie* change)
empezar = to begin (NOTE: this verb also has an *ie* change)
organizar = to organize
realizar = to make real, to accomplish
utilizar = to use, to utilize

VERBS OF PERCEPTION

See **PERCEPTION, VERBS OF**

VERBS which take the subjunctive

See **SUBJUNCTIVE MOOD**

VERBS, AUXILIARY

Auxiliary verbs *(los verbos auxiliares)* are used to form the compound tenses of other verbs. The main auxiliary verb in Spanish is *haber* (which is used by itself only in its impersonal form [*hay, había, habrá*, etc.], meaning "there is, there are, there was, there were," etc.). The other auxiliary verbs in Spanish are *ser*, which is used to form the passive voice, and *estar*, which is used to form progressive tenses.
See **TENSES, COMPOUND**
See also **PASSIVE VOICE, PROGRESSIVE TENSES**

VERBS, HELPING

See **AUXILIARY VERBS**

VERBS, IMPERSONAL

Impersonal verbs have no subject or object. Nothing or nobody is actually taking part in the action described by these verbs. They are used only in the third person singular.
E.g.: *Llueve.*
It is raining.
Hace frío.
It is cold.
Hay que trabajar.
You have (one has) to work.
Hay mucha gente.
There are many people.
Era necesario.
It was necessary.

VERBS, INTRANSITIVE

(Los verbos intransitivos). These are verbs which do not (and cannot) take a direct object.
E.g.: *Voy en un momento.*
> I am leaving in a minute.

> *Entras en la cocina.*
> You enter (in) the kitchen.

> *Ella llega siempre tarde.*
> She always arrives late.

> *Caímos en el hielo.*
> We fell on the ice.

REMEMBER: Some verbs are transitive in English but not in Spanish, and vice versa.
(A) TRANSITIVE ENGLISH VERBS WHICH ARE INTRANSITIVE IN SPANISH:
   (a) To enter = *Entrar en.*
   E.g.: *Entro en la casa.*
   > I enter the house.

   (b) To exit, to leave = *Salir de.*
   E.g.: *Salimos de la ciudad.*
   > We exited the city.

   > *Salimos de la escuela.*
   > We leave the school.

(B) TRANSITIVE SPANISH VERBS WHICH ARE INTRANSITIVE IN ENGLISH:
   (a) *Buscar* = To look for.
   E.g.: *Busqué mi libro por todas partes.*
   > I looked for my book everywhere.

   (b) *Escuchar* = To listen to.
   E.g.: *Escucho la radio.*
   > I listen to the radio.

   (c) *Esperar* = To wait for.
   E.g.: *Esperamos el próximo avión.*
   > We wait for the next plane.

   (d) *Mirar* = To look at, to watch.
   E.g.: *Miramos la fotografía.*
   > We look at the photograph.

See **VERBS, TRANSITIVE**

VERBS, IRREGULAR

See the heading for each verb.

VERBS, RECIPROCAL

(Los verbos recíprocos). These are always in a plural form (we, you, they) and indicate that the action is performed reciprocally (i.e., to, for, at, or on each other). They are accompanied by reciprocal pronouns (which are the same as the plural forms of the reflexive pronouns *[nos, os, se]*). For practical purposes reciprocal verbs are indistinguishable from reflexive verbs and ambiguity may result.
E.g.: *Nos miramos.*
> We look at each other.
   or: We look at ourselves.

> *Ellas se enviaron regalos.*
> They sent each other presents.
   or: They sent themselves presents.

To avoid ambiguity add the propriate forms of *uno (-a, -os, -as)* . . . *otro (-a, -os, -as).*

E.g.: *Se miran el uno al otro por la ventana.*
   They look at each other through the window.
See **VERBS, REFLEXIVE**

VERBS, REFLEXIVE

(Los verbos reflexivos). The action of a reflexive verb returns upon the subject. It is accompanied by the reflexive pronouns *me, te, se, nos, os, se,* which refer to the subject of the verb. A reflexive verb can:

(a) have a reflexive meaning:
   E.g.: *Me miro en el espejo.*
      I look at myself in the mirror.
(b) have a reciprocal meaning:
   E.g.: *Nos miramos por la ventana.*
      We look at each other through the window.
See **VERBS, RECIPROCAL**
(c) have a meaning with no reflexive or reciprocal content:
   E.g.: *Me callo.*
      I keep silent (I do not speak).
(d) be a substitute for the passive voice:
   E.g.: *El español se habla en muchos países de la América del Sur.*
      Spanish is spoken in many countries of South America.

NOTE:
Do not forget to conjugate the pronoun even if the verb is in the infinitive or the present participle.
SOME COMMON REFLEXIVE VERBS WHICH ARE NOT REFLEXIVE IN ENGLISH:

acordarse (de) = to remember
acostarse = to go to bed
apresurarse = to hurry
arrepentirse (de) = to repent
atreverse (a) = to dare
burlarse (de) = to make fun (of)
callarse = to keep silent
desayunarse = to eat breakfast
desmayarse = to faint
despertarse = to wake up
dormirse = to fall asleep
enterarse(de) = to find out
escaparse (de) = to escape.

fiarse (en) = to trust
figurarse = to imagine
fijarse (en) = to notice
irse = to go away
levantarse = to get up
negarse (a) = to refuse (to)
olvidarse (de) = to forget
parecerse (a) = to resemble
pasearse = to stroll, to take a walk
quejarse (de) = to complain
reírse (de) = to laugh at
tratarse (de) = to concern, to be about, to be a question of

CONJUGATION OF A REFLEXIVE VERB:
Callarse = "To remain silent."
PRES.: *me callo, te callas, se calla, nos callamos, os calláis, se callan.*
IMPERF.: *me callaba, te callabas, se callaba, nos callábamos, os callabais, se callaban.*
PRETER.: *me callé, te callaste, se calló, nos callamos, os callasteis, se callaron.*
FUT.: *me callaré, te callarás, se callará, nos callaremos, os callaréis, se callarán.*
CONDIT.: *me callaría, te callarías, se callaría, nos callaríamos, os callaríais, se callarían.*
PRES. SUBJ.: *me calle, te calles, se calle, nos callemos, os calléis, se callen.*
SUBJ. IMPERF. 1: *me callara, te callaras, se callara, nos calláramos, os callarais, se callaran.*
SUBJ. IMPERF. 2: *me callase, te callases, se callase, nos callásemos, os callaseis, se callasen.*
INFORMAL IMPERAT.: *cállate (tú), no te calles (tú); callaos (vosotros), no os calléis (vosotros).*
FORMAL IMPERAT.: *cállese (Vd.); callémonos; cállense (Vds.).*
PRES. PARTIC.: *callándose.*
VERBS, REGULAR *See REGULAR VERBS.*

VERBS, REGULAR
   See **REGULAR VERBS.**

VERBS, SPELLING-CHANGE

See under the relevant headings: **VERBS ENDING IN: *-CAR***
                                  VERBS ENDING IN: *-CER*
                                  VERBS ENDING IN: *-CIR*
                                  VERBS ENDING IN: *-DUCIR*
                                  VERBS ENDING IN: *-GAR*
                                  VERBS ENDING IN: *-GER*
                                  VERBS ENDING IN: *-GIR*
                                  VERBS ENDING IN: *-GUAR*
                                  VERBS ENDING IN: *-GUIR*
                                  VERBS ENDING IN: *-IAR*
                                  VERBS ENDING IN: *-QUIR*
                                  VERBS ENDING IN: *-UAR*
                                  VERBS ENDING IN: *-UIR* (except *-GUIR*)
                                  VERBS ENDING IN: vowel + *CER*
                                  VERBS ENDING IN: vowel + *ER*
                                  VERBS ENDING IN: *-ZAR*

VERBS, STEM-CHANGING

(1) In many *-ar* and *-er* verbs, the vowels *e* and *o* change to *ie* and *ue*, respectively, when they are stressed. When the stress does not fall on these vowels, they do not change.

   (a) E.g.: *Cerrar* = "To close."
PRES.: *cierro, cierras, cierra, (cerramos, cerráis), cierran.*
SUBJ. PRES.: *cierre, cierres, cierre, (cerremos, cerréis), cierren.*
INFORMAL IMPERAT.: *cierra (tú), no cierres (tú).*
FORMAL IMPERAT.: *cierre (Vd.), cierren (Vds.).*

   (b) E.g.: *Perder* = "To lose."
PRES.: *pierdo, pierdes, pierde, (perdemos, perdéis), pierden.*
SUBJ. PRES.: *pierda, pierdas, pierda, (perdamos, perdáis), pierdan.*
INFORMAL IMPERAT.: *pierde (tú), no pierdas (tú).*
FORMAL IMPERAT.: *pierda (Vd.), pierdan (Vds.).*

   (c) E.g.: *contar* = "To count, to tell."
PRES.: *cuento, cuentas, cuenta, (contamos, contáis), cuentan.*
SUBJ. PRES.: *cuente, cuentes, cuente, (contemos, contéis), cuenten.*
INFORMAL IMPERAT.: *cuenta (tú), no cuentes (tú).*
FORMAL IMPERAT.: *cuente (Vd.), cuenten (Vds.).*

   (d) E.g.: *Volver* = "To turn."
PRES.: *vuelvo, vuelves, vuelve, (volvemos, volvéis), vuelven.*
SUBJ. PRES.: *vuelva, vuelvas, vuelva, (volvamos, volváis), vuelvan.*
INFORMAL IMPERAT.: *vuelve (tú), no vuelvas (tú).*
FORMAL IMPERAT.: *vuelva (Vd.), vuelvan (Vds.).*

   (e) E.g.: *Jugar* = "To play."
PRES.: *juego, juegas, juega, (jugamos, jugáis), juegan.*
SUBJ. PRES.: *juegue, juegues, juegue, (juguemos, juguéis), jueguen.*
INFORMAL IMPERAT.: *juegua (tú), no juegues (tú).*
FORMAL IMPERAT.: *juegue (Vd.), jueguen (Vds.).*

(2) In some third conjugation verbs, the vowels *e* and *o* change to *ie* and *ue*, respectively, when they are stressed. When the stress does not fall on these vowels, they do not change. In addition, they also change the vowels *e* to *i* and *o* to *u* when they are unstressed and when the following syllable contains a diphthong.

(a) E.g.: *Sentir* = "To feel."

PRES.: *siento, sientes, siente, (sentimos, sentís), sienten.*
SUBJ. PRES.: *sienta, sientas, sienta, (sintamos, sintáis), sientan.*
INFORMAL IMPERAT.: *siente (tú), no sientas (tú).*
FORMAL IMPERAT.: *sienta (Vd.), sientan (Vds.).*
PRETER.: *(sentí, sentiste), sintió, (sentimos, sentisteis), sintieron.*
SUBJ. IMPERF. 1: *sinti-era, -eras, -era, -eramos, -eráis, -eran.*
SUBJ. IMPERF. 2: *sinti-ese, -eses, -ese, -ésemos, -eseis, -esen.*
PRES. PART.: *sintiendo.*

(b) E.g.: *Dormir* = "To sleep."

PRES.: *duermo, duermes, duerme, (dormimos, dormís), duermen.*
SUBJ. PRES.: *duerma, duermas, duerma, (durmamos, durmáis), duerman.*
INFORMAL IMPERAT.: *duerme (tú), no duermas (tú).*
FORMAL IMPERAT.: *duerma (Vd.), duerman (Vds.).*
PRETER.: *(dormí, dormiste), durmió, (dormimos, dormisteis), durmieron.*

VERBS, TRANSITIVE

(Los verbos transitivos). These are verbs which can take a direct object. Most verbs are of this type.
E.g.: *Comemos pan.*
　　　We eat bread.
　　　Habéis visto la película.
　　　You have seen the film.
REMEMBER: Some verbs are transitive in English but not so in Spanish, and vice versa.
See **VERBS, INTRANSITIVE**

VERY MUCH

NEVER translate this as *"muy mucho."* The correct form is the absolute superlative *muchísimo.*
E.g.: *Quiero muchísimo a mi mamá.*
　　　I love my mother very much.

VEZ (VECES) vs. HORA vs. TIEMPO
　　See *HORA vs. TIEMPO vs. VEZ (VECES)*

VIVIR

(Intransitive verb) = "To live."

PRES.: *viv-o, -es, -e, -imos, -ís, -en.*
IMPERF.: *viv-ía, -ías, -ía, -íamos, -íais, -ían.*
PRETER.: *viv-í, -iste, -ió, -imos, -isteis, -ieron.*
FUT.: *vivir-é, -ás, -á, -emos, -éis, -án.*
CONDIT.: *vivir-ía, -ías, -ía, -íamos, -íais, -ían.*
SUBJ. PRES.: *viv-a, -as, -a, -amos, -áis, -an.*
SUBJ. IMPERF. 1: *vivi-era, -eras, -era, -éramos, -erais, -eran.*
SUBJ. IMPERF. 2: *vivi-ese, -eses, -ese, -ésemos, -eseis, -esen.*
INFORMAL IMPERAT.: *vive (tú), no vivas (tú); vivid (vosotros), no viváis (vosotros).*
FORMAL IMPERAT.: *viva (Vd.); vivamos; vivan (Vds.).*
PRES. PARTIC.: *viviendo.*
PAST PARTIC.: *vivido.*

VOLVER

(Transitive and intransitive verb). See below for meanings.
PRES.: *vuelvo, vuelves, vuelve, volvemos, volvéis, vuelven.*
IMPERF.: *volvía, -ías, -ía, -íamos, -íais, -ían.*
PRETER.: *volv-í, -iste, -ió, -imos, -isteis, -ieron.*
FUT.: *volver-é, -ás, -á, -emos, -éis, -án.*
CONDIT.: *volver-ía, -ías, -ía, -íamos, -íais, -ían.*
SUBJ. PRES.: *vuelva, vuelvas, vuelva, volvamos, volváis, vuelvan.*
SUBJ. IMPERF. 1: *volvi-era, -eras, -era, -éramos, -erais, -eran.*
SUBJ. IMPERF. 2: *volvi-ese, -eses, -ese, -ésemos, -eseis, -esen.*
INFORMAL IMPERAT.: *vuelve (tú), no vuelvas (tú); volved (vosotros), no volváis (vosotros).*
FORMAL IMPERAT.: *vuelva (Vd.); volvamos; vuelvan (Vds.).*
PRES. PARTIC.: *volviendo.*
PAST PARTIC.: *vuelto.*
USAGE:
(a) (Transitive verb) = "To turn around (over, back)."
　　E.g.: *Vuelve la página.*
　　　　　Turn the page.
(b) (Intransitive verb) = "To turn (to), to return."
　　E.g.: *Mi papá vuelve de la oficina a las seis.*
　　　　　My dad returns from the office at six o'clock.
(c) (Idiomatic construction) *Volver a* + infinitive = "To + verb + again."
　　E.g.: *Ella volverá a tocar el violín.*
　　　　　She will play the violin again.
(d) (Idiomatic expression) *Volver en sí* = "To regain consciousness."
　　E.g.: *Volvió en sí en cinco minutos.*
　　　　　He regained consciousness within five minutes.
(e) (Idiomatic expression) *Volverse* + adjective = "To become."
　　E.g.: *La situación se vuelve peligrosa.*
　　　　　The situation is becoming dangerous.
NOTE:
Do not confuse *volver* with *devolver* (transitive) which means "To return, to give back."
E.g.: *Devolvieron los libros a la biblioteca.*
　　　They returned the books to the library.

VOLVER A + infinitive

(Verbal idiom) = "To + verb + again."
E.g.: *Ellas volvieron a leer el artículo.*
　　　They read the article again.

VOLVER EN SÍ

(Verbal idiom) = "To regain consciousness."
E.g.: *Volverá en sí en unos minutos.*
　　　He will regain consciousness in a few minutes.

VOLVERSE

(Reflexive verb) =
(a) "To turn (around):"
　　E.g.: *Se volvió para mirarla.*
　　　　　He turned around to look at her.
(b) When followed by an adjective = "To become."
　　E.g.: *Mi marido se vuelve imposible.*
　　　　　My husband is becoming impossible.

VOSOTROS (-AS)

(Personal pronoun, second person plural, informal). It is:
(a) the subject:
    E.g.: *Vosotros habéis ganado.*
        You have won.
(b) the object of a preposition.
    E.g.: *Iremos con vosotras.*
        We shall go with you.
NOTE:
This form is not used in Latin America, where *ustedes* predominates.

VOWEL

Vowels *(Las vocales)* are the letters *a, e, i, o, u,* and *y.* They represent a sound pronounced without any restriction of the breath.

VUESTRO (-A, -OS, -AS)

See **ADJECTIVES, POSSESSIVE**
See also **PRONOUNS, POSSESSIVE**

W

to WAIT FOR

= *Esperar* (Transitive verb).
NOTE:
The preposition "for" is included in the verb.
E.g.: *Esperaba el autobús en la calle.*
      He was waiting for the bus in the street.

to WALK

(1) "To take a walk" = *Dar un paseo* (Verbal idiom).
    E.g.: *Dimos un paseo con nuestros amigos.*
        We took a walk with our friends.
NOTE:
Dar un paseo en coche = "To go for a drive."
E.g.: *Dimos un paseo en el coche de Andrés.*
      We went for a drive in Andrew's car.
See **DAR UN PASEO** and **DAR UNA VUELTA**
(2) "To walk" (= "To go on foot") = *Ir a pie* or *andar.*
    E.g.: *Los niños van a la escuela a pie.*
        The children walk to school.

to WANT + verb

(a) If both verbs have the same subject: *Querer* + infinitive.
    E.g.: *Ella quiere ir a Salamanca.*
        She wants to go to Salamanca.
(b) If the two verbs have different subjects: *Querer que* + subjunctive.
    E.g.: *Ella quiere que yo vaya a Salamanca.*
        She wants me to go to Salamanca.

WEATHER

(1) Expressions describing the weather or the temperature use *hacer*.
  E.g.: *Hace viento.*
    It is windy.
    Hacía frío.
    It was cold.
    Hizo mucho calor el año pasado.
    It was very hot last year.
    Hace mucho sol.
    It is very sunny.
    Hará fresco mañana.
    It will be cool tomorrow.

NOTE:

Calor, fresco, frío, viento and *sol* are nouns. Therefore they must be modified by the adjective *mucho* (not the adverb *muy*).
  E.g.: *Hace mucho viento.*
    It is very windy.

(2) *Haber* can also be used impersonally to describe weather conditons, but only if the condition is visible, as in talking about the sun or the moon.
  E.g.: *Hay mucha luna esta noche.*
    The moon is shining tonight.

    Habrá mucho sol en Florida.
    It will be very sunny in Florida.

(3) Other weather expressions:
  (a) *Está nublado.*
    It is cloudy, overcast.
  (b) *Está despejado.*
    It is clear (skies).
  (c) *Hay neblina.*
    It is foggy.

NOTE:

Do not confuse these constructions with:
(a) *Tengo frío, tengo calor* (= "I am cold, I am hot"), used only for people.
(b) *Está caliente, está frío (-a)* (= ". . . is hot, is cold"), used only for objects.
  E.g.,: *El radiador está caliente.*
    The radiator is hot.

    El agua está fría.
    The water is cold.

NOTES:

(1) Since *caliente* and *frío* are adjectives they are modified by the adverb *muy*.
  E.g.: *El agua está muy fría.*
    The water is very cold.

(2) When talking about permanent and inherent qualities use the verb *ser*.
  E.g.: *El hielo es frío.*
    Ice is cold.

WHAT

(1) Interrogative adjective = *¿Qué?*
See **ADJECTIVES, INTERROGATIVE**
(2) Interrogative pronoun = *¿Qué?*
See **PRONOUNS, INTERROGATIVE**
(3) Relative pronoun (meaning "that which") = *el (la, los, las) que.*
See **PRONOUNS, RELATIVE**
See also **WHICH**

WHAT A . . . !

(Exclamation) = "*¡Qué* + noun!"
E.g.: *¡Qué hombre!*
  What a man!
NOTE:
If the noun is modified "*¡Qué* + noun + *tan* (or *más*) + adjective!"
E.g.: *¡Qué hombre más exigente!*
  What a demanding man!
  ¡Qué muchacha tan talentosa!
  What a talented girl!

WHATEVER

(a) (Pronoun) = *(Todo) lo que* + subjunctive.
    E.g.: *Puedes comer todo lo que quieras.*
      You may eat whatever you like.
(b) (Adjective) = *Cualquier(a), cualesquier(a)* + noun + *que* + subjunctive.
    E.g.: *Cualquier libro que sea, no me interesa.*
      Whatever book it may be, it doesn't interest me.

WHEN

See **CUANDO**

WHENEVER

= *Cuando quieras* (Conjunctional construction).
E.g.: *Llámame cuando quieras.*
  Call me whenever you like.
NOTE:
When *Cuando quiera que* has an indefinite meaning, it is followed by the subjunctive.
E.g.: *Cuando quiera que vayas al centro, cómprame el periódico.*
  Whenever you go downtown, buy me the newspaper.

WHEREVER

= *Dondequiera que* (Conjunctional construction).
E.g.: *Dondequiera que estés, llámame.*
  Wherever you are, call me.
NOTE:
When *Dondequiera que* has an indefinite meaning, it is followed by the subjunctive.
E.g.: *Dondequiera que estén, no lo quiero saber.*
  Wherever they may be, I don't want to know about it.

WHETHER

= *Si* (Conjunction).
E.g.: *No sé si vendrán o no.*
  I don't know whether they will come or not.

WHICH

(1) Interrogative adjective = *¿Cuál(es)?*
See **ADJECTIVES, INTERROGATIVE**
(2) Interrogative pronoun = *¿Cuál(es)?*
See **PRONOUNS, INTERROGATIVE**
(3) Meaning "The one(s) that" = *El (la, los, las) que.*
See **PRONOUNS, DEMONSTRATIVE**
(4) Relative pronoun = *Que.*
See **PRONOUNS, RELATIVE**
See also **WHAT**

WHICH ONE(S)

= *¿Cuál(es)?* (Interrogative pronoun).
See **PRONOUNS, INTERROGATIVE**

WHICHEVER

(1) (Adjective) = *Cualquier(a)*.
   E.g.: *Cualquier libro.*
      Whichever book (any book at all.)
(2) (Pronoun) = *Cualquiera . . . que.*
   E.g.: *Cualquiera de los libros que leas te interesará.*
      Whichever of the books you read will interest you.
NOTE:
Cualquiera . . . que is an indefinite expression and therefore is followed by the subjunctive.

WHILE + verb

(1) Meaning "During the time that" = *Mientras* + indicative.
   E.g.: *Escuchaba la radio mientras leía el periódico.*
      He listened to the radio while reading the newspaper.
(2) Meaning "Whereas (marking contrast)" = *Mientras.*
   E.g.: *Yo soy español mientras ella es colombiana.*
      I am Spanish while (= whereas) she is Colombian.

WHO(M)

(1) Relative pronoun = *Quien(es).*
See **PRONOUNS, RELATIVE**
(2) Interrogative pronoun = *¿Quién(es)?*
See **PRONOUNS, INTERROGATIVE**

WHOEVER, WHOMEVER

(Relative Pronoun) = *Quienquiera que* + subjunctive.
E.g.: *Quienquiera que venga podrá quedarse aquí.*
   Whoever comes will be able to stay here.
NOTE:
Quienquiera is an indefinite expression and therefore is followed by the subjunctive.

WHOSE

(1) (Interrogative pronoun) = *¿De quién(es)?*
   E.g.: *¿De quién es la pluma?*
      Whose pen is it?

      ¿De quiénes son las maletas?
      Whose suitcases are they?
NOTE:
When "whose" is followed by a verb other than "to be," the Spanish construction is quite
different from the corresponding English construction:
   E.g.: Whose car had the accident?
      De quién es el coche que tuvo el accidente?
      = Whose is the car that had the accident?
(2) (Relative pronoun) = *Cuyo (-a, -os, -as).*
   As any pronoun, it agrees in number and gender with the person or thing it replaces, not with
   the possessor.
   E.g.: *El niño cuya madre murió se llama Carlitos.*
      The child whose mother died is called Charlie.

WHY

(a) Meaning "for what reason?" = *¿Por qué?*
  E.g.: *¿Por qué no vienes con nosotros?*
      Why don't you come with us?
(b) Meaning "For what purpose?" = *¿Para qué?*
  E.g.: *¿Para qué vas a ir a Venezuela?*
      Why (for what purpose) are you going to go to Venezuela?

WILL

(a) When "will" is used as the future tense, use the future tense.
  E.g.: My father will go to Spain.
      Mi padre irá a España.

See **FUTURE TENSE**

(b) When "will" expresses the will, use the verb *querer*.
  E.g.: Gabriela will not obey her parents.
      Gabriela no quiere obedecerles a sus padres.

WITH

= *Con* (Preposition).
E.g.: *Trabajo con mi hermana.*
    I work with my sister.
NOTE:
In descriptions of persons or objects, use *de*.
E.g.: *La muchacha de los ojos verdes.*
    The girl with green eyes.
    La casa del balcón.
    The house with the balcony.

to do WITHOUT

= *Pasarse sin* (Verbal idiom).
E.g.: *No puedo pasarme sin postre.*
    I can't do without dessert.

to WONDER

= *Preguntarse* (Reflexive verb).
E.g.: *Me pregunto si vendrán.*
    I wonder if they will come.

WORD ORDER in a sentence

The normal word order is:
(a) in an affirmative sentence:
    Subject - verb - object or predicate
    E.g.: *Carmen come el postre.*
        Carmen eats the dessert.
        Mario es gordo.
        Mario is fat.
NOTE:
The subject is also often placed after the verb or dropped altogether.
(b) In an interrogative sentence:
    Verb - subject - object or predicate
BUT if the subject is very long it is placed at the end of the sentence:
Verb - object - subject

E.g.: *¿Come Carmen el postre?*
       Does Carmen eat the dessert?
BUT: *¿Come el postre la hija de Carmen?*
       Does Carmen's daughter eat the dessert?

WORD STRESS

(1) Most words ending in a vowel or with the consonants *n* or *s* have the stress on the next to the last syllable.
    E.g.: *CLAse, biblioTEca, ENtran, CarmenCIta.*
(2) Most words ending in a consonant other than *n* or *s* have the stress on the last syllable.
    E.g.: *ustED, aprendER, papEL, reLOJ.*
(3) Words whose pronunciation does not follow the above rules have a written accent on the syllable which is stressed:
    E.g.: *adiós, rápidamente, Hispanoamérica, jóvenes, lápiz, también.*

NOTES:

(1) The written accent is also used to indicate interrogative and exclamatory words:
    E.g.: *¿cuándo? ¿por qué? ¡qué idea! ¡cuánto trabaja!*
(2) The written accent is also used to distinguish between certain words spelled alike but whose meanings are different:
    E.g.:   *el* = the   BUT *él* = he
            si = if   BUT *sí* = yes
            mas = but   BUT *más* = more

See **ACCENTS**

to WORRY

(1) "To worry about" = *Inquietarse por* (Reflexive verb).
    E.g.: *Me inquieto por tu salud.*
          I worry about your health.
(2) "To cause worry" = *Inquietar* (Transitive verb).
    E.g.: *Tu enfermedad me inquieta.*
          Your illness worries me.

See **PREOCUPAR vs. PREOCUPARSE**

WOULD

(1) If "would" expresses the present conditional in English, the Spanish equivalent is the present tense of the conditional mood.
    E.g.: I would eat (if I were hungry.)
          Comería (si tuviera hambre.)

See **"SI" CLAUSES**

(2) If "would" has the meaning of "was willing," use the imperfect of the verb *querer.*
    E.g.: Peter would not study (because he was tired).
          Pedro no quería estudiar (porque estaba cansado).
(3) If "would" is used to indicate a repeated action, use the imperfect of the appropriate Spanish verb.
    E.g.: When I was young we would (used to) go to the beach every day.
          Cuando era joven íbamos a la playa todos los días.

See **IMPERFECT TENSE**

WOULD HAVE

"Would have" expresses the past conditional in English and Spanish.
E.g.: *Habría ido a Francia (si hubiera podido).*
      I would have gone to France (if I had been able).

See **CONDITIONAL TENSES**

WRITTEN ACCENTS

See **ACCENTS**

WRONG

(1) Meaning "Bad, wicked" = *Malo* (*-a, -os, -as*) (Adjective).

    E.g.: *Es malo mentir así.*

        It is wrong to lie like that.

(2) Meaning "Incorrect, mistaken" = *Incorrecto* (*-a, -os, -as*) (Adjective).

    E.g.: *Tu contestación es completamente incorrecta.*

        Your answer is completely wrong.

(3) The idiom "To be wrong [referring to a person]" = *No tener razón* (Verbal idiom) or *Equivocarse* (Reflexive verb).

    E.g.: *El profesor no tiene razón.*

        The teacher is wrong.

        El profesor se equivocó.

        The teacher was wrong.

Y

Y

(Conjunction) = "And."

E.g.: *El muchacho y la muchacha.*

    The boy and the girl.

NOTE:

The conjunction *y* changes to *e* before a word beginning with *i-* or *hi-*.

E.g.: *Margarita e Isabel.*

    Margaret and Isabel.

    Padre e hijo.

    Father and son.

YA

(Adverb) = "Already, now, at once, right away, soon."

E.g.: *Ya he leído este libro.*

    I have already read this book.

    Ya vamos a llegar a Madrid.

    We're going to arrive in Madrid soon.

YA NO

(Adverbial idiom) = "No longer, not any more."

E.g.: *Ya no puedo leer sin gafas.*

    I can no longer read without eyeglasses.

YA QUE

(Conjunctional idiom) = "Since, due to the fact that."

E.g.: *Ya que eres tan inteligente, me puedes ayudar.*

    Since you are so intelligent you can help me.

YEARS OLD

Age is expressed by the idiomatic construction *Tener . . . años (de edad).*

E.g.: *Gabriela tiene veinte años (de edad).*

    Gabriela is twenty (years old).

YET

= *Todavía* or *aún* (Adverbs).

E.g.: *Todavía la veo en mi imaginación.*

I see her yet in my imagination.

NOTE:

The negative "Not yet" = *Todavía no.*

E.g.: *Todavía no han llamado.*

They have not called yet.

YOU

(Pronoun)

(1) The formal "You" =

(a) *usted(es)* (abbreviated *Ud., Uds.* or *Vd., Vds.*) when it is the subject or object of a preposition.

(b) *lo, la (a Vd.); los, las (a Vds.)* when it is direct object.

(c) *le, (a Vd.), les (a Vds.)* when it is indirect object.

(2) The informal "You" =

(a) *tú, vosotros (-as)* when it is the subject or object of a preposition.

(b) *te, os* when it is direct or indirect object.

See **PRONOUNS, PERSONAL**